CW00430470

Naylor Brothers

MG PARTS Ltd

TA TB TC TD TF SPRITE MIDGET B BGT
BGT V8 C CGT TA TB TC TD TF SPRITE
MIDGET B BGT BGT V8 C CGT TA TB TC
TD TF SPRITE MIDGET B BGT BGT V8 C
CGT TA TB TC TD TF SPRITE MIDGET B
BGT BGT V8 C CGT TA TB TC TD TF
SPRITE MIDGET B BGT BGT V8 C CGT TA

Thousands of Parts to keep Thousands of Cars
BGT V8 C CGT **Running** TD TF SPRITE
MIDGET B BGT BGT V8 C CGT TA TB TC
TD TF SPRITE MIDGET B BGT BGT V8 C
CGT TA TB TC TD TF SPRITE MIDGET B
BGT BGT V8 C CGT TA TB TC TD TF
SPRITE MIDGET B BGT BGT V8 C CGT TA
TB TC TD TF SPRITE MIDGET B BGT
BGT V8 C CGT TA TB TC TD TF SPRITE
MIDGET B BGT BGT V8 C CGT TA TB TC
TD TF SPRITE MIDGET B BGT BGT V8 C
CGT TA TB TC TD TF SPRITE MIDGET B

**MG Spares Manufacturers and Suppliers of
Quality Parts and Expert Advice for Your Car**

BRITISH MOTOR
HERITAGE APPROVED

Access

VISA

ACCESS AND VISA WELCOME

Member of the Classic British Sportscar Spares Group

*Comprehensive,
Fully illustrated
catalogues covering:*
- *MG T Series 1936-1955*
- *Sprite & Midget 1959-1963*
- *Sprite & Midget 1964-1980*
- *MGB & MGB GT 1962-1980*
- *MGB GT V8 1972-1975*

Naylor Brothers MG Parts Ltd Regent House Dockfield Road Shipley West Yorkshire BD17 7SF Tel: 0274 594071 Telex: 517402 Fax: 0274 531149

THE MAGIC OF THE MARQUE

MIKE ALLISON

This book is dedicated to MG enthusiasts everywhere, both living and dead, but especially to all those who helped to build MG cars, for creating the Magic; also to those who have run and maintained MG cars as well as to the spouses and families who have given their support, thus keeping the Magic alive.

Dalton Watson plc
Russell Chambers
The Piazza
Covent Garden
London WC2E 8AA

First published 1989

Designed and produced by
The Pen and Ink Book Company Ltd.
Huntingdon, Cambridgeshire

Printed by Scotprint Ltd, Musselburgh, Scotland

British Library Cataloguing in Publication Data

Allison, Mike
  MG.
  1. MG cars, to 1985
  I. Title
  629.2′222

    ISBN 0-901564-82-6
    ISBN 0-901564-87-7 Leather

Contents

Preface

MG Sports Cars are renowned the world over. Indeed, there is probably no one in the so-called Western World who cannot recognize the simple octagonal badge which for over fifty years has been synonymous with the public ideas of what a sports car represents. There is something magical about a car so well known, especially when it is remembered that only just over a total of one million cars were built bearing the badge prior to the closure of the Abingdon plant.

Perhaps now in the last twelve years of the twentieth century the origins of the magic are getting a little clouded, and the time has come to look at MG cars and examine how this magic arose, indeed if there is any at all.

Although the earliest MG cars were built in the third decade of the century, public imagination was first caught by the exciting deeds of the small cars of the early 1930s, and it was to the 1931 special car EX 127 that the adjective 'magic' was first applied, when it was called 'Magic Midget'. Literally dozens of race and record achievements followed, the cars setting the standards of performance in their classes for the day. There was actually little 'magic' as such – all achievements were the result of hard work in preparation and good driving – but there is no denying that in their day, the Midgets and Magnettes were the cars to beat in all types of competition.

In 1935 commercial pressures closed the competition department, and production changed to a new range of cars which had their origins in more mundane Morris cars, and yet sales of cars bearing the Octagon continued at previous levels. The new MGs were every bit as successful as their predecessors had been in terms of sales. Attempts were made to export MGs, and to a degree this was successful, bringing the cars to all corners of the British Empire.

After the Hitler war it was necessary to 'Export for Survival', and the little plant responded, culminating in the huge sales of cars all over the world, and especially to the United States of America, right up to the end of the 1970s. The fact that the Abingdon plant was eventually closed out of economic necessity is something of a mystery. The furore over the closure of the old factory by British Leyland in 1980 resulted in an appreciation that the MG name really meant something in terms of potential sales, far more than a bland 'S' or 'GT' label, and we now have a situation where the Rover Company, as successors to British Leyland, are still producing cars with the MG badge, the only marque name now so honoured. Surely there is a little magic in this too?

The fact of the matter is that the MG name has bred something of a cult. The MG Car Club has been in existence for nearly sixty years, and is the only one make club which can fill a grid of its own marque cars in each of eight or nine races at a single meeting! Furthermore it remains the only marque club which caters wholly for the needs of its membership, whatever the model of MG owned.

What is it that generates such enthusiasm, which for want of a better term I prefer to call 'Magic'? Speaking personally, it started for me during the Second World War when, as a small boy, I was captivated by the sight of what must have been a P-type. As soon as I was able, I had a P-type of my own, by which time the car was twenty-three years old, and after a succession of heartbreaks I finally got it going properly. Since that time I have owned and driven many MGs, indeed examples of just about every model, and while I would be the last to claim that MG cars are perfect examples of motor engineering, one must say that there can be few cars which offer so much pleasure for so little prime cost. I would add that this is not a blinkered view of a rabid MG enthusiast, for in the course of my work I have been privileged to drive a wide variety of cars of all types, and while many of these are very nice, most were originally much more expensive than their MG contemporary.

One of the biggest features resulting in the huge sales of MG cars over the years has been performance, but performance alone does not sell cars: witness the last few years of MGB production, when we were constantly told by the wiseacres of the motoring press that the car would not sell because it was too slow . . . and yet it did! A glance at the tables at the end of the book will show that right up to 1978 there was very little drop in sales, so what generated these sales? It was not sentiment – was it a little magic? Probably the fact that the car looked the part helped, and here lies an important feature contribution to MG sales throughout: there has seldom been an ugly MG.

The J2 is, and the MGB GT will probably become, a 'classic' car design generating a whole new breed of vehicles aping the general layout. I can hear dissent at the suggestion of seeing the latter car in this light, but it was the first hatchback car . . .

I state here that the book does not seek to be a history of the MG factory, merely a record of the products. What I have attempted to show in this book is that MG cars have always provided a standard by which their competitors are judged, in terms of design and performance, and that this was not all that has contributed to the *Magic of the Marque*. The chapter headings have tried to bring together models with similarities, or a continuous story. I have tried to be factual, but there are opinions expressed from time to time which are wholly my own, viewed from the point of view of an ex-employee, perhaps coloured by feelings within the factory expressed by colleagues at the time. Historians have tried to record their interpretation of the facts; perhaps it might be interesting to know what *we* felt.

I hope that you will enjoy reading the book, and that if you are not an MG enthusiast then you will appreciate why so many people are.

Mike Allison
Newbury, Berkshire
November 1988

Acknowledgements

Another book could be written listing the helpers and help given in the compilation of this book. However, constraints set by the publishers mean that I must be brief, and I will start by apologizing to anyone who feels aggrieved at being left unmentioned: I appreciate all help given and thank everyone, for without your help no book would be published.

First and foremost, I thank my former colleagues at the MG Car Co. Ltd, for helping me with data and reminiscences which form the backbone of the text. Amongst those who have helped considerably are John Thornley, Tom Viner, Grace and John Lewis, and Henry Stone. It is a matter of sadness that many of those who helped are now no longer with us, so I record with pride that I knew and worked with such people as Cec Cousins, Reg Jackson, Alec Hounslow, Bill Lane, Sam Nash, John Knight and Roy Brocklehurst, all of whom supplied anecdotes related in the text.

The help afforded by the Rover Group, and British Motor Heritage, must be recorded, for many of the prints used are from their files. In this connection the assistance given by Anders Clausager is greatly appreciated.

A large vote of thanks to the officers and members of the MG Car Club for the considerable help given, especially to the Club Executive for permission to use material and photographs held in their files. Special mention is made of help given by John Bates, Martin Brent, Ron Cover, Ron Gammons, Phil Jennings, Warren Marsh, and Paddy Willmer, who gave up time to answer many questions, and supplied data and photographs.

A large part of the photographic material in this book appeared in *The Magic of MG* by the present author. In addition, I gratefully acknowledge use of the following photographic sources: British Motor Heritage Trust, the MG Car Club, Philip Bayne-Powell, Ron Cover, Barry Foster, Fred Scatley, and many others too shy to identify their work on prints used. If I have not identified other photographers I apologize.

Wilson McComb must be thanked for helping me to harness enthusiasm into useful channels, and teaching me to differentiate between recorded fact and deduced opinions. I hope that I have been able to keep the two separated herein.

Lastly, most especial thanks are due to my wife Anne, who has always supported me in my hobby and work, and without whose support on all eight sides there would be no book.

Nuvolari wins the 1933 TT. The Bryan de Grineau picture which used to hang in the boardroom at MG.

Above: Racing at an MG Car Club meeting: K1 Special leads a C-type.

Below: 1927 14/40 two-seater.

Right: MGs return to Brooklands: headed by the ex-Whitney Straight K3.

Magic of the Marque: a series of pictures taken during 1988 at MG Car Club events by Ron Cover.

Right: Old Number One: still active at Silverstone.

Below: The 14/40 at Brooklands.

Far right: A TC drives up the Brooklands Test Hill.

Top left: 1930 M-type Midget.

Bottom left: 1950s MG-engined Parson Special.

Top right: A 1933 K3 with a 1934 NA, two historic MGs which are still actively campaigned.

Bottom right: Ex-Kenneth Evans trials N-type, whose supercharger seems somehow to have migrated!

Above: J2 Special off up the Test Hill.

Top right: 1935 PB Midget on the Brooklands home banking.

Bottom right: 1934 PA Midget in much the same place.

Main picture: 1956 ZA Magnette.

Inset: TF Midget with appropriate numberplate.

Top left: MGA Twin-Cam Coupé.

Bottom left: MGB with hood up: odd that most post-1962 MGs are seen this way!

Top right: A customised MGB GT V8.

Bottom right: A standard PA Midget.

Main picture: 1930 M-type.

Inset: A row of 1930s racers.

Oxford and Cowley

For the past thirty or forty years various writers have attempted to dispel the many myths, half-truths and downright lies told about the early days of MG, and I intend to follow this tradition in the hope that, perhaps with the passage of a few more years of repeating the truth, this will become accepted into folklore! To some extent I have done my share of myth-spreading, but that was some time ago, since when considerable additional information has come to light, including data provided by retired MG employees after publication of the original edition of *The Magic of MG* many of whom had been too reticent to volunteer information before publication. Unfortunately it was not possible to incorporate this information in any of the reprints, but I am happy to put the record straight now, although it is sad that many of those who helped with information are no longer able to see their contributions in print.

Perhaps the hoariest story of all is that MGs were always two-seat sports cars, made of special parts mainly octagonal in shape, and assembled at Abingdon. In fact the earliest cars were modified Morris cars, part Oxford and part Cowley, of no real sporting pretensions, being available in two- and four-seat forms, both open and saloon. Most people associate MG cars with the old Oxfordshire town of Abingdon, but just as now, when the cars bearing the MG octagon are built in far-off Birmingham, so it was in the beginning, for the earliest MGs were made in and around the town of Oxford, about ten miles away. The octagon itself was not prominently present on an MG for a number of years following commencement of production; but now we are getting to areas which require definition, so let us start at the beginning and trace the early days of MG as far as they affect the cars, and look at the cars in some detail.

Morris Garages Ltd were the Oxford distributors for Morris cars and were owned, like the car manufacturing plant, by William Morris. As did most large garages, they produced as a side line and to special order bespoke bodies for those customers who wanted something a little more special. We do not know for certain whether this took place before Cecil Kimber joined the company, but it seems quite likely. However, one thing is quite certain and that is that without 'CK' there would have been no 'MG': the two pairs of initials were synonymous for the first twelve years of production. On the other hand, it is unlikely that Kimber would have started the ball rolling without the basic enthusiasm that existed for sporting cars at the repair shop associated with Morris Garages Ltd, even though he was keen on fast motoring.

In fact right from their beginnings, Morris Garages sought for ways to serve the needs of the Morris car owner, and had produced a range of specially designed luggage, car rugs and other goods, which might now be referred to as necessary accessories, or 'bolt-on goodies'. Kimber was appointed to the position of General Manager in 1922, and found that a significant part of the work of the Service Department was in the maintenance and tuning of all types of car and motor-cycle for wealthy students and local residents. There was also a market for a car which was slightly better equipped than standard, and it is likely that these two activities inspired the idea of a sporting Morris car, although it is doubtful whether any conscious decision in that direction was taken for at least another year. Indeed the market for such work was very small in reality, and hardly likely to impress a hard businessman like William Morris.

Morris Motors were already producing a Sports Cowley in 1921, offering special tuning in the form of aluminium pistons (cast iron was the material used in the touring cars) and large bore exhaust as well as a higher final drive ratio which, combined with the lighter body, gave the car a spirited performance for its day. Morris Garages certainly helped to improve on this performance for owners in and around Oxford. However, sales of the Sports were not brisk, and the model was dropped in 1922, but it was possibly this which caused Morris Garages to look seriously at the subject of sporty car production.

The bodies for Morris Garages to fit to Oxford and Cowley chassis were made by the nearby coachbuilding firm of Charles Raworth and by the better-known concern of Carbodies at Coventry. The body styles were of a wide range, providing more appointments than the standard Morris offerings. One innovation was the use of two-tone colour schemes: one of the earliest known applications of this, certainly for a British manufacturer, if not in the world. While these cars may have had a greater 'Jones appeal' they were very expensive compared with the standard Morris product, and there was little effort on the part of Morris Garages to disguise the car's ancestry; indeed, the fact that they were based on such a respected name as the Morris car may well have helped sales.

With the demise of the Cowley Sports, Kimber ordered six two-seater bodies from Raworth and started to market a car which was later referred to as an 'MG Sports Morris', often affectionately known by employees as the 'Chummy'. The car was based on the 12 hp Cowley model but bore some family resemblance to the later 'Bullnose' MG models, having a similar windscreen and the scuttle ventilators which became a characteristic of the whole 14 hp range. It also had lowered suspension and a raked steering column. However, the car was still a Cowley with improved looks, and at £350 was too dear compared with its parent. This view was put forcefully when Morris Motors introduced their 'Occasional Four', a very similar style of car at £215 for 1924.

It was in a Chummy that Kimber won a Gold Medal in the 1923 Motor Cycling Club Land's End Trial. Following this, sales of the special-bodied Morrises picked up a little, although hardly enough to get excited about – the balance of the original six Chummy bodies sticking around for some time. The introduction of the Morris Occasional Four was countered by offering a specially tuned version at the old price, still £350, and then with a much better-looking body on the 14 hp Oxford chassis... the die was cast!

The Cowley Sports — almost certainly what inspired Kimber towards a sporting Morris-based car.

A typical early-1920s Morris Garages body: this one is on an F-type Morris Oxford Six, probably 1923 or 1924.

This was the Hughes-bodied Morris Oxford built for Jack Gardiner.

This was Billy Cooper's car, which featured at Brooklands meetings. The body was built by Carbodies.

The first 14 hp sports car was built to the special order of one of the Morris Garages employees, Jack Gardiner, who had recently inherited a sum of money. The body was apparently made by the side-car manufacturer, Hughes of Birmingham, and Cecil Cousins, one of the earliest employees, could remember delivering the chassis to them for the body to be mounted, describing it on tape to me as 'a bloody cold ride in February'. This car appears to have been a one-off, but it was described as an 'MG Special 4-seater Sports' in a contemporary photograph.

Kimber ordered three each of a handsome two- and four-seater body from Carbodies, similar in style to the Hughes body and mounted these on chassis which had been fitted with decambered springs and Hartford shock absorbers at the rear, a lowered steering column, which incidentally was mounted on the chassis and not the engine as on the Morris Oxford. A special carburettor, possibly an SU sloper as fitted to the contemporary Bentley, was fitted. The scuttle of the body was considerably lower than on the standard Morris, which made it necessary to crank the gearlever to miss the dashboard in the reverse and second gear positions. It was found possible to fit the Cowley radiator, which was smaller than the Oxford unit, with no loss of cooling efficiency, and a number of other detail changes were incorporated. The earliest cars were unpainted, the aluminium panelling being highly polished, and set off with polished wheel discs, which also hid the artillery wheels! The result was quite stunning, the car being particularly good-looking. Not only did the car look good, however, but its handling was far superior to the standard Morris car, thus starting one of the principal attractions of MG cars down the years.

These cars were probably the first to carry the now famous MG octagon, but it was to be found on step plates hidden in the door shuts. The earliest known use of the octagon was in an advertisement for the Chummy in 1924. These early advertisements did stress the sporting achievements of the car, while calling it '...an exceptionally fast touring motor car, capable of 60 mph on the flat...'

One of the earliest cars was sold to Billy Cooper, a regular trials competitor, who had bought one of the original Chummies, and he entered it for a high speed trial at an MCC meeting at Brooklands, when it succeeded in gaining a first-class award. It received considerable attention and admiration and sales enquiries were received at the Queen Street showroom in large enough numbers for the embryonic factory in Alfred Lane to become embarrassed for lack of space.

At this time the cars were built largely 'after hours'; there was no actual production area, the chassis being received from Cowley and then modified to take the new body in the small mews garage in Alfred Lane just behind the Radcliff Infirmary in the centre of Oxford. When the chassis was prepared it was then driven to Coventry to have the body mounted, and then driven back to Oxford for finishing off. Cars were built to order, not for stock, but at this time the total staff involved in car production was only three or four, so things must have been quite lively!

Late in 1924 Kimber had his famous special trials car built, this being done at the service shop at Longwall, and finished just in time for the 1925 Land's

No story of MG is complete without 'Old No.1', regarded by most as the first MG sports car. It was built at the Longwall Street depot for Kimber in early 1925.

A 1925–6 production four-seater, displaying the change to steel upper panels in the body. These were painted either blue or dark red, but the lower panels were still polished.

End Trial. Whether this was done as a prototype or merely to satisfy an urge to design something extra special is not known. It was basically a Morris, although it used a special ohv 1.5-litre engine built by Hotchkiss who also built the standard Morris unit. The transmission was standard Morris with oil-immersed clutch and three-speed gearbox. The chassis was specially built from Morris components but featured semi-elliptic springs all round, with overslung axles. The whole car was clothed with a body which can only be described as a sports car. It was capable of speeds approaching 80 mph and when driving it one appreciates that it *is* a sports car, proving to be the first of many. After a minor problem with the chassis, which had to be hurriedly repaired by plating, Kimber was able to win a Gold Medal in the Trial, and success in this event produced sufficient publicity for the aforementioned lack of space at Alfred Lane to become acute.

Kimber appealed to Morris for more space, and this was made available at the Bainton Road works of Osberton Radiators, in the north of Oxford, the move being made in September 1925, over a weekend, according to Cousins! At this time also a couple of electric drills were added to the works inventory, which made drilling the holes in the chassis a little easier than it had been using a breast drill of the type known throughout the motor trade as a 'gut-buster'! The staff was up to a dozen or so, and production was increasing!

A policy of steady improvement of the marque was followed, and during 1925 the carburettor was changed to the more readily available Solex MHD, and at the same time the throttle pedal was moved to the right, rather than being centrally mounted as on the Morris. The handbrake was moved to the right-hand side of the cockpit and the Barker headlamp dip system was introduced, as an optional extra, which provided an additional lever to the driver's right. The upper parts of the body were made in steel instead of aluminium, necessitating the painting of these, while the lower panels were still unpainted aluminium and were polished. The mudguards were of steel, and were painted to match the red or blue upper parts, while the polished wheel discs remained. A saloon was offered, with vertical rear panel, and these were finished in two-tone paint colours as pioneered by Morris Garages. Two-tone finishes were to be a feature of MGs through the years, and did much to increase the appeal of certain models.

For the 1926 season further detail changes were introduced, and it was no coincidence that most of these were offered on the standard Morris Oxford, so that a Clayton-Dewandre B-type vacuum servo was added to the braking system, and the electrical system was improved a little. MG improvements included the standard fitting of the Barker dip, which was a purely mechanical system, and a screen wiper, although this was also hand-operated. A new, additional body style was the salonette model, which was a four-seater, with two doors and fitted with a rear-mounted boot. This was formed to a point, rather like the prow of a ship, but became known as a 'duck's tail' – among other less polite sobriquets around the works! This model was fitted with balloon tyres as standard, in place of the high pressure beaded-edge type which did give a rather harsh ride on country roads. These tyres were offered as an option on other models, and the body of the open cars was increased by two inches in width.

Much more drastic changes were to follow late in 1926 for the 1927 model year. Morris wanted to drop the old bullnose radiator, which had been fitted to Morris cars since 1913 virtually unchanged in design, to give the cars a more up-to-date look. At the same time he also wanted to improve the carrying capacity of the basic chassis, which was Edwardian in concept. However, as far as possible, it was intended to keep the mechanical components unchanged, and in this way keep the selling price stable. In fact the new chassis was, up to a point, what MG needed, but the improved stability which resulted from extra stiffness of the frame was at the expense of increased weight, and it proved very difficult to get the redesigned MG to be as fast as its predecessor. Furthermore, Morris Motors were having great trouble getting their brakes to perform adequately, and had designed the most incredibly complicated compensating system, which also featured the enormous C-type servo. However, this had the result that the brakes of the new MG were actually less effective than those of the previous model, which led ultimately to a pure MG design for the 1928 model, as we shall see.

Other improvements introduced to the MG in 1927 included a seven-gallon fuel tank, with a reserve tap and a gauge, and automatic windscreen wipers, still mechanical but driven off the gearbox. The introduction of the reserve tap to the fuel system allowed the discontinuance of the spare fuel can which had hitherto been supplied, but had provided a stowage problem on the MG. A spare fuel can carried on the running board of a standard Morris might look alright, but was out of place when carried on the more stylish MG! Rear springs were now half-elliptic, but all springs were decambered compared with the Morris, and balloon tyres became standard on all cars. The engine was now mounted on rubber blocks, this being allowed by the additional chassis stiffness. The higher rear axle ratio used on the 'Bullnose' MG was retained.

Above: The 1925–6 two-seater photographed on a building site, possibly at the Bainton Road factory.

Below: The interior of the 1925–6 two-seater: the speedometer is rather unwisely placed in front of the passenger. Note the MG octagons in the door shuts.

A 1926 salonette, with boat tail, photographed at an MG Car
Club meeting in 1969. This car is nicely original, apart from its
radiator badge.

The 1927 two-seater, showing how well the 'flat' radiator was adapted to the lines of the car. Side panels were 'engine-turned' instead of polished.

So far as the bodywork was concerned, every effort was made to retain the illusion of a sports car, but the angular radiator made the styling exercise very difficult. The body finish broke new ground, for while the two-tone finish was retained, the lower panels of the open cars were engine-turned and varnished, which must have been more durable than the polished aluminium. An MG octagon appeared on the radiator for the first time on this model, although not an enamelled badge, but a metal stencil form mounted halfway down the radiator block.

It was during 1927 that Morris Radiators let Kimber know that he was outstaying his welcome, so that Kimber was forced to approach William Morris for finance to build a new factory dedicated to the production of MG cars. At this stage the bare chassis were still being driven to Carbodies for body mounting, so that actual space for production requirements was fairly modest. The estimated sum required for building new premises was £10,000. This was agreed to, so a site was acquired at Edmund Road, just off the Cowley Road, and less than a mile from the parent Cowley works, and the factory was built very quickly in six months, and occupied by September. There now started a determined effort to establish for MG an identity separate from Morris Motors, and in November 1927 Kimber was offering an MG warranty rather than the Morris one.

For 1928 the biggest improvement made was to the brakes, a typical piece of H.N. Charles thinking: simple, yet practical. Out went the servo and the compensation devices, the pedal pulling on a single cross-shaft which was connected by a single rod to each wheel brake. The handbrake worked, as before, through a separate linkage to additional shoes in the rear drums. The result was surprisingly effective: the brakes performed better and were easier to maintain. The basic layout was retained right through to 1936, when hydraulic brakes were introduced to MG, and was copied by Morris in 1930 on their 14 hp cars, although Cowley sported fluid operation very shortly after this date. Additionally, the brakedrums were fitted with shrunk-on aluminium cooling fins, which enhanced the looks, if they did nothing for either heat dissipation or stopping power! They did help in Kimber's quest for providing MG with an identity separate from the parent Morris. The now-familiar enamelled radiator badge appeared for the first time on the 1928 model.

This 'separate identity' became something of a fetish with Kimber, who wanted to establish with the public and – probably more importantly – the press that MG was not a wing of the Morris car factory, but a manufacturer whose products were unique and easily recognized. He made considerable efforts to 'prove' this, and once the Edmund Road factory was built he encouraged tours by anyone who cared to visit. The production procedures adopted showed that the chassis was built up from scratch, and not a modified unit, while the engines were stripped and rebuilt, the cylinder

The road test car, with door open to display the more ergonomic control panel.

heads and ports being polished to a high standard. Once built up, the chassis was given a rigorous running-in schedule on rollers, said in a contemporary report to be the equivalent of 750 miles' road use! Certainly care was taken to ensure that cars were received by customers in good shape, but it may just be that it was found difficult to achieve the desired road performance. Indeed, all cars were given a full power test on a machine known as the 'Comparator', probably invented by H.N. Charles; this was an early dynamometer, and was used at both Edmund Road and later at Abingdon up to 1936.

During 1928 was introduced the first of many octagonal instrument panels, and the car became known as the 14/40 Mark IV MG Sports. Reasons for the revised name and the mark number are difficult to find, and at best are inconclusive. Cousins thought that the Mark IV was introduced for the fourth year of production, but could not explain the '14/40'. Certainly 40 bhp could never have been coaxed out of the engine on a reliable basis, even given the extremes to which MG went during vehicle assembly. At this time, however, current advertising by MG was claiming that 40 mph averages were possible for the car, at a time when this was not an easy achievement, and this is my personal explanation. Whatever the reason, the 14/40 Mark IV is now a very good example of the vintage touring car, especially in its 1929 form with neat wheels and MG hubcaps. However, the side-valve engine was

The 1927 four-door tourer was a handsome car.

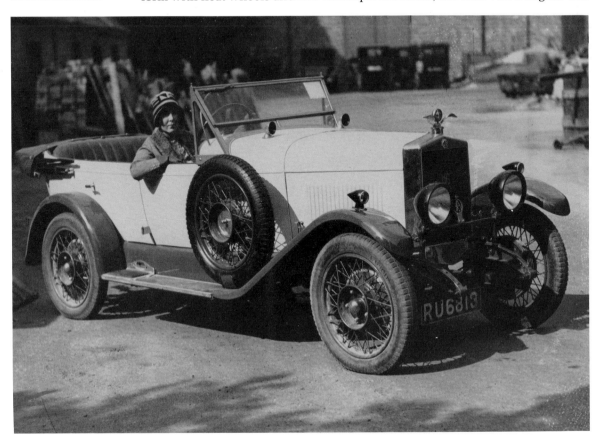

a little stretched in its capability, as well as not being appealing to the buyer of what was a rather expensive car with sporting pretensions.

By 1929 other models were in production and the days of the 14/40 were numbered, production finally coming to an end with the move to Abingdon. While the 14 hp cars were not designed as competition cars, in addition to trials successes they were used in rallies and MCC events, and it was a 1927 car which became the first to win a race, in Argentina of all places.

Rear view of a similar car. The MG plate was a false one, although later, London MG dealer University Motors bought all the numbers to sell at a premium on new cars.

Above: The 1927 two-door salonette featured two-tone colour schemes and was well appointed.

Left: The interior, displaying access to the rear compartment.

Below: The actress Madeleine Carroll poses with a 1927 salonette.

Above: The salonette with 'boat tail' as it was described officially.

Right: The instrument panel of the 1927 cars was well thought out, with gear lever in the centre, but handbrake to the right of the driver. The additional 'gear lever' on the right controlled the mechanical headlamp dipper!

Below: Around the factory the name of a part of the duck's anatomy was used to describe it.

It is odd to reflect that MG started in business as a coachbuilder, for by 1927 they were selling chassis to other coachbuilders! This rakish two-seater was by Jarvis.

The 1928 chassis, now featuring the MG enamel radiator
badge. Note the scuttle fuel tank with its rigid mounting. It is
also possible to see the improved braking system.

The demonstration four-seat tourer for 1928.

Above: 'Old Speckled Hen' was a fabric saloon with a striking stippled finish on its lower panels. It remained at the factory as a hack for quite a few years.

Left: The sobriquet somehow stuck, for the Abingdon brewery, Morlands, has named one of its products after 'Old Speckled Hen', here pictured with a traction engine.

Below: The metal-panelled saloon of 1928, displaying two-tone colours — and here strongly reminiscent of the contemporary Riley Monaco. Selling prices were similar, but the MG's larger engine probably gave it the edge on performance and silence of running.

For the 1929 season the wheel style was changed; here is a
nice saloon version of the 14/40 Mark IV.

The only known flat-radiator saloon survivor, now in the
Bressingham collection.

A 1927 Drophead coupé, with dickey seat — often referred to as a 'mother-in-law seat'.

Right: The control room of the Mark IV, showing the octagonal instrument bezels; there was even an MG crest on the throttle pedal!

Mark IV two-door saloon — with dickey — surely an unkind banishment for complaining passengers!

2

Vintage Splendour

The MG Six was introduced at the 1928 Motor Show, almost certainly bred of a desire by Kimber to move the appeal of the marque up-market, and to continue the break from obvious Morris parentage shown in the now ageing 14 hp range ... at least this is the view taken by most historians, which I shall examine in more detail in the next chapter. Suffice it to say that at the 1928 London Show there also appeared another new model, at the other end of the price scale.

It was during 1927 that Morris had announced their Light Six car, powered by a six-cylinder ohc 2.5-litre engine. Hitherto, Morris engines all had side valves, so that the new engine appeared to herald something of a revolution in Morris design thinking. The Light Six did not reach production, however, and it is not know for what reason, although chassis design was not in step with the advanced thinking of the basic engine conception. The formula did reach production in a Morris car as the Morris Six in 1928, a model which became the Isis the following year and stayed in production until 1935, enjoying a modest production success until it was overtaken by a return to the inevitable side-valve-itis which afflicted Cowley engine designs until after the war.

The engine design may have been inspired by Kimber, but was certainly designed by Frank Woolard's team at Morris Engines, Coventry. Unlike those fitted to other contemporary engines, the counterbalanced crankshaft was of fairly generous proportions and carried in four main bearings. It was pressure-fed from a large external oil pump, and all its bearings were white-metal-lined bronze bushes. The connecting rods followed normal practice for the period, being of H-section and with a split small end and white-metalled big end bearings. The pistons were of light alloy, split-skirt, with the gudgeon pin located with a pinch-bolt.

The camshaft was in the cylinder head, driven by a system of gears and chains which, if complicated, at least had the merit of running in a degree of silence unknown at the time. Valves were operated by L-shaped rocker fingers, and were arranged at an opposing angle of about 25 degrees. Porting on the original design was on opposite sides of the head, and the only restriction was the use of a single carburettor which was rather small. Drive was taken through a cork-faced clutch, running in oil as on all Morris cars up to that time, to a three-speed gearbox.

Kimber was able to convert one of the prototype engines and fit it to a chassis of MG design. This prototype car used more MG design thought than any of the 14 hp cars had, and the result was a good car, not so much in the pure engineering sense but in that it offered excellent value for money. The engine suffered a little, the cylinder-head-mounted single carburettor giving way to two SUs, mounted low down on the cylinder block and, even worse, under the exhaust manifold. Quite why this was done is not understood, for it now meant that the fuel had to be induced to cross the cylinder block, and then up into the head through two small-diameter transfer ports. No doubt some degree of pre-heating of the charge was achieved, but it did little to raise the power output of the engine, between 55 and 60 bhp being realized, which was quite good for 1928. The drive to oil pump, distributor, dynamo and water pump was redesigned to incorporate different components from the Morris. The Morris cork-insert clutch was retained as was the three-speed gearbox, and drive was taken by torque tube to a conventional rear axle assembly ensuring good lateral location.

The chassis was formed of channel section, with plenty of cross-members. Both axles were of MG design, although the torque tube and gears were of Morris origin. Brakes had drums of generous 12-inch diameter and with alloy fins. They were operated by Perrot shafts, these being operated by cables as on the later 14/40 cars. The Perrot shafts gave way quickly to simple backplate levers operated by cables, which proved much easier to maintain and more effective in stopping power. Marles steering gear was used and the steering box was chassis mounted. The wheels were initially similar to the late series 14/40, but most production cars were fitted with Rudge centre-lock wheels which were to become a standard feature of MG cars for the next twenty-five years. The radiator calls for special mention, for it crystallized the development which had taken place on the 14/40 unit from 1927 and became so familiar on all MG cars right up to 1953, with its stylish chromium-plated shell.

Bodywork was commodious and luxurious, if a little on the narrow side, appearing initially in open and closed four-seat forms, and later a smart two-seat with dickey. Very full instrumentation was offered, including a tachometer and a clock; there were even interior lamps for the instruments on all models, and at the rear in the saloons. The model was known immediately as the MG Six, and shortly afterwards was being marketed as the 18/80 hp MG Six.

The cars were all priced well below the true luxury cars, and sought to compete in the Alvis and Lagonda market. Offering more performance than either of these marques, they were well spoken of by the press. The problem was that even at a 'reasonable price' there were not many buyers in the £500 market at a time when there was an economic recession and when the average annual income of workers was around a fifth of this figure, most people having a much lower income. Furthermore, those who could afford £500 could probably spend £1,000 or more with equal facility, so that potential buyers might be expected to be fastidious, and perhaps the cars were not as refined as some of the more exotic marques at the higher figures.

Chassis improvement was proceeding, and a far better complete chassis package became available in late 1929. The frame was of heavier construction, and used axles of wider track, with enormous 14-inch brakedrums. The radiator shell now featured vertical shutters which were thermostatically controlled by the water temperature, which helped to ensure that water temperature was kept at an optimum level. Automatic chassis lubrication was featured, employing a small pump which was

Opposite top: A 1929 18/80 saloon with boot. This picture is heavily retouched to disguise the bolt-on wheels.

Centre: Prototype four-seat tourer without boot, but with bolt-on wheels.

Bottom: A similar car but with boot – again retouched to disguise the wheels.

The interior is very similar to the 14/40s, but gives considerable space.

Bottom: 1929 two-door salonette.

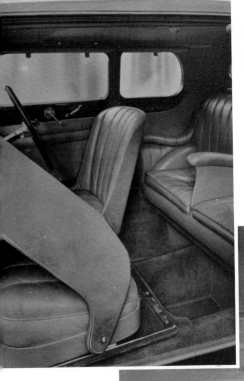

energized by the motion of the car on the road, and supplied oil to all the vital points via a maze of small-diameter tubing. The oil-immersed cork-insert clutch was retained, and this transferred power to a four-speed gearbox which was featured for the first time on an MG, with a central remote control gearlever which fell to hand nicely, and set a standard for most subsequent MG models. This car was marketed as the 18/80 MG Mark II, the older model continuing production as the Mark I. It suffered a little with being a heavy car and in consequence not quite such a spritely performer, and even more by being £100 more expensive that its older brother.

The Mark II broke new ground in its chassis numbering system, all previous chassis having been identified by a simple numeric series, but the new car was given a prefix 'A', and the first number allotted was 0251, which also happened to be the telephone number of the factory! This system was followed through to the TD, after which a BMC system was used.

In fact the Mark II was a much better appointed car than the Mark I, some of the bodies taking advantage of the wider chassis and being internally more spacious. Initial appearances made it difficult to prove this, and the latter car sold better on the basis of lower price, and the fact that it always offered a brisker performance, in spite of the maligned three-speed gearbox. The increased weight of the Mark II meant that the additional gear was essential, and that to some extent the car needed to be rowed along on the gearbox to extract the best performance, while the Mark I was a good performer even in top gear, which was more in keeping with the general character of the car.

During 1930 the Speed Model Mark I was sold with a guaranteed speed of 80 mph, which could probably not be achieved by any standard Mark II.

With the introduction of the Mark II, and the increasing volume of production of the Midget, which was completely assembled at Edmund Road, as opposed to the 14 and 18 hp cars which were bodied at coachbuilders, space was again at a premium, and it was soon obvious that a new factory with more space was needed. The Pavlova Leather·Works at Abingdon had a spacious building available, and again Kimber approached Morris for permission to buy, this time for £100,000. The building had been used for making leather coats and saddles during the First World War, but had not been used for about ten years prior to the purchase by the MG Car Co. Ltd. It did not take long to move all the impedimenta of car production from Cowley, and it was in full production early in 1930.

By this time the staff was growing in number, and H.N. Charles, who had been working as a part-time design consultant to Kimber in addition to his full-time job at Morris Motors, finally transferred permanently with the move to Abingdon as Chief Designer. It is worth while recording at this point that there was no drawing office until Charles moved across, and that no actual drawings of the 14 hp cars were ever completed, while those for the 18 hp cars were completed during 1934–36! The rate at which new models started to appear from this date made it impossible to keep up with the paperwork, something which would be unthinkable now.

In 1930 the ultimate variation on the 18/80 theme appeared, as the 18/100 Mark III Tigress model. Conceived as a road racing car in the old Bentley tradition, it was based on the Mark II chassis and featured many of the Mark II details. The engine had a true crossflow cylinder head, for the first time on an MG, twin downdraught SU carburettors, with unique 'egg-cosy' damper chambers, being mounted on a manifold on the offside of the head, and a three-branch exhaust manifold carrying away spent gases from the nearside. There were two sparking plugs per cylinder, fed by a very complicated distributor, and dry sump lubrication was featured. All internal engine components were said to be balanced, and crankshaft and connecting rods were machined all over. The gearbox ratios were improved, although the layout was very similar to the Mark II, and a very large fuel tank was fitted. The bodywork conformed to the requirements of international road racing, while a Brooklands regulation exhaust was fitted.

It was hoped that 100 bhp and 100 mph could be offered and it was intended that the Tigress be sold as a ready-to-race car for long-distance sports car racing, but in reality it showed up the inherent frailty of the basic engine design, which could not be persuaded to give much more than 80 bhp and then suffered with deficiencies in the crankshaft oil supply. The only official outing by a works car ended when it swallowed a carburettor part, over-revved and ran a bearing or two – Cecil Cousins colourfully described the engine as being completely blue inside!

Factory development of the 18 hp range was not stopped immediately, and quite a lot of work appears to have been put in with the help of Shell Oil, using a Mark II car fitted with a Mark III engine at Brooklands. They eventually obtained over 90 bhp, but never with the degree of reliability

Three views of the rear boot, showing the built-in rexine cover for luggage. It was normal at the time for luggage to be exposed; the enclosed boot was yet to be developed.

Front end of the chassis of MG 18 hp six.

which would have been needed to compete on level terms with the much simpler and successful design of Georges Roesch in his Talbot. All development work was therefore stopped before the start of 1931, with production of the Mark I ceasing that year, and the Mark II a year later, although new Mark IIs could be bought from stock until well into 1934. Only five Mark III cars were completed, parts being remaindered in special editions of the Mark II or sold off as spares. All of this underlined the fact that the buying public were not of the opinion that the 18 hp MG was what they wanted.

In fact the 18/80 had a fairly successful competition history in both Mark I and Mark II forms, especially in long-distance rallies, Sir Francis Samuelson competing in the Monte Carlo Rally in 1929 in a Mark I and 1930 in a Mark II. Other drivers competed with some success in all types of rally and trial, but perhaps the most remarkable story is that of Morgan Marshall of Bristol who ran in countless MG Car Club and MCC events in his Mark I Speed Model between 1936 and the early 1980s, and logged well in excess of 350,000 miles!

The 18/80 range was a good example, in hindsight, of poor market research before production: they were built to satisfy a real market, but one of limited size and in which there was fierce competition. The Mark I and Mark II cars were good examples of the large vintage car, and were certainly priced keenly when viewed against their competitors. Indeed it is tempting to think of the 18/80 range as being an early attempt at what William Lyons became

Left: Front suspension of the 1929 car, showing Perrot brakes.

Below: Instrumentation for an 18/80 followed this pattern, with seven dials.

Bottom: The complete MG Six chassis.

The 1930 Motor Show chassis. In later years, MGs were to become well known for their sectioned displays.

so good at with his Jaguars twenty years later, producing a high specification car for a comparatively low price. In 1928–31 the market was not so readily available, owing to the general economic depression, and competition was perhaps a little too fierce. However, the cars did demonstrate that MG were in the business of producing good cars at a very competitive price, and they must have worried producers of the more expensive small production models quite considerably, especially those firms which offered smaller engines, less appointments and less performance for more money!

By this time MG were tasting considerable success in a quite different market area, and came to realize that the days of what we now call the vintage car, with its large lazy engine and open body, were over and that commercial success lay in a quite different field.

Above: The early prototype MG Six Chassis No. EX100, which had started life as a Morris straight eight prototype, using a Wolseley engine.

Left: The fabric-covered two-door salonette, and …

Below: The metal-panelled salonette of 1930.

The very handsome 1930 Mark I saloon.

Interior view of the four-door saloon, showing the high degree
of finish.

Above: 1930 four-door tourer, with boot.

Below: 1930 four-door tourer with hood up. Actually the car was snug in this form, and by the standards of the period thoroughly practical transport.

Above: The large 18 hp car did not altogether lend itself to a two-seater body, but this was the result: not at its best-looking with the hood up!

Below: The two-seater with hood down was better-looking, however, even if the dickey seat made it plain that 'two is company, three is none!'

In the early 1960s the MG Car Co. rebuilt this Mark I Speed Model.

Bottom: The final form, now retained by the British Heritage Motor Trust.

This Mark I Speed Model competed in the 1931
Monte Carlo Rally.

Miss Amy Johnson, the aviator, was presented with this Mark I salonette by Lord Nuffield in recognition of her achievements.

The car had a distinctive and appropriate radiator mascot.

The Mark II prototype.

Above & below: 1930 Motor Show Mark II chassis, showing how much more rugged the car had become.

Right: The gear lever of the four-speed box featured a Yale thief lock, anticipating Saab by at least thirty years!

Mark II two-seater, very similar in style to the Mark I.

The Mark II sold best in four-seat tourer form. This particular
car exists to the present day.

The Standard Mark II saloon, which was on offer until well into
1933. It was well appointed, at £695 it needed to be!

Mark II saloons standard…

... and non-standard. This one was built to the order of Colonel Grahame Deakin.

Motoring artist Gordon Grosby had this Mark II de luxe saloon, now in
Jerry Goguen's collection.

Coupé version of the Mark II by Carbodies.

Coupé Mark IIs.

A one-off, to the order of Eastbourne MG dealer Harold Parkinson.

Bottom: Special two-seater by Carbodies, which still exists.

To prove that not all
18/80s were
handsome! Wealthy
enthusiast Mrs
Gough had this car
built in 1931 to
special order, and
one wonders what
Kimber thought of it!

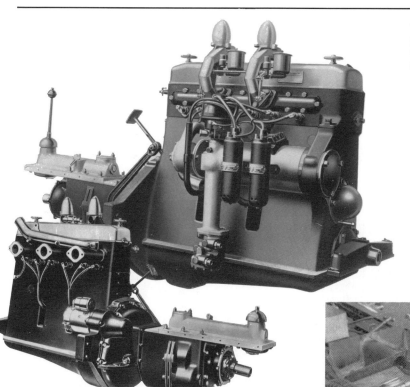

The engine developed for the racing Mark III. Note the special SU carburettors and distributor, and the twin plug head. Power output was disappointing, however.

The 1930 Double Twelve 18/100 Mark III, or 'Tigress' was finished in cream with brown wings. It was a good-looking car, but was old in conception and proved slower than its opposition.

The 1930 Olympia
Motor Show Tigress,
which survives.

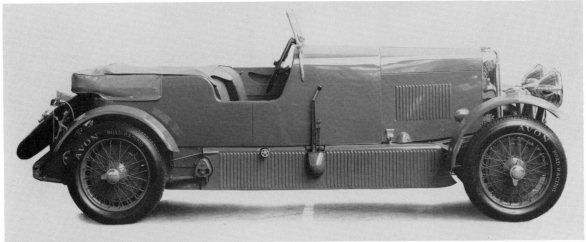

The Rothschild car — the
other Mark III survivor.
Both cars are owned by
Christopher Barker.

3

The Early Midgets

As related in the previous chapter, the 1928 Motor Show saw the introduction of the 18/80 range of MGs at the high end of the price spectrum, while right at the other end was offered the MG Midget. In point of fact neither car was being produced, and the Midget on show did not even have an engine fitted. In the manner of the day, manufacturers often tested reaction to a model design by showing a prototype, and if they took orders, they produced. W.O. Bentley's autobiography reveals that this happened even at the highest planes of manufacture.

The Midget was a direct linear descendent of the Morris Minor, which no doubt Kimber had seen at Cowley, and which was also making its début at the same 1928 Show. Morris cannot have failed to notice the success of the Austin Seven which must have been having an impact on sales of the Cowley range by 1927, by bringing new car motoring to a whole new range of potential buyers. The price of the Morris Cowley was pared to the bone, and the selling price of the Seven was still some £50 less. Until 1927 there was no suitable small engine available to Morris, nor perhaps the finance to design a new unit: there was certainly little spare capacity to produce it. Morris must have therefore cast his eyes around for a small car to act as direct competitor to the baby Austin.

Wolseley were a much respected company but financially insecure, and were available to anyone with capital. Morris bought the company, it is said, to stop Austin doing so, but it is quite likely that Morris saw some potential in the Birmingham factory which had produced some very high quality medium-sized cars, including a 10 hp model which had been in production for some years, and – even if he did not appreciate it before the purchase – it soon became obvious that he had gained access to a very good design team, which actually had an 8 hp engine on the stocks, together with a whole range of closely associated engines. None of these had actually reached production in 1927.

The Wolseley B4 engine was a straightforward derivative of the old 10 hp engine, which in turn owed its advanced design with ohc to the Hispano-Suiza Type W4a aeroplane engine which had been made by Wolseley under licence during the First World War. The B4 was a simple four-cylinder engine of 57 mm bore and 83 mm stroke, giving a capacity of 847 cc. The crankshaft had two main bearings, the front one being a ball-race and the rear a white-metal-lined bronze bush. End float was taken by the front bearing housing through an extension, and between the thrust point and the actual bearing were a bevel gear and a skew gear. The latter drove the oil pump and ignition distributor, while the former drove a vertical shaft which transmitted the drive through another pair of bevels to the overhead camshaft. A novel feature was that the lower part of this shaft was formed by

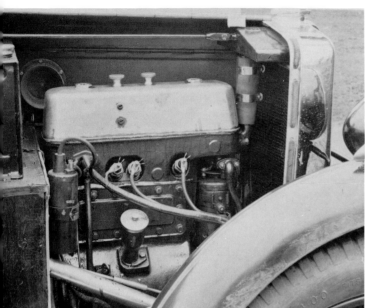

The offside of the M-type engine, displaying the ignition system. The front oil pipe was later altered.

Right: The nearside of the M-type engine, showing the simple manufolding of the 'AA' cylinder head. Note the guarantee plate, which marks this car as Oxford-built!

The M-type chassis, which was simple but effective.

the dynamo armature while the upper part of the shaft was enclosed in the cylinder head, just enough being exposed to couple with the upper end of the dynamo armature using a spring steel coupling. The dynamo was bolted rigidly to the front bearing housing, the electrical services being taken from the side of the casing.

There were several advantages to mounting the dynamo in this position, the principal one being that the heavy armature formed a damper to vibrations emanating from the camshaft drive. There were, of course, no ancillary drives to worry about, but a number of problems did arise, and for many years, as the cars got older, oil got into the dynamo, usually leaking from the housing above, and was liberally spread around the engine compartment by the coupling. Most of these problems were caused by the then-frequent need for engine decarbonization, and the lack of skilled fitters in the retail garage trade to carry out this work. It is easy to sneer at this now, but at the time the Minor was introduced the motor car itself was still barely forty years old, and the majority of garages at that time had been blacksmiths only a few years previously. Furthermore, there was no formal education in motor engineering available for aspiring mechanics, and any apprentice to the trade was taught the blacksmith's art rather than mechanical fitting. The intricacies of ohc drives posed rather different problems from the shoeing of horses or the manufacture of iron gate fittings!

The valves in the cylinder head were slightly inclined to each other at 6 degrees, but unfortunately space considerations dictated that this angle was the 'wrong way' to make the combustion chambers hemispherical. These

The original M-type with external front brake cables.

Although the boot was large, well over 50 per cent of the space was occupied by the spare wheel!

RX5971 was used by H.S. Linfield of *Light Car*, who wrote praising it greatly in several articles.

A 1930 car with hood up, which made for a dry head but cramped driving!

were in fact roughly diamond shaped, and did, in spite of initial appearances, give quite reasonable gas-flow. The valves were operated by the camshaft, using finger followers. Considerable derision has been poured on the camshaft, and it must be admitted that there was no timing overlap, but the conservative nature of the cam timing was very much in the nature of things for the period. Porting was on the nearside of the engine with three exhausts and two inlets, and fairly straight, and a one-piece cast iron

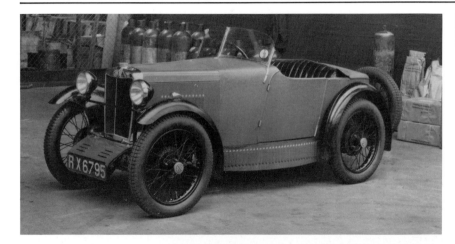

RX 6795: the car which made 100 consecutive ascents of the famous Beggars' Roost Hill.

The prototype Coupé — hardly stylish.

manifold was used in which the exhaust take-off was at the extreme front end, and the inlet manifold was formed below and carried a single 1-inch SU carburettor. The ignition distributor was mounted low down, adjacent to the dynamo at the front, but easily accessible.

Oil was fed to the engine from an external double-gear oil pump, which brought oil from the sump and delivered it to an oil strainer before it was passed to the front main bearing, and thence by external galleries to the rear main and to the cylinder head. There was a large external oil strainer – it was hardly a filter – but it did stop the passage of leaves and similar-sized pieces of unwanted material through the engine! Used oil was returned from the head to the sump by way of two external return pipes. The whole engine had a very clean exterior appearance and looked workmanlike. Initial trials had shown it could produce some 20 bhp, or roughly double the output of the Longbridge side-valve unit, although it was admittedly 100 cc, or about 12 per cent, larger in capacity.

It took Cowley less than six months to design a chassis and running gear and mount a fabric body which was functional rather than pretty! Orders for

The 1929 Morris Minor, from which the M-type MG was derived.

1929 M-type with weather protection up. To say the least, it was not easy to get into the car!

the car, imaginatively called the 'Minor', were instantly forthcoming, and it was in production very quickly, with a two-seater being offered at the magical £100 price. It cannot have taken Kimber long to realize that what Cowley had achieved he could improve upon, and the MG Midget body was designed and built within a few weeks, and offered at £185. If orders for the 18/80 came in with great public interest being shown, orders for the Midget flooded in, and it was soon obvious that MG were on to a winner.

Production actually started in earnest in March 1929. Mechanically the car was almost pure Morris Minor, although the spring camber was decreased, Hartford shock absorbers fitted, and the rake of the steering column was lowered, very much in the manner of conversion of the old 14 hp cars to MG specification. However, the rest of the original Morris Minor was there: the 6-volt electrical system, even the tiny scuttle-mounted fuel tank with gravity feed of fuel to the carburettor, the dreadful fabric universal propeller shaft couplings and the horrible transmission handbrake. Complete chassis were received from Morris Motors, modified as needed, and then mounted with the little two-seater body, all work being carried out at Edmund Road. Each car was run on the Comparator, and a speed in excess of 60 mph was obtained for each car before despatch.

The press were euphoric in its praise, extolling the wonderful virtues of the car. Road test cars had a top speed of just about 65 mph, with a high level of road holding to enable high average speeds to be maintained, and low fuel consumption. If it seems odd now to regard such performance as good, reflect that the top speed of the 14/40 was only 65 mph while that of the comparable Austin Sports was *well* under 55!

In late 1929 a tiny two-seat saloon was added to the range, called the Midget Coupé, which was beautifully appointed but sold in large enough numbers to display that some of the public wanted a closed sporting car, suggesting that the modern generation of sporty saloons is not as 'modern' in conception as we may have thought. The whole concept, whether open or closed, was in reality designed as a sporty rather than a sports car, but its overall performance certainly earned its reputation as a 'real' sports car. A number of publicity stunts were carried out, including 100 consecutive ascents of the famous Beggars Roost hill without stopping the engine, mirroring a similar stunt by a Singer on Porlock Hill. Furthermore, it was not long before examples were found competing in all types of motoring competition and winning awards. Success in MCC Brooklands Members' Day meetings soon opened up a possibility of the little car running in a real race, and a number of cars were prepared for the 1930 Double Twelve race.

Already in production models the brakes had been improved by adopting the MG cable system in place of the Cowley-designed rod and cable system, and the transmission brake was done away with at the same time. For the Double Twelve a new camshaft was designed which gave a small amount of overlap, and an outsize downdraught carburettor was fitted, still fed by gravity from the scuttle-mounted tank, although now of larger capacity. A slightly modified body to comply with the race regulations was concocted, and the regulation Brooklands exhaust system gave the finishing touch to the purposeful little cars. Power was up to around 27 bhp, and one of the teams

The Early Midgets

1929 Sportsman's Coupé: the original fabric-bodied version.

1931 model Coupé with metal-panelled body.

Interior views of the Coupé, which has lately been referred to as the 'Mini Cooper' of the period: actually it was a well-appointed saloon of small scale in the mould of the 18/80s.

The Double Twelve M-type, which gave MG the racing success which they had sought with the Mark III.

A row of Coupés outside the Edmund Road Factory, showing that there was no such thing as standard in 1930!

of cars took the Team Prize. There were great celebrations at Abingdon, almost as though the M-types had won the race outright, and the 18/100 which had made its racing début at this race was quietly pushed into a corner.

A replica of the team cars was catalogued, and around twenty were sold, the asking price being £245, an enormous 32 per cent higher than the standard car, but advertised as having 'every nut split-pinned and ready to race'. However, it is difficult to see how this was meant as a serious attempt to sell a *racing* car, since with a mere 850 cc they would have been forced to run in the 1100 cc class, where they were no match for the Rileys and Amilcars. Two cars did in fact run at Le Mans, and one at Spa, but these forays only underline the truth of this statement.

One result of the Double Twelve car was that the new camshaft timing was standardized on the production cars, the first instance at Abingdon of competition improving the breed. Over the next five years this was to become something of a byword at MG and while to a very real extent it was true, it is equally true that competition activities hastened the demise of the ohc engine. However, in the mid-1930s optimism reigned supreme.

In order to compete with the Austin Seven, MG needed to reduce their engine capacity to 750 cc, but more than that they needed a target to demonstrate that the Midget was being built by people who knew what they were doing. Austin had made several unsuccessful attempts to make the Seven the first 'baby car' to exceed 100 mph, which would be quite a landmark; indeed it was less than five years previously that an AC car had been the first of 1500 cc to exceed the magic 'ton', so to do this with half the capacity seemed then to be attempting the unreasonable. H.N. Charles thought it was possible, but was certain that a complete new chassis was essential for such high speed. He also felt that the Minor chassis was not really suitable for a sports car, and already various drivers had found that the Midget, with its short wheelbase, would spin all too easily, and then was inclined to roll over, due to its high roll centre. The higher the speed the more nervous the car would become, so a lower centre of roll was considered essential. There is little doubt that the Abingdon design team had a good

By 1932 the M-type was out of date, but was offered with metal-panelled body, as shown here. By the end of 1932 it was superseded by the J2.

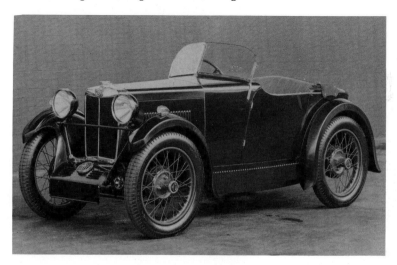

A University Motors special folding-top Coupé, described as the 'University Foursome'. Surely a blatant piece of copywriter's misrepresentation!

One of the most attractive of the special-bodied M-types, the Jarvis: at £255 it must have represented a buy at least as attractive as the works Double Twelve car.

The Montlhéry Midget, or C-type. Altogether more workmanlike than the M-type. The early unsupercharged version.

Above: A race-stained car: probably Norman Black's Irish GP-winning car of 1931.

The supercharged car which was subsequently sold to the Evans brothers, starting a five-year association with MG Cars.

look at a variety of chassis designs, and while photographs appear in the Cowley photographic files of a French car called the Rally, the eventual design was no slavish copy of this design and incorporated several features of original design. Indeed, close study of the photographs of the Rally show only that it was underslung at the rear, and that there were precious few similarities beyond that between the Rally and the eventual MG chassis.

Coded 'EX115' the overall chassis design was to form the basis of most MG chassis for the next ten years. The frame was a simple ladder type, with parallel sides separated by tubular cross-members, the outer ends of which also formed the fulcrum points for the suspension springs. The springs themselves were pivoted at the front end, while the rear ends slid in bronze trunnions. This system, of which there are several contemporary examples including Aston Martin, has the advantage over conventional swinging shackles in that it does not allow lateral movement of the axles across the line of the frame. It has the disadvantage that, as the bronze trunnions wear, the springs can move sideways, and they then become noisy which is the reason MG eventually stopped using them. The frame was swept over the front axle, but passed under the rear. Hartford shock absorbers were provided to damp spring movements.

Design of a complete car, coded EX120, followed rapidly once the chassis layout was finalized. The engine was arranged rigidly on a three-point mounting in the frame to stiffen the front end, and the whole chassis was therefore seen to fulfil the requirement of a low centre of gravity. Initially there is little doubt that the car was seen as an '850' and a straight replacement for the M-type. Thoughts of a 750 must have occurred around mid-1930, but design of a suitable crankshaft was not rapid enough to build a suitable engine for a 100 mph record attempt, which was becoming urgent owing to the effort being expended at Longbridge to achieve the same result sooner. A cylinder block was therefore bored to 54 mm, rather than the standard 57, and a standard crank and rods assembly was prepared, but the crankpin journals were reground to give a stroke of 81 mm, which could be accomplished easily on an unfinished forging, and then it was finished off by being polished all over and carefully balanced. The cylinder head was prepared in such a way that friction was, as far as practicable, eliminated, needle roller bearings being used for the camshaft. Reg Jackson, who was in charge of the preparation of this engine, told me that there was no component which was not polished, and that the engine would turn without aid under the closing pressure of a valve spring. It was capable of running at in excess of 7,000 rpm, an exceptionally high crankshaft speed for the period.

A body which bore a passing resemblance to the M-type was hastily concocted for the car from spare sheet metal. A four-speed ENV gearbox was used, probably as it was the only unit commercially available at short notice: the Wolseley four-speed was still a year away from production. It was rather large for the power outputs envisaged, the same gearbox being found in the 2-litre AC of the period; however, it had good ratios and was one component which seldom gave any trouble. With a small supercharger fitted, 100 mph was achieved at Montlhéry in January 1931, and the speeds reached were all

The original presentation of the C-type, with radiator cowled. This proved unsuccessful in racing and was not continued after the initial batch of fourteen cars.

The prototype four-seat Midget, D-type.

improved upon at Brooklands two months later, followed by 101.1 miles in one hour back at Montlhéry in September. All this was carried out in the twelve months since the first assembly of the chassis frame! But that was not all that was achieved.

William Morris cannot have failed to be impressed with the news value and free publicity which firstly the Double Twelve and then 100 mph had generated, and this was probably instrumental in the development of the C-type racing car. John Thornley was at pains to point out in his famous book, *Maintaining the Breed*, that the primary job at Abingdon was the production of cars for sale for use on the highways; indeed he says that it was always appreciated at Abingdon that there were few buyers for pure racing cars, so it was important that a road car was developed in parallel with any racing project. However, the success of the Montlhéry exploits led very quickly to the production of the C-type, while the D-type lagged behind by some five months and its introduction was timed to coincide with the new small six-cylinder car.

The C-type was a production version of EX120. The new short-stroke crankshaft was available, although not fully counterbalanced until later in 1931; in fact one of these was used in the Brooklands repeat of the 100 mph runs, and so the bore of the engine reverted to 57 mm. Another camshaft was designed, with timing which was found to be so good that it became the standard for most of the ohc cars produced subsequently, and referred to henceforth as 'standard timing', although the C-type engine was the only one with the AA head so fitted. The single downdraught carburettor was inherited from the 12/12 M-type, but a large fuel tank was fitted at the rear of the car, fed by electric fuel pumps. The body was a two-seater, and had a

The D-type.

D-type instrument panel.

The production version of the D-type, which has attractive lines, making up for the overall lack of performance!

The J-type engine, as fitted to J1 and J2 cars.

The J-type chassis.

The J3 engine, showing its small supercharger. The engine had shorter stroke than the J1 and J2, giving a 750 cc displacement, and used up the original batch of C-type crankshafts.

shapely cowl over the radiator. The scuttle was brought to two cowled humps, a feature which became so typical of the sports car shape for the next twenty-five years. The rear of the body was shaped to a point, like the M-type. The new car was priced at a very competitive £295, a mere £50 (or 20 per cent) more than the Double Twelve replica, and this for a brand new design which was destined to be a great success in competition.

The actual racing successes of the C-type will not be chronicled in detail, but at its first outing in the Double Twelve at Brooklands in May 1931, it won not only the Team Prize, but also the race outright. Racing was the primary purpose of the C-type, and its power output was increased by 40 per cent by supercharging, and in this form it was able to win the TT in September, just in time for the introduction of the D-type at the London Motor Show in October.

The D-type Midget had a slightly longer wheelbase than the C-type, but was in all essentials identical in layout, having the more sensible 12-volt electrical system, and having the underslung chassis and Rudge wheels. The engine and three-speed gearbox were taken from the M-type, which was still in production, although a neat remote control was fitted to the gearbox. No two-seater was offered, the bodywork being either an open or closed four-seater. Fuel was brought from a rear-mounted tank by an electric SU fuel pump. The whole car was very pretty, if a little short in bonnet length, but suffered from a distinct lack of power, for it was quite heavy. The

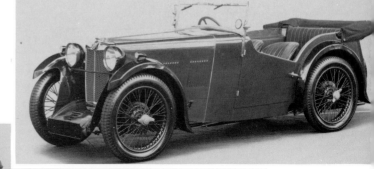

The J1 tourer, showing what a handsome little car it was.

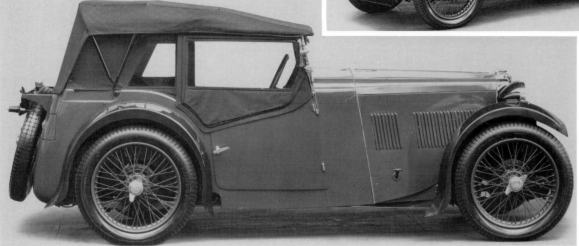

The J1 saloon was quite good-looking, but the short bonnet gave it a stunted side-on appearance.

decision to keep the M-type in production, now with a metal panelled body, was probably coloured by the fact that development of the C-type was leading to greatly increased power, and a completely new car was by this time already on the horizon.

Supercharging the C-type had brought up a number of new problems, of which overheating and mixture distribution were the most chronic. It will be recalled that the cylinder head had but five ports, and all these on one side of the casting. The combustion chamber shape was cross-flow, and so the incoming charge from the carburettor had to double back to gain entry to the valve head. Charles no doubt got to know the road from Abingdon to Ward End quite well at this time, and a new design of cross-flow head was produced, with opposed porting (referred to as AB as opposed to AA for the earlier type) and having eight ports altogether. Water passages were revised, and a power increase of 20 per cent was achieved unblown. Needless to say, the head was immediately made available to all C-type owners, who were acting as unpaid testers! Power produced by the supercharged engines was increased by rather more, and about this time triple valve springs were introduced along with the legendary steel gasket, which solved the head gasket problems which had arisen.

The J2 Midget. The original 1932 version is considered by many to be one of the classic sports cars of all time.

The J2 dash panel was functional, with all controls easy to reach.

From side and rear views, the J2 was uncompromisingly a sports car.

The J3, which was only differentiated from the J2 by the larger front cowl, hiding the supercharger.

The J4 — no doubt that this was a racing sports car: its front cowl, larger than on the J3, hid a large Powerplus blower, while the exhaust supplied was to Brooklands Regulation pattern.

JB1047 was the works demonstration J3 but, fitted with a J4 engine, it took several long-distance records.

Engines were regularly run to well over 6,000 rpm, the official maximum, and were on the whole fairly reliable. A new design of connecting rod, eliminating the small-end clamp bolt and introducing a fully floating gudgeon pin overcame connecting rod failure, and was introduced into production during 1932. Oddly enough, 1932 saw the number of MG successes dwindle, but this was largely due to the fact that most races were run on handicap, and success tends to make the handicapper more severe!

By the end of 1932 the whole Midget range was due for rationalization, and the M, C and D-type cars gave way to the J-series. It is nice to think that the J-types were just built up for the Motor Show, but the truth is a long way from that. It is fairly certain that work on the M-type replacement, a two-seater car, had started alongside the C and D-types, but that increased power with long-term reliability was not found easy to achieve. Furthermore, it is more than probable that work on the AB cylinder head for the C-type could only be justified if built in large enough numbers for normal production. The new head was first used in the British Racing Drivers' Club 1,000-mile race at Brooklands in May, and was so successful that it was in full production within six months.

The J-type chassis followed the pattern set out in the D-type, but the engine and gearbox, not to mention the new two-seater body, were quite different. The engine retained the crankcase layout which had proved so successful, and the cylinder head was the AB C-type unit, with the standard valve timing and two SU carburettors, as used latterly on the C-type unblown racers. The four-seat bodies, both open and closed, were similar to the D-type, the open car featuring the humped scuttles and doors with a deep cut-away along its top edge: this model was called the J1.

The two-seat body was simple, with cut-away door tops, humped scuttles and a large fuel tank mounted vertically outside the rear of the body. The spare wheel was mounted behind this tank, and the whole car looked every inch a sports car; indeed its outline is undoubtedly one of the classic car shapes: simple, functional, but above all good to look at. This model was of course the legendary J2 Midget.

Late in 1933 all J2s were offered with a revised mudguard pattern, referred to as 'swept wings'. Opinions are divided as to the resulting aesthetics.

Two J-type Coupés — above from the Czechoslovakian firm of Uhlik, and below from the London
Van den Plas company.

There was a supercharged version of the J2 available, called the J3, the engine of this being 750 cc, with the same bore and stroke as the racing cars, but without the counterbalanced crankshaft, presumably using up the batch of early C-type cranks. The bodywork was closely similar to that of the J2 and was obviously intended as a road car, removing the criticism that the C-type had not been a practical car for road use, with its doorless body. This proved a formidable car in the milder sporting events, such as rallies and trials, and one example actually took long-distance records, although with a J4 engine fitted, while retaining its smaller blower.

The real racing car was the J4, which was similar in outline to the J2, but had no doors, and had a full house racing engine employing the very latest thinking, developing a great deal of power and proving a very fast car. The J4 featured the split track-rod steering which will be described in detail in the next chapter, and braking was improved by fitting 12-inch drums which went some way to checking the speeds of which the car was capable. However, the car was exploring the limits of the chassis design, and was not an easy car to drive to its limit. An unblown version was catalogued as the J5, but no cars were sold in this form.

The press went overboard in their praise of the new cars, and speeds of around 80 mph were reported for the J2. We now know that there was an element of 'hotting up' applied to the engine of the road test car, and although standard cars would just better the 70 mark with the windscreen erect, the degree of tuning applied to the press car was hardly excessive, having slightly raised compression, and it was no real problem for owners to get their cars to achieve the road test figure, putting only the fatigue life of their crankshaft at risk!

The rather skimpy nature of the front wings, which allowed for a generous washing of the cars' occupants with rain water when negotiating turns in wet weather, was coming in for criticism. This feature was countered by the introduction in late 1933 of the swept wings, similar to those fitted to the Magna and Magnette models, but these tended to detract from the general sporty look of the original design, not quite harmonizing with the rest of the body.

J2s were soon featuring in trials, and quite a few were raced with success. The only problem was that if pressed for too long at very high speed the poor two-bearing 'bent wire' crankshaft suffered from vibration and broke. This was further complicated by the fact that even the production engine was by this time in a fairly high state of tune, developing roughly twice the original design power for the crank, and it would also fatigue crack if run at low revs under load. You just could not win, and the factory issued a service instruction to the effect that the cranks should not be reground in service. This was acceptable since a new one was only £5 10s 0d! A factory modification was introduced to eliminate crankshaft roughness, which incorporated an additional front ball-race, but this did not stop the crank from breaking. In truth, it was obvious that a new engine design was needed, but work was proceeding apace with a completely different sort of car... perhaps this might provide an answer?

4

Magnas and Magnettes

The move to Abingdon saw the end of the old side-valve cars, and production was now based on the very successful 8 hp Midget and the limited market 18 hp cars, one selling for just under £200, the others ranging upwards in price from just over two-and-a-half times that figure. Kimber would obviously like a car to fill the gap, but what could do it? The standard Morris range was still bolstered by the 12/14 hp side-valve range, which even in Morris form was not selling as well as it had: there was simply no getting away from the fact that the cars were old-fashioned. It is true that they had improved both in looks and in specification, but a more up-to-date car was still a couple of years away. Wolseley on the other hand had a range of cars which might fit the bill, with the 12 hp Hornet and 16 hp cars, which became the Viper model in 1931, as primary contenders. Both of these were powered by six-cylinder engines having recognizable connections with the Midget engine, which was made by Wolseley anyway. They both featured the vertical dynamo camshaft drive, but the Hornet engine was a straightforward six-cylinder derivative of the M-type engine, having the same bore and stroke, while the 16 hp engine was, at 2025 cc, a little too near 18/80 size for comfort: the 18 hp car was only selling slowly, so would a 16 fare any better?

At this point it would be pertinent to look at the reasons why six-cylinder engines were popular in the 1925–35 period. Four-cylinder engines were fairly harsh running units, a fact which was highlighted by the use of solid mountings of engines into the chassis. Also the transmissions of cars were notoriously difficult to operate, with heavy clutch operation and non-synchronized gearboxes making for a lazy style of driving, in which one aimed to complete a journey with a minimum of gear-changing. This, in turn, led to heavy flywheels which tended to emphasize the uneven running of the engine, especially at low crankshaft speeds. One solution to the problem was the adoption of the smoother running six-cylinder engine, which by 1930 was enjoying a considerable vogue, following the example set by Continental manufacturers, who found that low gearing and high-speed small capacity engines could be combined successfully to propel large bodies.

We do not know when the decision was taken at Abingdon to produce a small six-cylinder car, but it was announced in the press in September 1931. The Wolseley Hornet was not an inspiring car when viewed as a sports car: indeed this it was not, being in effect a long Morris Minor, even retaining the three-speed gearbox. The Hornet at this stage was aiming at the sort of market which looked for basic appointments coupled with a degree of refinement, which even in 1930 was the growing market area, so in consequence it was selling briskly, way above the levels envisaged at Abingdon; so there was a real market for the small six sports car having

The F-type Magna chassis, clearly showing its close resemblance to the C and D MG Midgets. It is far removed from the Wolseley Hornet, from which the engine was derived.

family connections with the Midget. Once again the Kimber appreciation of filling a market slot with an improved version of the original at a substantially higher price was the inspiration, and it is likely that design started at around the same time as that of the Montlhéry Midget in late 1930.

If the Hornet was a stretched Minor, then the Magna was a stretched Midget, but the derivative in this case was not the M-type but the C and

The L-type Magna was different from the F-type, especially in the engine department: note the opposed port cylinder head fitted to the 1100 cc engine.

D-types which, in turn, derived from EX120. In this respect the car may be considered a true MG rather than a modified Hornet, which other writers seem to be at pains to make it. Apart from the engine and the steering box, there is no major component common between the Magna and the Hornet, and the latter car was to have a new engine by the end of 1931 when the Magna was introduced. There was the delightful ENV gearbox from the C-type which enabled good use to be made of the flat torque curve of the engine. The frame was ten inches longer than the D-type but the axles were similar. The car ran on centre-lock Rudge wheels and a choice of close-coupled open or closed four-seat body was offered, similar to that of the D-type but with a much longer bonnet.

The engine was closely similar to the Hornet unit, and has been referred to as an 'M-type plus two cylinders'. This is an over-simplification, however. For while it did have a more than passing resemblance to the M-type unit, it was far more robust in construction, both crankshaft and camshaft running in four main bearings. As in the M-type, the front crank bearing was a ball-race, with the end thrust being taken in the front housing which also enclosed drives to the camshaft, distributor and oil pump. The two intermediate crank bearings were bronze-backed white-metal-lined shells carried in duralumin housings which were clamped to the crankshaft before it was fed into the crankcase from the front, where they were an interference fit, and then located in position using long through bolts: a system which was to serve well for the next six years. The rear main bearing was a white-metal-lined bronze bush similar to that of the Midget. The rear crank journal was fed through from the rear end and fitted to the crankshaft on a taper with key location, as on the Midget. The whole assembly was very rigid, but a little small in diameter of journals. The early engines had, unlike the Midget, duralumin connecting rods with bronze-liners for the white-metal big end bearings. These needed very careful assembly, and were not very successful: in 1932 replacement of bearings was a regular chore!

The F2 Magna of
1932: if anything,
more handsome
than the J2, which
had a similar body.

The cylinder head was pure Wolseley, having all the ports along the nearside, and there were only nine in total, four inlet and five exhaust. The camshaft was of similar proportions and timing to the original M-type, which was a mixed blessing. Twin carburettors were fitted to the large one-piece cast iron manifold, with the exhaust being taken from the front like the Midget. The engine was a very tidy-looking unit, and this was enhanced by the fitting of steel cladding plates on each side, which did little for the over-worked cooling system: indeed I have seen only one engine on which these plates were retained. Cooling must have been a problem on the F-type engine, since it was provided with a fan, the only ohc car to be so equipped as standard. Drive was taken from a clutch similar in design to the M, but with more friction area, to the massive ENV gearbox already mentioned and thence by a Hardy Spicer propshaft to a conventional rear axle. Axles and brake gear were directly interchangeable with those of the D-type.

The car was well received by the press critics of the time, who praised its ability to pull from 5 mph in top without snatch, as well as its gearbox, and – surprisingly – its brakes, which achieved a 30 ft stop from 30 mph without making the car swerve! In truth, the F-type was not a bad car; it suffers in hindsight from the fact that all its direct successors were better which is the fate of many initial designs. True, the engine was not especially powerful, nor was it in itself capable of a significant improvement when tuned – at least not with reliability, but the designs which followed it proved beyond doubt that the basic essentials were sound. Furthermore the rate of development at Abingdon at this time was nothing short of phenomenal.

No sooner was the model in production than the MG design staff were trying to improve the power. Late in 1931 an engine with higher compression, 12/12 valve timing and larger carburettors was tested and gave 47 bhp, an improvement of some 27 percent over standard, but deficiencies in the cooling system were shown up, as well as the weakness of the dural main bearing housings and connecting rods, which resulted in a revision of the cooling system, the provision of steel main bearing casings and the use of J-type connecting rods during 1932. Later in 1932 a two-seater version of the F was introduced and called the F2, being very similar in appearance to the J2 except that it was also fitted with 12-inch diameter brake gear, which was just becoming available to the owners of the C-type racing cars. The four-seat cars were also fitted with the larger brakes, this model being called the F3.

A far more important consequence of the engine trial in late 1931 was that at this stage Charles must have visited Wolseley to see what they could do to improve power output without impairing reliability. This was brought to a head by the fact that Wolseley were going to chain drive for their camshafts, in the interests of shortening the rather long engine, thus enabling them to shorten the bonnets of their cars, most of which carried capacious saloon bodies. Now in 1931 a sports car *had* to have a long bonnet, so Abingdon had every reason to follow this course, and it is quite likely that Charles just did not *want* a chain drive. If anyone wonders why, let it be said that chain drives at this time were not notable for quiet running or reliability. In the case of the 18/80 these inherent problems were overcome by the use of a

The F1 Magna of 1931, as originally introduced. It had a rakish line —
indeed, it looked fast. In the manner of the old 14/40, it could cover
ground well, but absolute performance was not really present.

The Abbey-bodied coupé on an F1 chassis.

Below: The Stiles-bodied threesome was a popular model, and several survive.

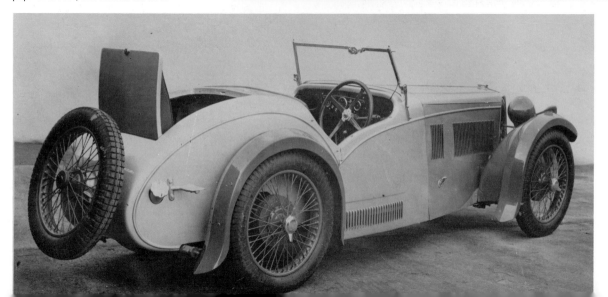

three-stage drive, which if anything was more complicated than the shaft drive. If the vertical dynamo had its problems, Abingdon obviously felt that the devil they knew was better than some unknown demon!

Interestingly it was only after the war when Jaguar produced their XK engine that designers took chain drives for ohc engines seriously. Although several had been tried, and some enjoyed limited success, mass production cars had not been notably successful, chiefly, I believe, for the lack of a suitable reliable chain tensioner to take up the stretch of the long chain associated with ohc during service, and even the Wolseley ended as a 'lost cause' in 1935, when they were forced to adopt simpler engines. It is interesting to record that they reverted to shaft drive for their new ohc engine which was introduced after the war.

On a more practical level, of course, Wolseley were not interested in the four-cylinder engines, which were by this time being produced for MG only, Morris having reverted to side-valve operation for the Minor. So it is quite possible that MG opted for the vertical dynamo so that the Midget and Magna engines had as many common parts as possible and that they did not have to foot the bill for designing a new camshaft drive for the Midget engine!

The prototype saloon F1.

It is quite likely that Charles's attention was being focused on the next international capacity class for competition, the 1100 cc class, into which the new car should slot in logical progression from the success of the Midget. Also it seems likely that he saw the engine as needing to be supercharged from the outset. It appears that Robin Jackson, no relation of Reg Jackson of MG, had worked on a supercharged version of the Magna during the early part of 1932, but this was not an especial success. The engine was eventually bought by Richard Bolster and installed in his GN-based special, but

The production version of the F1 — better-looking, and well appointed.

Lord Howe posing with his car, finished in black with roof panels in his personal shade of blue.

although it was initially fast, one of the duralumin connecting rods broke, and the engine was scrapped. This story has a happy ending, for the car still exists, now fitted with a modified later Magnette engine.

The result of discussions with the Ward End engine designers was that MG got an engine to suit H.N. Charles's requirement, retaining the basic crankcase design, but dispensing with the ball-race at the front, substituting a plain bearing, increasing the crankshaft dimensions and improving the oiling arrangements to the crankshaft, increasing the size of the oil pump and

The L2 Magna, considered by many the best-looking MG — but roadholding was not up to Midget or Magnette standards.

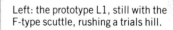

Above and below: The L1 Magna was a
nice-looking car.

Left: the prototype L1, still with the
F-type scuttle, rushing a trials hill.

incorporating full-flow oil filtration. Connecting rods were redesigned, and the flywheel was made considerably lighter. However, if the bottom of the engine was improved, the lessons learned from the J-series engines allowed for the cylinder head to be transformed! Porting of the new cylinder head was of the cross-flow type with six inlets and six exhausts, and of generous proportions. The basic layout of the valve gear was retained but increased in dimensions which allowed for lower contact pressures and, in theory, would improve reliability. Dubbed the K-series, this engine, put alongside the F, showed that there was practically nothing interchangeable apart from nuts and bolts, and even these were coincidental, since few sizes shared the same job on the two engines!

Here starts one of the more complicated phases of MG nomenclature, for the K-series engine immediately appeared in no less than three guises, known in the factory as KA, KB and K3, and these were shortly followed by the KC! All four units retained the 57 mm bore of earlier engines, but had a 71 mm stroke, giving a displacement of 1086 cc. This allowed the engine to fit into the 1100 cc international class for racing and record-breaking purposes, which must have been a primary objective. The new smaller displacement engine was to appear in a new range of chassis named the Magnette, presumably a small Magna. The cars were much more robustly built than their predecessors, and one feels that Kimber had his eyes on the up-market area typified by the Riley range of small saloons and tourers. While the products of the Coventry factory were very nicely built and featured several advanced designs, the prices were high.

The KA had a special camshaft of 'slower' timing than the now standard MG engine, this being done for the engine to be installed in a saloon car, and coupled without intermediate clutch to a preselector gearbox made by ENV to Wilson patents. Because of this, the engine idle speed needed to be less than 500 rpm, otherwise the car tended to creep unless checked with the brakes – the standard valve timing will not allow for such a low idle speed. It had magneto ignition and triple SU carburettors, which made the maintenance of this low speed somewhat tricky, but that is another story! For those not familiar with the operation of the preselector gearbox, it is simple to use in that one selects a gear and *then* uses the clutch pedal to engage it, thus obviating the need for careful synchronization of hand and foot operation which bedevilled most early motorists. Needless to say, the operation required some finesse and was foolproof, but like all foolproof mechanisms it bred a new generation of fools! However the Wilson gearbox enjoyed considerable vogue until the coming of the true automatic transmissions.

The KB had the standard valve timing, and carried a twin-plate clutch to drive through a four-speed gearbox of the same type as now fitted to the Wolseley Hornet, although fitted with a remote control which at first glance looks like that of the ENV box fitted to the F-type. In all other respects the KA and KB engines were identical.

These two engines appeared at the time of the 1932 Motor Show. The KA was fitted exclusively to a so-called 'pillarless' saloon of pleasing lines mounted on a long wheelbase chassis, while the KB was available in short

Kimber's Folly! The L1 Continental Coupé, which was a
nicely appointed car which few wanted. The order for 100
reputedly took 100 weeks to sell!

The L1 Saloon was not as handsome as the F, but was more practical.

The University Motors foursome on an L-type chassis: at least one survives; the author built up the chassis for its owner a number of years ago.

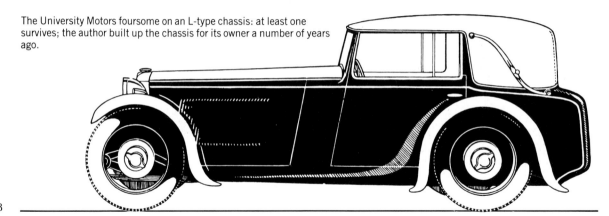

The original Magnette was a saloon, and
JB550 was the first one. It was a pillarless
saloon, well appointed, but a little
overweight, necessitating low overall
gearing.

and long chassis open forms. The two chassis were basically similar in layout to the F-type, but of much heavier construction. The track was six inches wider at 4 ft, the wheelbase being 9 ft on the K1 and 7 ft 10 in. on the K2. Both cars featured 13-inch brakedrums, while the brakes were still cable-operated.

One of the more revolutionary features was the adoption of a split track-rod system in the steering gear, which was designed by Charles to help to overcome the conflicting forces imposed by the more conventional layout, commonly known as 'kickback'. In this system the steering box operated a transverse draglink which, instead of operating directly on the nearside steering arm, bore on a slave idler arm mounted near the centre of the axle beam. Two short track rods connected this idler arm to the steering arms attached to the stub axles. It was undoubtedly a clever solution to an age-old problem which bedevilled beam axle steering layouts, and was used on all MG racing cars in 1933–34 as well as on all K-series cars.

The long-chassis open car had a capacious four-seater body, while the K2 carried a more conventional two-seater body. All the K-type cars had graceful swept wings, but were nowhere near as handsome in two-seater form as the J2 Midgets or the F2 Magnas announced at the same time.

The KC engine appeared in early 1933, not in a K-type but in a new car, the L-type Magna, this being a replacement for the F-type. The KC was presumably designed as an economy version, since it sported only two carburettors, and had coil ignition. It also had a cheaper dynamo and a number of other detail differences, but in all essentials was a K-type. The L-type chassis was very similar in all details to the F2/3 which it replaced, although the gearbox was similar to that fitted to the K-type, but using the Wolseley remote control as used in the J-type. With its long swept wings the L-type car was pretty, and in two-seat form better-looking than the F, but in four-seat and saloon form, however, it was not as successful in looks.

Cecil Kimber in his special Corsica-bodied K1, which was supercharged, and capable of 100 mph — at 6,500 rpm!

Abbey-bodied K1 hard-top Coupé.

KN chassis fitted with a
Whittingham & Mitchell Coupé body.

The K3 engine was fitted to the most famous of all the pre-war MG models and probably the most successful 1100 cc racing car of all time. Basically a supercharged K2, the K3 car was conceived from the outset as a serious class contender in competition: as John Thornley remarked in his *Maintaining the Breed* it could 'leave no doubt that it was designed to go fast, keep right way

Abbey-bodied K1 Coupé.

The K1 Tourer was a spacious car, a genuine four-seater.

The K2 two-seater had a similar mechanical specification to the K1 originally, but later in 1933 was fitted with the KD engine, of 1271 cc, two carburettors and pre-selector gearbox.

up, and keep on going'. It could be a proud boast of MG that no driver has ever been killed in a K3, if that were not seen as tempting fate.

The chassis frame was closely similar to that of the K2, but incorporated an additional cross-brace behind the gearbox. The brakedrums were special, having cast iron liners screwed into the elektron drums, but the rest of the running gear was common with the more mundane Magnettes, although the wheel hubs were slightly longer for the racing cars. The gearbox was a preselector, and for a racing car it enabled instant gear control, and instantaneous changes of ratio with little effort from the driver – beyond remembering which gear was preselected!

For 1933 the K3 could be bought with the standard two-seater body, with a large fuel tank carried behind, and bearing a very close resemblance to the J4 Midget. The coachbuilt body was fairly heavy in standard form, but various

The 1933 K3 Magnette, an uncompromising competition car. JB1474 was the Birkin/Rubin Mille Miglia car, while JB1475 was driven by Lurani and Eyston. Both cars survive.

The K3 chassis — these pictures of the 1934 car show the Marshall supercharger and pre-selector gearbox control.

cars through the year carried lightweight and superficially similar bodies – truly the age where the road car and race car looked very similar! Indeed the works actually produced a lightweight body for racing which was known at the factory as the 'skimpy', and had no wooden frame. In general the coachbuilt body was used for long-distance events, such as rallies and the Mille Miglia, while the skimpy was used for track racing and road events such as the TT.

The K3 engine as originally conceived used all standard components found in the other variants. In fact all the time the factory were involved directly in racing, standard crankshafts and connecting rods were used, and replaced after every race. Subsequently many cars were fitted with Laystall cranks and special connecting rods both of standard design and later to improved specification. Special valves became available fairly early on, and these were used in conjunction with triple-valve springs for sprint use, although in long-distance racing double springs were generally used, in an attempt to prevent drivers from over-revving too much. Really, the principal difference between the K3 unit and that fitted to a production car was the way in which it was assembled. The production units were mounted in the chassis as received from Birmingham. The units destined for the racing cars were completely stripped at Abingdon and then carefully rebuilt by the racing shop; Reg Jackson told me once that between 50 and 100 hours were spent on this operation for every K3 engine, and that this was repeated every time the engine was returned to the Works – is it surprising that the cars went so well?

Late in 1933 the K-type engine took on another variant when it reverted to the original bore and stroke, increasing the capacity to 1271 cc and became the KD. This was offered in the whole touring K-type range, and was generally coupled with the preselector gearbox. The standard valve timing was used, and the objections of excessive 'creep' were overcome by the simple expedient of using a clutch between the engine and gearbox which disconnected the drive when neutral was engaged. This system is much more elegant than fluid or centrifugal couplings, which were never very reliable, or suffered constant slippage, and one wonders why other manufacturers did not take up the idea. The KD engine also featured twin carburettors, but unlike the L-type unit these were carried on a manifold with greater separation, another lesson learned by racing the cars, in this case the L-type, which ran successfully with the new manifold in the JCC Relay Race at Brooklands. The chief advantage of the KD engine was that it gave 25 per cent more power than the KB or KC units, and this did give the Magnettes a new lease of life.

However, this was short lived, for less than six months later a new cylinder head was available, and further improvements were available for the cylinder block and crankshaft. These were a direct result of racing the K3s. A complete new engine was available. Meanwhile developments in the chassis department had resulted in a completely new frame and system for mounting the body, and in March 1934 the N-type Magnette was announced.

The N-type engine was said in 1934 to have a capacity of 1286 cc, but I have found at least one contemporary reference to the KD having this capacity,

Jensen built this body for W.E.C. Watkinson on a
1934 K3. The body is now fitted to a K2.

The 1934 K3 was even more uncompromisingly a racing car than the earlier model.

The KN Magnette Saloon, dubbed 'hot stuff' by the press, was the final flowering and the best of the variations on the K-theme.

and personal experience has shown the stroke of all 'long' crankshafts measured to be 83 mm, which gives a capacity of 1271 cc. It now seems that the extra millimetre of stroke was introduced in a crude attempt to distance still further the products of Abingdon from those of Birmingham! Be that as it may, the new engine gave a further improvement of 25 per cent in power output, and the N-type was much lighter than the K had been, so that it resulted in a very lively little car. The clutch was a single-plate type, actually very similar to that which had been used on the KD-powered cars, but was connected to a Wolseley gearbox similar to that in the L-type and operated directly by the foot pedal.

The chassis deserves special mention since it was the first MG frame since 1930 not to be a simple ladder frame. It was wider at the rear than the front, cross-members being large-diameter tubes. At each side were mounted short outrigger members carried on Silentbloc bushes, and it was to these that the body was attached, being supported at the rear on other brackets insulated from primary chassis shocks by Silentblocs. The result of this was that the cars were very comfortable to ride in.

The NA chassis, displaying the body outriggers, and the much improved engine, to prove the last of the ohc units in production pre-war.

The engine detail, exhaust side.

The KN chassis.

Bodywork styles offered were two- and four-seaters, with a long sloping tail enclosing the fuel tank. A few cars were built using the old K2 slab-tank bodies and these were known around the factory as NK or ND, the latter designation now being used. These cars were sold to those who intended using them in trials, but in fact the standard two-seaters were probably lighter and were actually more successful in competition. A standard two-seater car was road-tested at a speed of over 80 mph while the journalist MacGinnis stated that he had maintained high speed in a four-seater for many miles. Truly the Magnette was a sports car with a great performance for its time.

The K3 continued as an 1100 cc racing car, with a body which featured a long tail including a massive fuel tank, and a Marshall supercharger in place of the Powerplus previously fitted, which gave less boost but needed less lubrication, which in turn allowed the engine to run with a smaller appetite for sparking plugs. Power output was kept up by increasing the static compression ratio, and the cars were faster than those of the previous year for reasons of lighter weight, coupled with improved braking power. This was achieved by using another simple system, anchoring the outer cable to a lever which operated on one brake shoe when the inner cable pulled on the other, thus ensuring that a maximum of effort was applied to the brake shoes. However, the days of the K3 were numbered; nothing is static in the world of motor racing, and better designs were being fostered by the very success of the K3, but by other manufacturers.

Meanwhile the true competition version of the N-type was the NE, a car built specifically to win the 1934 TT, the regulations for which banned superchargers for the first time, and therefore the K3. Not only were MG successful, but in winning they became the first marque to win the TT in successive years, and the first to win it three times.

The NE was basically an NA chassis and running gear, with an improved engine power output brought about by a better camshaft and larger

The NA two-seater was a handsome car, if somewhat tall, but very comfortable to ride in.

carburettors. The old twin-plate clutch took the drive to a close ratio gearbox, later to be standardized on the N-type road cars, but otherwise the car was identical in running gear to the standard car. The bodywork used was made to comply with the race rules, which oddly precluded the use of the standard two-seater body as this was too wide! A larger than standard fuel tank was enclosed in the tail, and I will upset a few people by saying the result was a good-looking car – which just goes to prove that beauty is in the eye of the beholder. The NE was capable of 100 mph while the engine was revved in the race to well in excess of 6000 rpm which, if nothing else, underlined the road test reports on standard cars which claimed that 5500 rpm could be used safely.

The two-tone colour scheme enhanced the NA's looks.

Around the time of the TT the N-type appeared in two new body styles, the 2/3 seat Allingham Coupé, which resurrected the dickey seat, and the closed Airline Coupé which was a really attractive car. At the same time the K-type pillarless saloon reappeared as the KN, dubbed by a press wit 'hot stuff', powered by the N-type engine, and quite a fast little saloon with a 75 mph top speed and good acceleration. The KN also appeared in open form, using up stocks of the K1 tourer body, these apparently being mainly sold by the London MG distributor University Motors as the 'UM Speed Model Magnette'. During 1935 the model range was rationalized, and only the two-seater, four-seater and Airline were catalogued, together with the KN saloon. The KN was unchanged, but the N-type had a revised scuttle line,

The 1935 N-Magnette, now referred to as the NB, with reversed colour scheme and reversed door hinges!

The four-seat version of the NB revealing the lower scuttle line.

AXN637, an Allingham, was driven by W.E.C. Watkinson in the 1934 RAC Rally.

slatted radiator grille, and doors were hinged at the front. This variant was announced at the same time as the PB Midget, and the revised Magnette was known at the factory as the NB although it was never marketed as such.

As related in the next chapter the wind of change was blowing through Abingdon, and the days of the high revving ohc engines were numbered; however, the sixes continued until well into 1936, and the N-type was the last of the series to remain in production. Late in 1935 three special cars were built for the Three Musketeer trials team based on the Magna/Magnette range, but these were not strictly production cars.

The Allingham Coupé, built by Whittingham J. Mitchell, was a listed body style, and a handsome car. The tail concealed a dickey seat which was enclosed by the hood — quite a novel feature.

Two views of the Abbey-bodied NA, which was a rarity. The factory produced a similarly styled car in limited numbers, known variously as 'NK' or 'ND', and used up K2 bodies.

The Cresta-bodied NA, built by Cresta Motor Works of Worthing in small numbers.

An ugly coupé based on the N chassis from Abbey: one of their rare poor body styles for MG.

A good-looking special from Sportcar AG of Zürich.

On the whole the Magna and Magnette range were good cars offering a lot of performance for a modest price. They were easier to drive fast than the Midgets, but rather heavier. This latter feature allowed them to carry four people with greater ease and less oversteer than the Midgets and so the four-seat variants proved the more popular. The N-type was probably the best of the ohc cars, taken all round, but this is said with some caution by one who owned such a car for many years!

5

The Midget Grows Up

Chapter 3 dealt with the origins of the Midget series of cars, and broke off with the suggestion of something new to come in order to eliminate the crankshaft failure which afflicted the J-type engine when the state of tune was raised. This is not to say that every crankshaft was about to break, or even that the cars were inherently unreliable: far from it, but crankshaft failure was an embarrassing problem and MG Design were not unaware of this, or the fact that the engine was not the smoothest-running unit available. It was an equally valid point that while racing was an activity to be used for advertising purposes, the only way to increase power outputs of the 750 cc engines was to increase engine speeds, and if this was done then a much stronger crankcase design was necessary.

During 1933 the Magnette engine had demonstrated that it was capable of sustaining high crankshaft speeds, even in touring cars, for long periods of time with little sign of stress, and so preliminary sketches of a four-cylinder engine based on the 1100 cc unit were made. In effect this 'cut out' cylinders four and five, but left in all the desirable features such as larger crank and cam bearings and a centre main bearing for the crankshaft. A new crankshaft was drawn, but for the touring car this was still non-counterbalanced, known colloquially as the 'bent wire' shape. Early trials, which seem to have taken place around August or September 1933, were encouraging, and the prototype chassis was soon running. This was to become the P-type and was in effect a much stronger J. Both front and rear axles were similar to those of the J, but the brake gear was enlarged to the 12-inch drums already in use in the L Magna and J4 racing Midget. The frame was slightly longer and made of much heavier material. The bodywork – either two- or four-seat – was open, no saloon was offered, and the general layout was a tidied up version of the later J2s, with swept wings. The fuel tank for the four-seater was enclosed in the rear of the body, and the instrument panel was improved. Perhaps the only black mark was that the gearbox was given a very poor set of ratios for a sports car, which left a large 'gap' between second and third gears. However, this was praised by the trials-driving fraternity, for the very low bottom gear meant that the standard P-type could climb hills which previously had required a lot of power or an ultra-low final drive ratio.

With its beautifully smooth engine the P-type soon won its devotees, while its much improved brakes meant that it could be driven on the roads at averages similar to almost any contemporary car, irrespective of engine size. Actual performance was in truth about the same as that of the J-types, principally due to the increased weight of the new car. The price was still the same at £222. It was on sale in March 1934, and for once there was no waiting for the first examples to be seen, since production had started two months earlier.

Three views of the P-type chassis: comparison with the shot of the J chassis in chapter 3 will show that while the chassis frame was similar, it was the engine and brake gear which contributed most to the increased weight.

The standard P-type two-seater is a much cleaner car than the swept-wing J2.

The three-quarter view of the P-type shows what a nice little car it was — and it was small... a true Midget.

Coincident with the introduction of the P-type came the announcement by the factory that, provided the boost pressure did not exceed 5/7 psi over atmospheric, the new car guarantee would not be invalidated if a super-charger was fitted. Belt-driven supercharger kits became available from a number of manufacturers, and although fuel consumption suffered if all the performance was used, the performance increase was worthwhile, maximum speed being increased to as much as 90 mph, while acceleration times were transformed. The fitting of superchargers by trials competitors became commonplace, and some of these used well above the recommended boost pressures, with few ill effects, apart from an appetite for valves, pistons and rings, due to the poor quality fuel then available. One thing was quite certain, crankshaft failure was a thing of the past!

At the autumn London Motor Show, the small saloon slot was filled with the attractive Airline Coupé: a really smooth looking small GT car having two seats, it featured an opening roof, but was rather expensive at £290. It was something of a sensation at the Show, and this little car remains one of the more attractive MG saloons of all time.

It was a bare two months after the P-type that the Q-type racing Midget was announced. Although called a Midget, and using a 750 cc version of the new engine, in truth it owed more to the Magnette range. Chassis side-members were similar to those of the short chassis K-type but they were closer together, while the axles were similar to those of the N. The body was close in shape, although not identical, to the 1934 K3.

The engine had a counterbalanced crankshaft of the same stroke as the J4,

The PA Airline Coupé was a truly attractive little car and, while a trifle heavy, in PB form had a good turn of speed.

but this was fitted into the P-type block, necessitating a longer connecting rod, while the P-type cylinder head and valve gear were used. The supercharger was a high pressure Zoller unit giving in excess of 25 psi boost (2.67 bar for those who think in today's 'absolute' units), a figure which had never previously been used, and the specific power output of the engine was not approached by a racing engine for many years. With well over 110 bhp the Q-type was very fast, and very hard on its transmission. A preselector gearbox was used, as on the K3, but this was connected to the engine through a non-operating clutch which merely slipped when the torque applied was too great a surprise for the rear axle! This reduced, but did not eliminate, the likelihood of rear axle failure.

The bodywork was similar to that of the 1934 K3 Magnette, although the fuel tank was enclosed inside the rear panelling; certainly the two cars bore a close family resemblance, not only with each other, but also, when viewed from the front, with the other cars in the MG range.

Priced at £550, the Q-type should have sold in large numbers to those interested in racing. The problem was that not many people were able to afford such an outlay for a racing car, which, although reasonable, was no small amount by the standards of 1934, and the fact was that those who could afford such a sum were usually in the position to afford considerably more and buy a more exotic machine capable of attempting overall honours, rather than a mere class win. However the car was very fast, and won a number of races as well as setting several 750 cc class sprint records; it really did point to the fact that the limit of roadholding had been achieved for a conventional chassis.

1934 had seen the effectiveness of independent suspension demonstrated by the Mercedes-Benz Grand Prix cars, and several manufacturers were producing road cars so fitted, including BSA and Alvis in Britain, the latter having produced an independently sprung front-wheel drive Grand Prix contender as early as 1928. Chassis stiffness was not sufficient in many of these early attempts at providing independent suspension systems, and it was to be perhaps fifteen years before the full advantages were truly seen, at least with mass production examples. Following on 'knife and fork' experiments by Reg Jackson and his crew in the racing shop, possibly as early as the autumn of 1933, H.N. Charles began working officially on independent suspension systems fairly early in 1934, and at least one P-type was built up with independent front suspension. The result of this work was more far-reaching than a lash up on a standard chassis, however. It was to be another decade before so much original thought was put into chassis design by a British manufacturer.

Working from first principles, Charles decided that for a suspension system to work properly a good, firm, rigid base was required. Previously designed chassis had been rather lacking in this respect, and it had been necessary in consequence to use road springs of very high rate and little camber to achieve the good reputation which MG had built up. The frame for the new car, designated the RA-type, was an electrically welded unit of Y-shape, and immensely strong, although very light by the standards of 1935 at 57 pounds. Suspension was by double wishbones at front and rear, and the springing

A PB pictorial: a nice car in typically British rural setting.

The Q-type Midget. It extracted 110 or more bhp from its 750 cc engine, the highest specific output achieved from any car pre-war.

The cockpit was, well, snug; Alec Hounslow told a story of the passenger having a grab handle on the floor to hold himself in place! The shape of the car was right, but the chassis was not up to the power available.

The R-type Midget. The chassis was well thought out, and able to make use of the power of the Q-type engine. The car was nice to look at, but perhaps a little heavy. Rear suspension geometry was the only serious design error, and plans were available to improve that: but...!

117

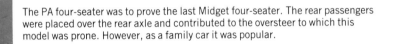

The PA four-seater was to prove the last Midget four-seater. The rear passengers were placed over the rear axle and contributed to the oversteer to which this model was prone. However, as a family car it was popular.

The PB displays its slatted grille. Apart from that and its tank filler cap, it was virtually indistinguishable from the PA.

medium was a long bar, held in torsion. Slight deficiencies in design were that the rear wishbones were of equal length, and that the shock absorbers were a fluid damper of insufficient size for the job. The engine, its supercharger and the gearbox, all of very similar type to that fitted to the Q-type, sat in the arms of the 'Y' in front of the driver, while the final drive was bolted to its tail and behind the driver. The initial bodywork was a neat single-seater, the car being an uncompromising racing car.

Rear view of the PB — probably the nicest of the pre-war Midgets from a practical point of view: it looked good, it was comfortable (at least by the standards of 1935), and it went well.

A special-bodied P-type by Hami of Zürich, with streamlined grille and tail.

Another special, this from Abbey, based on the PB but hardly an attractive car!

It would be nice to think that in 1935 there was a whole range of fully independently sprung touring cars waiting to go into production, but beyond the R-type racing car there were only rather woolly plans: perhaps a larger racing car, in the Magnette series, and a saloon car based on a similar chassis, of which a rough prototype was actually built, but enthusiasm seems at this point to have outstripped actual design capability. Furthermore, the R-type was offered for sale at £750, but this cannot have covered the cost of production: apart from the engine and gearbox there was practically nothing on the car which was already in production, and history proves that nothing was to be, for William Morris was in the process of selling his private interest in MG, Wolseley and SU to the Nuffield Organization, and when their accountants looked at the overall picture, they did not like what they saw and wielded the axe in the heaviest way possible. Late in July 1935 it was announced that all competition activities were to be stopped forthwith, and the staff were dispersed to other activities or dismissed. The Design staff were all assigned to new jobs on the Design staff at Cowley. Production was continued, but responsibility for buying components routed through the Cowley Buying Department. Most other activities were to be continued, so that the Sales, Service and Customer Relations aspects were still carried on at Abingdon, and to the outside world business was continuing unchanged.

It is not always appreciated that the first new model to be announced by the new regime was the PB Midget, in September 1935, although actual design work had commenced some time before that model's release of course. It had been fairly obvious to Abingdon that the products of the Singer Car Company were taking sales in the sports car field. The Singer 'Le Mans' boasted a 972 cc ohc engine, which had a far better torque curve than the P-type, and was therefore drawing a measure of success in the trials results, as well as being more appealing to the buying customer for road use. Increasing the P-type bore size was deemed feasible following an alteration of the casting coreboxes, and at 60 mm the displacement was 939 cc. After a minor hiatus with piston rings, power was raised by a satisfactory 20 per cent, and the corresponding torque figure was in the same league as that of the Singer, and so there was little opposition from Cowley to continuing with the planned introduction of a PB which was an *improved* as opposed to a *new* model.

The PB was improved in detail compared with the PA, as the P-type now became. In addition to the change in engine size, better indirect gear ratios were fitted, and the steering gear was changed to the more satisfactory Bishop Cam type. The propellor shaft was changed to a Hardy Spicer needle roller type, and instrumentation was improved, while the radiator was given vertical slats for the first time since the 18/80 Mark II, a feature which was to be present on all MGs until the late 1960s. The PB was offered at £222, the former price of the PA, while the price of the latter was reduced to £199 10s 0d. All three body styles of the PA were offered and such was the appeal of the larger engine that twenty-seven PA cars were converted by the works to PB specification in order to sell them. In fact the PB was a far nicer car to drive than its smaller brother, many enthusiasts stating that it was the best of the leaf-sprung Midgets. Be that as it may, the PB was at its best when supercharged, a point put forcefully by the 'Cream Cracker' trials team during 1936.

Less than a month after the announcement of the PB came the first completely new model from the new Cowley-based Design Department which will be considered in the next chapter, and it took less than twelve months for the new MG Midget to be designed, tested and announced: the speed of introducing new models had not changed! It was now obvious that a really radical change had taken place, for while the PB had used obvious Abingdon design thinking, the new Midget was to use as many components as possible from the Morris range.

The R-type Midget

Chassis design was modelled on that of the P-type, although track and wheelbase were both increased to the dimensions of the N-type. However, gone were the overhead camshaft, and the high-speed engine, gone was the vertical dynamo, the cable brakes and even the compact size. The new Midget boasted an engine size greater by 21 cc than that of the Magnette, which was continuing, incidentally. The engine was derived from the Morris Ten, and was to be shared with the new Wolseley 10/40, although in MG form it had twin SU carburettors. Valves were still overhead, but operated by pushrods from a camshaft running within the cylinder block and driven by a chain, of all things! As if this was not enough, cylinder head porting was back to the AA type dropped three years before. The dynamo was mounted at the side of the engine, and driven by rubber belt. Due to the larger displacement, power output was up to 50 bhp, a rise of 16 per cent compared with the PB, but was some 12 per cent less than the N-type. However, the power was all developed at a modest engine speed, and the ability of the engine to pull strongly from very low speeds was soon appreciated. The clutch was the cork-insert type which ran in oil, so beloved of the Cowley designers, but since the engine was mounted on flexible rubber mountings, the operating linkage from the pedal could no longer be direct, and a compensating linkage was introduced, which was initially a cable operating on a simple lever. While the gearbox ratios were not too bad, it also featured synchromesh for the first time on a sports MG, so that the gear-changing was no longer the precise art it had been on the 'cammy' cars.

The engine and gearbox were not the only changes, for Charles's pioneer work with independent suspension was all forgotten, and the new Midget had the familiar ladder frame – well, nearly familiar, for in fact it lost nearly all of the cross-members which had characterized previous Midgets, the few remaining being of simple channel section rather than of tubular section, resulting in considerable loss of rigidity. One redeeming feature was the introduction of boxed front side-members, which were actually essential in view of the fact that the engine was mounted on flexible rubber mountings. The suspension was the familiar flat leaf springs, pivoted at the forward ends and with sliding trunnions at the rear ends. Front and rear axles were rigid, of course.

The physical size of the car was actually as large as the Magnette, although it was much lower in side profile. Hydraulic brakes, operating in smaller drums than the P-type, were featured for the first time on a sports MG. The whole package was offering more car in every sense than the P-type, but at the same price. The simpler mechanical specification promised lower maintenance costs, so that customers should have been satisfied and, in general, they were. In broad terms the performance of the standard car was better than either the J or the P-type, although fuel consumption was not as good: in fact the overall performance was on a par with the N-type Magnette, but slightly lower in all departments, especially in handling and road-holding, although contemporary road tests were too polite to point this out!

In spite of several shortcomings, however, the essential Abingdon ingredients were present, and it was not long before the MG personnel accepted the new T-type Midget as an MG giving a high degree of 'fun'

The TA chassis of 1936 was actually less strong than that of the P-type, even though it was boxed at the front. The engine was mounted on rubber blocks, which took away some of the rigidity of the early cars, but helped to make the new generation of Midgets feel more pleasant to drive.

motoring for a reasonable price, a feeling which was soon echoed by the buying public. Eventually even the highly critical trials fraternity accepted the new T-type Midget as a good car which achieved everything the P and J-type cars did in standard tune, with a good deal less fuss. The problems started when they tried tuning the engine, which did not like high crankshaft speeds, these being prevented in effect by poor port design, great rotating weight of the crank and flywheel assembly, heavy valves and the rather conservative valve timing. It was not long before the factory devised methods of tuning the engine which soon became available to owners who wanted to apply them. The factory-supported MG Car Club trials teams used modified T-types from the 1937 season, employing superchargers and larger engines as the seasons progressed. In fact, when supercharged, special crankshafts and clutches were used, and it looked from the outside as if the whole cycle of events might be repeated with competition leading to improved design, even if full-scale participation in sporting events might officially be frowned upon.

For the 1938 season the Cream Cracker team appeared with large-engined cars, using less-modified units from the VA model rather than the specialized blown T-type engines of the previous year. These cars proved very successful – almost too successful, for interest and opposition gradually dwindled in this sport which was to become dominated by purpose-built cars over the years.

There was a whole series of modifications introduced during the production run, mostly mechanical, at the behest of Cowley. During 1938 a Drophead Coupé, similar in style to the larger model Coupés, was introduced. This body was built by Salmons of Newport Pagnell, and was referred to as a Tickford Coupé. Really practical, this was arguably the first

The TA body was much longer than that of previous Midgets, and it was altogether a more popular car for this reason.

The instrumentation of the T-series was similar to earlier cars.

The TA Midget in rear view retained its good looks.

successful attempt to make the small sports car a comfortable form of transport. It was extremely well appointed, but in consequence was quite a bit heavier than the standard Midget. At £269 it found a ready market, and killed off the Airline body which had been offered, for the new Coupé gave the option of an open car when the weather was kind.

In August 1939 the 1940 model Midget was announced. Dubbed the TB, it featured a new engine and gearbox, but was otherwise unchanged. It would not be correct to say that any influence arose from MG in the design of the new engine or its associated transmission: these all came directly from the Morris 10 Series III and Wolseley New Ten which were announced at the same time. It did, however, bear only very superficial resemblance to the unit it replaced. In MG form it was known as the XPAG unit, which was to feature so prominently in MG fortunes for the next fifteen years. The new engine was of slightly smaller capacity, gained by decreasing the stroke considerably, although the bore was actually increased: one result of this was that the RAC rating went up from 10 to 11 'horsepower' with the decrease of capacity! A new camshaft giving more valve overlap was featured, and the whole engine showed signs that the high revving MG was to return to currency. This was assisted by the use of a counterbalanced crankshaft. The quoted power output was up to 54 bhp at a rousing 5400 rpm: high-revving sports engines were indeed returning to Abingdon!

A Borg and Beck dry clutch was at last used, and the gearbox was improved, with better ratios and a more effective syncromesh mechanism than that of the TA. Little else was changed in the new model but it was soon obvious that whatever the TA lacked, the new TB had: basically sound, it had a good cylinder head design to go with the robust lower half of the engine. Only one thing was wrong, and that was nothing to do with MG, or Cowley, for a criminal lunatic plunged the world into a major war, and thoughts at both Abingdon and Cowley were turned to the production of quite different vehicles.

The TB Midget of 1939, which was to have such a short life.

The Tickford Coupé was a popular body style for the pre-war T-Series; equipped with the three-position folding hood, it allowed the best to be made of uncertain British weather!

A prototype TA Tickford with improved tail treatment which was not produced in large numbers.

The TA was also produced in Airline Coupé form, but this was superseded by the Tickford.

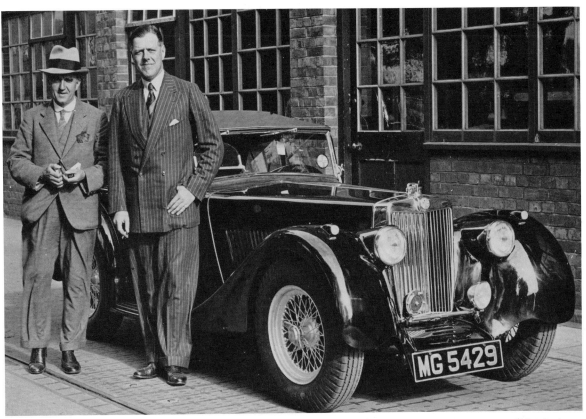

A one-off TA built for Lord Ashley by Offord, here being collected from Cecil Kimber at Abingdon in 1939.

6

Pre-war Comfort

More dissent exists amongst MG enthusiasts when discussing the S-V-W range of cars than any other of the pre-war models, and is rivalled only by that surrounding the post-war Magnettes, or possibly the Longbridge MGs of the eighties.

As already mentioned, at the time of the purchase of MG from Sir William Morris by the Nuffied Organization early in 1935, there were at Abingdon only some rather woolly plans for an S-type Magnette on the lines of the R-type Midget. There was also a prototype T-type saloon in existence, with all-round independent suspension, powered by an engine of unknown capacity built by a contractor outside the Nuffield group, but said variously to have six cylinders or to be a V8, depending upon whose story one believes. Cecil Cousins was adamant that it used a Blackburne engine, in which case it could have been a twin ohc six cylinder 1.5-litre, as used by Frazer-Nash and others, or the 2.5-litre six-cylinder unit of basically similar layout as used by British Salmson. Either way, accepting the story to be true, use of an engine from outside the Nuffield empire must have been the last nail in the coffin for MG Design: not only was there plenty of spare capacity at both Ward End and Morris Engines in Coventry to satisfy the supply of engines for the production at Abingdon, whatever design was finally decided upon, but any move outside the Nuffield Organization would have brought purchasing and supply problems.

Many rash charges have been directed at the Nuffield Organization for the change in design policy, but it really is difficult to see how else they could have reacted. In 1935 there were two distinct lines of design thought within the Organization, best described broadly as 'Ward End thinking', and 'Cowley thinking'. A third string, which we will call 'Abingdon thinking' was growing in strength and importance by 1935, and it was this proliferation of thinking in the Design departments which caused the senior management in the Nuffield Group to look at what was being produced and to put some thought into a more unified strategy of design. Let us now look broadly at these divergent design patterns and the changes which were wrought.

Ward End was the home of Wolseley, and their designs were based on cars which had been designed in the mid-1920s using a series of ohc engines, and while these might have been forward-looking when conceived, they were beginning to look 'old hat' ten years later: their chassis design was definitely out of date, using small section frames with little cross-bracing, and long road springs with large camber and little damping, which ensured that the ride of the cars was soft, even comfortable, but that the control of the car was distinctly limited, especially if put into the context of a sports car. The trend towards the all-steel body was bringing increased weight to the cars, which

Pre-war Comfort was emphasizing the poor nature of the suspension control, and while the cars were no worse than others of the period, it was obvious that new designs were needed. The one redeeming feature of the Wolseley Company was their pioneer work with hydraulic brakes.

Cowley thought was also based back in the previous decade, with side-valve engines, not to mention their adherence to three-speed gearboxes and a virtual lack of suspension control, but their body design was starting to move towards all-steel construction, and the first step on the road to the modern one-piece body/chassis unit was being considered, while hydraulic brakes were also featured on most models. Furthermore there can be no denying that Cowley was delivering cars which the domestic motorist wanted, at a price he could afford and at a surprisingly high quality standard, thus ensuring low running costs.

Abingdon thought was strongly attached to the Wolseley line so far as engines were concerned, but was more highly developed; indeed the power outputs and the way these were applied to the products of the small factory must have had much admiration from designers at both Ward End and

The MG Two Litre, or SA, had a very rugged chassis which was able to carry the luxurious coachwork fitted.

Right: The nearside of the SA engine compartment, showing how uncluttered it was, with most essentials accessible. The cylindrical tank to the right was the reservoir for the built-in jacking system.

Cowley. However, it was bringing quite an unfavourable backwash from the motor trade who found the designs were too complicated for the average garage mechanic to work with. Unlike both Ward End and Cowley, Abingdon chassis design was very forward-looking, the only blind spots appearing to be the reluctance of Abingdon to consider steel body construction and their insistence on using mechanical brake actuation. If this appears surprising, do remember that hydraulic brake design was still in its infancy, and that fluid actuation in itself does not make the brakes more effective: indeed road test figures of the NA and PB showed the brakes at least as effective as those of the TA. Where hydraulic brakes scored was in the lack of constant adjustment which was necessary with mechanical brakes to keep them effective, due to general wear and cable stretch.

In addition to this there were increasing problems developing in the trade with respect to the complications of spare parts storage for the large number of models which the three companies were producing, supposedly from the same engineering group but operationally autonomous. A unified line of design thought was obviously needed, one which was up to date in terms of engine, chassis and body thinking, and yet was economic to build (which would keep the selling price attractive) and above all one which would give reliability in service, as well as answer the criticisms raised above. Whether or not they were successful is not for this book to discuss, and we will now look at the products of the Abingdon factory and show the family connections with the products of other branches of the Nuffield Organization.

The MG Design team were moved lock, stock and barrel to Cowley in the early summer of 1935, and were set to work on the design of a new car based upon a six-cylinder engine of just over 2 litres capacity. Wolseley and Morris designers were to produce their own versions, all working in the same drawing office, and while there was a far closer interchange of components possible, there were also many fundamental differences by the time the new models were all announced. The MG Two-Litre, as it was originally called, was aimed more at the luxury carriage market, at one time filled by the 18/80 range, and like that model it was intended that the new car would have slight sporting pretensions. Therefore there was no real change in production policy, it merely reverted to that of 1928: the accent was to be less on 'sports' and more towards the car as a means of transport, retaining some of the appeal of a sporting character. It may be of interest that the Wolseley version appeared in a number of guises eventually, one of these being known as the '18/80' in 1937!

The car had a chassis design which was pure Abingdon and was not shared with either the Morris or Wolseley models, and featured springs with limited movement and good damping, by double-acting hydraulic shock absorbers. The chassis rode low, but was overslung at the rear. The frame was boxed, which resulted in a good, torsionally stiff, base for the car, and enabled the suspension to do the work of absorbing the movements of the road wheels to a degree not experienced in an MG, or indeed any Nuffield product, before. That the marque differences were to be maintained was underlined by the fact that neither the Morris nor the Wolseley models which shared the same engine had a chassis frame which offered anything like the stiffness of the new MG.

The engine was the first component shared with other cars in the Nuffield range, and was fitted to the Wolseley 16 hp 'Super Six'. It was a long-stroke unit of 2062 cc with overhead valves operated from a camshaft located low down in the cylinder block by pushrods and rockers, the camshaft being chain driven. The crankshaft ran in four main bearings and was counterbalanced. All bearings were still of the white-metal type. Full-flow oil filtration was featured, and most oilways were by external pipes. Valve porting reverted to the old AA pattern, there being six exhausts and four inlets, so that manifolding was quite efficient with twin cast exhaust manifolds, and a cast aluminium inlet manifold with twin downdraught SU carburettors. The carburettor intakes were silenced with a large inlet filter for the first time on an MG. Drive was taken through the Morris cork-in-oil clutch, which as usual meant a heavy flywheel, but had the merit of providing a very smooth take-up of drive, which was not always found in dry clutches, even in the mid-1930s. A four-speed gearbox, but no syncromesh as yet, with a neat remote control took the drive, via a long propeller shaft, to a conventional rear axle.

Wheels were Rudge centre-lock type on all production examples, although the original prototype had wire-spoked wheels of obvious Morris parentage. Brakes were hydraulically operated using the Lockheed system, featuring single leading shoe, while the handbrake operated on the rear wheels only by cables applied by a centrally mounted fly-off lever. Another innovation was the introduction of the Jackall in-built car jacking system, which stopped the need for grovelling under the car with a portable jack when one had the then-all-too-common experience of a tyre puncture.

The bodywork showed the influence of Cecil Kimber's thinking, and was very well appointed, with full instrumentation as well as arm rests, door pockets and burr-walnut facings. Seats were leather-covered to add that finishing touch. The overall effect was one of considerable style, and while it showed a great change in the design thinking at MG there was no denying that the car offered a great deal for the money, and a car which was right up to the minute in styling. In fact, the selling price of £375 for the saloon was £24 cheaper than the KN saloon it was said to replace, but it offered more internal space, better appointments, more comfort, more effortless performance, and all at the same fuel consumption; furthermore, its styling was a great leap forward when compared with that of the old Magnette.

Announced in good time for the 1935 Motor Show, orders were received at a gratifying rate, but unfortunately the heavy hand of Nuffield no longer permitted the rapid start of production which had been the feature of the old Abingdon days, and it was not until some seven months later that the first cars were being delivered to customers. This was most unfortunate, since the Coventry firm of SS Cars had announced a similar-looking car, and were much quicker into production and certainly won some of the sales which the new MG had hoped for. Once production did get under way, the press received the car well, and in terms of road performance, handling and comfort it set new standards for cars in its price range.

The prototype Two Litre, fitted with Morris wheels, but otherwise unmistakably MG.

The production version, showing the striking resemblance to the contemporary SS car.

The model was current from early 1936 right up to the outbreak of the
Second World War in September 1939, so it is hardly surprising that a large
number of modifications were incorporated into the specification by way of
improvement. The first of these was the introduction of a slightly larger bore
engine, this being introduced essentially to standardize pistons with the
four-cylinder car, but also as the smaller bore engine was dropped from the
Morris/Wolseley range. The revised engine came together with a better
gearbox having syncromesh on third and top gears.

The Two Litre embarking on the Kyle of Lochalsh ferry.

In addition to the saloon, a capacious four-seat open tourer built by Charlesworth was offered at £399, the price of the old KN saloon, while the price of the Morris Bodies-built saloon quietly crept up to £389. During 1938 a 'folding head foursome coupé' was announced, generally referred to as the Tickford and built by Salmons of Newport Pagnell, later to become the home of Aston Martin cars. Very well appointed, this version was sold for £415.

By early 1936 the T-type Midget was in production, and it did not take too much stretch of the imagination to realize that the N Magnette's days were numbered. In fact the so-called 12/48 hp Wolseley was already in production when the 'one-and-a-half litre' MG was announced in time for the 1936 Motor Show. The capacity of the engine was just over 1.5 litres, but was a four-cylinder of the same bore and stroke as the revised SA engine, so if that was called two litres at least there was logic in the name, although we now refer to it as the VA. The engine shared much in common with its larger sister, which must have helped storemen and mechanics alike. The general layout was very similar, although the carburettors were conventional semi-downdraught, with intakes silenced with a large air filter. The cork-insert clutch and gearbox, with synchromesh on the top *three* ratios, were also present, while the chassis was a smaller version of the SA in most respects. All the extras found on the larger car were present: the built-in tool tray, Jackall jacks, and full instrumentation. Even the body was similar in style to the larger car, so that it seemed that, taken all round, the new regime was having the desired effect, and producing cars which were in demand.

The VA was said to be the replacement for the Magnette, but the two cars cannot be compared, for they are totally different in concept. The VA is a touring car in the best tradition; indeed it helped to set standards for the future, while the NA was a sports car of the old style and perhaps might be viewed in hindsight as the ultimate flowering of the true 'vintage' style of sports car. In some respects the VA was a retrograde step, for its engine was undeniably agricultural, a low-revving plodder, which would achieve a reasonable road performance by virtue of large displacement and sensible gearing, rather than the ohc six-cylinder unit which with some 20 per cent

Two examples of the Two Litre in typical pre-war MG publicity shots.

less capacity developed 5 per cent more power. Road test figures showed the new car to possess great charm, with performance figures ahead of most of its price competitors, but not in the sports car league: the top speed was good, but the acceleration was not exactly sparkling! The VA was offered with open four-seat and saloon bodywork, both made by Morris Bodies, and with the popular Salmons-built Tickford Coupé style becoming available during 1938. Prices were £280 for the open car, £325 for the saloon, and £26 more for the Tickford.

Like the SA, the VA was progressively modified while it was in production, perhaps the most significant modification being the introduction of a dry clutch, which improved the liveliness of the engine considerably, owing to the reduction in flywheel weight. Also introduced in the VA, for the first time on an MG, were shell-type thinwall bearings, which would eventually reduce overhaul costs. Late VAs are in fact very pleasant cars to drive, even in modern traffic, only the ride and internal heat betraying the age of the car.

By 1938 the SA was getting long in the tooth while the design was being perfected. The engine was due to be dropped from the Nuffield range and replaced by one of a larger bore, giving a capacity of rather more than 2.5 litres. When fitted to the Morris the model was known as the Morris 18, and the Wolseley version became known as the 18/85. A fully counterbalanced crankshaft, and thinwall bearings were featured, while MG modifications to this basic power unit included water-heated oil temperature control, and the obligatory twin carburettors, now semi-downdraught. Power output was up by over 20 percent, which allowed for a considerable improvement in both performance and general specification. The new car, introduced at the 1938 Motor Show, was dubbed the '2.6-litre' or WA, and caused a minor sensation. It really was a fine car, offering a considerable amount for a price of under £450 for the saloon, while the Tickford Coupé was also offered at just £25 more. With two 18 hp MGs on sale there can be little doubt that the SA would have been dropped from the range during 1939 or 1940, but in the event both cars ceased production in August 1939, along with the VA and TB models.

It is interesting to reflect that during 1939 experiments were under way on a new small saloon of 10 hp with independent front suspension. This did not see the light of day for another eight years, but it might well have appeared in 1940 but for events which changed the production at Abingdon from cars to machines of war.

The S-V-W range of cars therefore stands out from the general run of pre-war MG production which was, even in 1939, still founded on sports cars. How can we now assess the importance of these models? The correct answer is, of course, that we cannot. However, it is tempting to place the cars on a parallel with Jaguar cars of later years, for they offered a considerable specification at a relatively low price. For MG, and of course for the Nuffield Organization, what they did was to fill a market left vacant by the demise of the 18/80 cars but at a much more attractive price, and produce a series of cars which diverted the attention of the insurance companies away from the out-and-out racing image which the ohc models had produced.

Furthermore, something that is not generally appreciated, the cars provided a commercial success, for the total sales of the three types outsold the T-series Midgets by roughly two to one. Truly, there were more buyers for touring cars than for sports cars; the clever point was in giving the cars the MG identity to maintain marque loyalty when the young sportsman became a successful businessman with a family to transport. For the Nuffield group this was important, for the former user of an MG Midget might not be interested in a Morris 12 or a Wolseley 12/48, but would be attracted to the VA with its better handling and appointments for a small extra price – surely the basis of the original Kimber thinking with the early Morris Garages cars of the mid-1920s?

The SA Tickford Coupé built by Salmons of Newport Pagnell, was a particularly attractive body style.

The four-seat tourer was the rarest of the standard body styles fitted to the SA chassis. Built by Charlesworth, it had ample seating space for four, while the rear seat passengers were not as exposed to the elements as they had been in the earlier cars.

The large size of the SA made it easy for the specialist coachbuilders to make good-looking cars. This was by Keller of Switzerland.

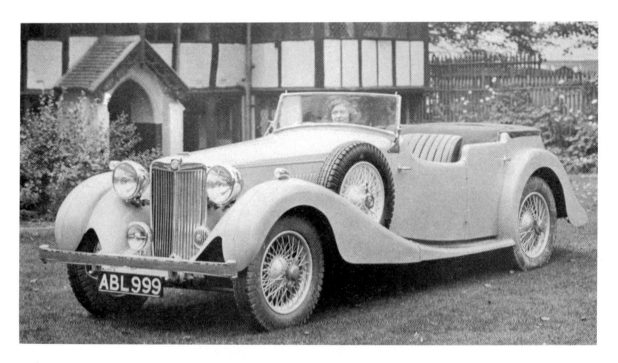

A WA four-seat tourer prototype. The WA was known at the time as the '2.6 litre MG'. Development of this car took place over eighteen months, far longer than it had taken to produce any of the earlier models.

The 'One-and-a-half litre', or VA, saloon was an attractive car...

Even from rear view. This car was run by Mrs Kimber.

An open tourer leading a saloon.

The tourer version of the VA, which was said to be replacing the Magnette N-type, but really sought a completely different market.

The Tickford-bodied VA was a little tail-heavy when viewed together with its longer sister, but was nevertheless a well-appointed car.

Top: The WA saloon in
production form, wearing
the shaded headlamps
necessary as an air-raid
precaution after
September 1939.

The fixed tool kit was a
feature of the whole
S-V-W range, this one
belonging to a WA.

Left: The WA saloon in
happier days…

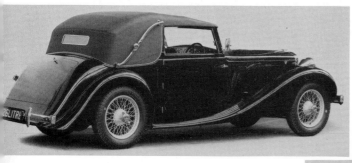

The Salmons Tickford Coupé provided the WA with perhaps its most attractive variant.

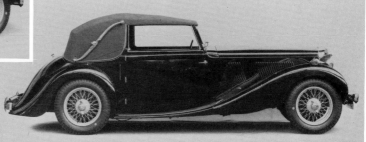

Pre-war Comfort

The interior of the Tickford Coupé was well appointed and spacious; note the octagonal instruments.

Another Keller-bodied car, this time a WA which in side elevation could almost be a Mercedes!

A one-off body by Salmons with a profile which suggests a Derby Bentley, but with a price ticket more than £1,000 lower.

Midgets for Export

At the outbreak of the Second World War in 1939, production of cars had given way at Abingdon to production and maintenance of machines of war, as it had at most other engineering plants over the whole country. A very wide variety of jobs had been undertaken, ranging from servicing guns and production of aircraft parts to overhauling tanks. No job was too large or too small or too difficult for the men and women at the MG.

However, the actual work done was not the only important outcome of the war effort. Reg Jackson, at one time foreman of the racing shop, became Chief Inspector of the works during this time, and ran a qualified aircraft standards inspection team, and later modelled the car inspection systems on what he had learned from the aircraft industry. These systems, which were progressively brought up to date with the passage of time, were eventually found to meet in principle most of the exacting 05/21 Standards set by the organization of British Leyland in the 1970s. He was rightly proud of the achievements of MG during the war, as indeed were all other members of staff.

As the requirement for war equipment decreased during 1945, thoughts were turned at Abingdon to resuming car production. The easy course would have been to resume production of the pre-war models, as did other parts of the Nuffield Organization and indeed other car manufacturers. The situation at Abingdon was rather different, however. While a Morris, Austin or Hillman car might be viewed as an essential form of transport, the more exotic forms of transport would not be so popular in a war-torn country in which the political climate had changed a good deal since 1939. In addition to the rebuilding of a country devastated by intense bombing, the new government was bent on changing the whole social order, and while many of the changes introduced were good for the country, many others merely cost a great deal of finance and resources, and introduced vast civil service empires with nothing to do but make life awkward for those who were producing goods or wanted to start doing so. There were certainly shortages of essential materials, and it was necessary to ensure that efforts at rebuilding the country were directed towards the general public and their welfare – motor cars could not figure high on a priority list. So it proved: political ideals could not be sacrificed and the mountains of paper which had to be processed in order to obtain materials for any purpose ensured that the rebuilding of the country was retarded.

The VA and WA models would obviously not find favour with those who determined which companies would receive vital supplies, and would in any case duplicate to some extent the products of Cowley, spreading supplies across too wide an area. It was therefore decided that production would be centred around an updated TB Midget, which would be produced

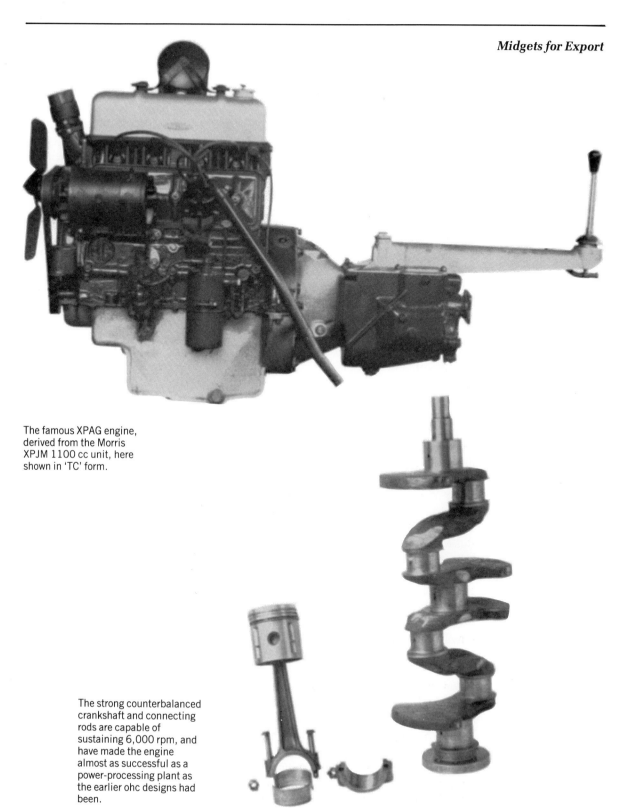

The famous XPAG engine, derived from the Morris XPJM 1100 cc unit, here shown in 'TC' form.

The strong counterbalanced crankshaft and connecting rods are capable of sustaining 6,000 rpm, and have made the engine almost as successful as a power-processing plant as the earlier ohc designs had been.

in small numbers, but sufficient to ensure that the small workforce would be gainfully employed.

The car featured changes to the chassis, incorporating swinging shackles for the road springs. This eliminated one of the best features of the chassis design of the pre-war Midgets, but swinging shackles had been successfully employed on the S-V-W range of cars, so on the face of it they should have been equally successful on the Midget. This overlooked one important design feature of the Midget: the chassis frame itself was fairly flexible, unlike that of the larger cars, and the rubber-bushed shackles did impair the ultimate handling of the car. The modification was introduced for two reasons: the first being the practical one that the sliding trunnions needed constant oiling to prevent rapid wear and, in consequence, noisy operation. The second reason was the more fundamental one that phosphor-bronze was simply not available in large enough quantities to ensure uninterrupted production!

In the engine a timing chain tensioner was introduced, but was otherwise unchanged, and the transmission was likewise unaltered. The body was altered in detail, but the car was still recognizably an MG Midget; indeed it was very close indeed in most respects to the TB, and so it was dubbed the TC-Series. The first examples were built before the end of 1945, and production started in earnest early the following year.

Initially the price was set at £375, but this went up fairly quickly due to the effects of increasing levels of taxation which were imposed by the Government. There were constant stoppages in production due to materials shortages caused in the main by the complicated paperwork systems introduced by the plethora of civil service departments. The surprising thing is that Abingdon managed to produce over 1,000 TCs in 1946. It became obvious that materials would become available in those companies who were exporting, and so markets were found in the British Empire, principally in South Africa and Australia, but also in a former colony, the United States of America. Production of the TC increased and in spite of its out-of-date design it sold well through the next three years. The final build tally of 10,000 units in just over four years far outsold any previous MG model. Incidentally, just a fifth of that number went directly to the USA, far less than we now tend to believe.

Thoughts during those four years must have turned frequently to producing a car of more modern concept, and almost certainly the production of the lovely little Y-type saloon (covered in detail in the next chapter) alongside the distinctly vertical TC must have caused a certain amount of amusement. No one knows when the decision was made to update the Midget, but my guess is that not even the Cowley Design Office would have been happy with the TC. The strictures imposed by the Government must have had a considerable impact, however, and the Midget would certainly not have been a high priority production vehicle. The prototype TD was built during the latter part of 1948 in the traditions of pre-war Abingdon, without any initial design work: a Y-type chassis was shortened, and a TC body mounted on it. It took about six months' work to get this into a production form, and actual production commenced during the summer of 1949.

The TC Midget displays its obvious pre-war heritage; it was in production for four years, like the
pre-war TA and TB — but over three times the number were produced!

Midgets for Export

The chassis owed much to the Y-type, and was very strong in torsion. The frame length was shorter, which resulted in the wheelbase being some five inches less. The front suspension was almost identical in layout, but with different spring and shock absorber settings. Rear suspension was quite different, the chassis passing over the rear axle and the leaf springs having a very large degree of camber. Spring deflection was controlled by lever-arm dampers, and no other control of chassis roll was used. The engine, gearbox and rear axle units were similar to the Y-type, although twin carburettors were retained from the TC. There were the two leading shoe front brakes from the Y-type which improved the braking considerably. Perhaps the horror of horrors for the traditionalist, however, was the introduction for the first time on a sports MG of disc wheels.

The engine was derived directly from that of the TC, although the air intake cleaner was changed to the currently popular oil-bath type. The gearbox was improved in the synchromesh department, even if the ratios were slightly wider. The clutch mechanism, however, featured the double compensated mechanism of the Y-type, which was neither simple nor elegant, providing as it does no less than eight pivot points to wear and a cable to stretch! The whole car was a workmanlike unit, however, and destined to be an even greater success than its predecessor, selling at almost three times the rate. It was the TD which was the first MG to sell in real quantities to the United States.

With the appointment of John Thornley to the position of Managing Director of the MG Car Co. Ltd, coupled with a change of political climate in the country, things at Abingdon improved immeasurably. Production was no

Comprehensive weather equipment ensured the TC was as snug in bad weather as possible.

The TC was equally at home on racing circuits — this one was competing at Silverstone over twelve years after it was produced, and still looking remarkably standard.

longer hampered by constant shortages and the paperwork systems designed to create these. Works-supported cars started to appear in competition events, and for some time it was possible to run a near-standard TD in sports car events, just as before the war one could run a J2 or P-type, for this was the period before the scientifically designed racing specials. Perhaps the first step along this road was taken unwittingly by Abingdon when they produced the TD Mark II, a 'homologation special' if ever there was one, with a mildly tweaked engine, improved suspension and a few detail modifications, which allowed the 1250 cc TD to keep pace with the 1500 cc HRG and Jowett opposition of the period!

Incidentally, the naming of the car 'Mark II' has for years caused confusion, for there are two types of TD engine, of which the second has a prefix 'TD/2' contained in its engine number. This is quite definitely not a 'Mark II', for the two engine 'type' prefixes merely denote a change of cylinder block, cylinder head, gaskets and clutch assembly which have no interchange ability of parts: a real 'Mark II' has the prefix 'TD/3' in its engine number!

By 1952 sales of the TD were showing signs of falling, while George Phillips had appeared at the 1951 Le Mans race with a very smooth-looking special based on the TD, which had caused quite a few raised eyebrows as to the possibility of a really modern MG. Abingdon were to get put down at this suggestion, for 1952 was the year of the formation of the British Motor Corporation, an amalgamation of the Austin Motor Company of Birmingham and the Nuffield Organization. The new head man of this grouping was to be Leonard Lord, who was no friend of the Nuffield group, and when a complete outsider came to the Austin Company with a proposal for a new

The TC was the first MG to be exported to the USA in any significant numbers, but was only produced in right-hand-drive form.

The MG TD was a far more rugged piece of engineering than the earlier T series cars had been, and was closely related to the Y-type saloon. It was an excellent conception: only the disc wheels causing real criticism!

The TD front suspension, which carried through to the MGA almost unchanged, and is even recognizable to an MGB owner!

The TD Mark II. This featured an updated engine and fuel system, improved front suspension and bucket seats.

The hood of the TD was obviously derived from that of the TC.

The driving compartment of the TD can clearly be seen here, and was considerably more comfortable than that of earlier Midgets.

sports car based on Austin components, the MG project was shelved, and the Austin-Healey 100 was introduced. Quite why BMC decided to pay royalties for the use of the name of a rival, but very small, company will probably remain one of the great mysteries of motoring history, although there may have been sound commercial reasons for the decision, as outlined in a later chapter. Whatever the reason it certainly stopped development of new sports car designs at MG for two years, while an important saloon model did appear.

A new MG sports model was essential to bolster the falling sales, especially in the USA. The newly formed BMC were attempting to launch a new marque, which was laughable really, for all that the Americans knew of Austin were the A40 and A90 Sports models which had been a dismal flop: what they wanted was a new MG model, a marque they loved: yes, *loved*, in a way which was totally lost on the moguls at Longbridge. A face-lift TD was sanctioned, and this was hastily cobbled together by the production team at Abingdon, and irreverently referred to at the time as a 'TD which had been kicked in the face'.

That the new sports car has grown to be loved by so many is one of the great motoring mysteries to those who were at Abingdon at the time, for it is the TF that we are discussing! The TF was basically a TD with a lowered and smoothed bodyline and slightly improved interior fittings, even if the instrument panel harked back to the short-lived WA saloon. Mechanically it featured a pressurized cooling system for the first time on an MG sports car, which enabled owners to forget the daily chore of topping up the radiator in hot climates. The air intake silencer was replaced by small pancake-type units, which may have looked the part, but were in fact less efficient than the oil-bath type they replaced. The car was not really a sales success at the time, offering no increase in performance or comfort, and yet it is now the car which many people think of as the archetypal 'square-rigged' MG, and the one upon which, in the 1980s, a whole minor industry has grown in the production of look-alike (well, nearly!) cars based on other out-of-date, or even up-to-date, cars.

Perhaps none of us at the time were particularly perceptive, but there was a new MG model announced at just about the same time which was to introduce a new range of engines to the marque; but as the new Magnette was a saloon car, few took any notice of it, apart from reviving the use of a hallowed marque name! In retrospect it is easy to see this as a case of history repeating itself, for had not the original Magnette fathered a range of exciting sports cars?

By 1955 the TF was seen even at Longbridge to be a flop, but the best that could be devised in the short term was to increase the engine size to 1500 cc, and so the short-lived 'TF 1500' was born. However, things were developing apace at Abingdon, and it was around this time that the Design Office returned to Abingdon, to be led by Sydney Enever, who had been one of the racing mechanics and, later, Jackson's right-hand man in the record-breaking attempts of the later thirties.

All the T-series MG models have much the same performance in standard tune, which for a production life of fourteen years in total was not

The TD special which George Phillips drove at Le Mans in 1951. It proved very fast — too fast, for the engine blew up — but this car was the starting-point for the next generation of MGs.

Left: The TD was offered with wire wheels as an optional extra, but very few cars were so equipped. This one has a later modified set fitted, as have most cars seen these days.

Right: A Mark II TD doing what it ought to! This one in Kenya many years ago.

The TF chassis was clearly derived from that of the TD. Note the pressurized cooling system, and the sham radiator cap!

Rear view of the TF chassis, showing the scuttle hoop which improved steering feel over the TD.

particularly creditable. However, when reviewing the figures it is important to put these into the context of their time and remember that technical advancement was not especially notable within the motor industry of that period, and the advancing age of the cars was not really apparent until around 1953, after some twelve years of production, so that within the context of their time the T-series cars were a success both commercially and technically.

What these cars achieved they did from a very simple specification, and it was this fact more than any other which ensured their success, for they were uncomplicated to maintain and therefore could be sent to almost anywhere in the world and be run without the need for constant specialist attention. Furthermore, it was possible to tune the XPAG engine – indeed this was officially blessed by a booklet, containing tuning hints, issued by the factory, and the cars could be made significantly quicker to provide a good basis for a competition car. For contemporary competition, right up to the mid-fifties, a tuned T-type was *the* car to beat in its class. By 1953 a whole new breed of specialist car producers were coming into being, such as Lester, Kieft, Tojiero and Cooper, with superb chassis design ensuring light weight, allied with sensible suspension geometry. Strange to relate, many of these cars were powered by the XPAG engine, although the light construction allowed for frequent chassis breakages, which let the heavier MGs into the results more often than might otherwise have been the case. This new breed of competition car sounded the death knell for the modified road car in motor sports, since the specialist cars had superior power-to-weight ratios; but the final nail in the coffin for MG T-types in competition was the introduction of the Coventry Climax ohc engine, which ensured that the lightweight cars now held *all* the advantages.

With the benefit of hindsight, many more people have an affection for these models than for any other MG, and there is hardly anyone in the civilized world who does not regard a T-type MG as a 'real' MG. Furthermore, no range of cars did more for the reputation of the little company, or indeed of Great Britain, in the post-war period. The importance of the T-type cars within MG history can never be overstated.

8

Post-war Saloons

History has a strange way of repeating itself, and nowhere is this more true than in the history of the MG car. Right at the start the first MG had been derived from an ordinary Morris Oxford, the 18/80 from a touring Morris, the M-type from the Morris Minor, and so on, each model having its roots in a fairly mundane touring car. In 1939 the Cowley design team were working on a 8/10 hp car to replace the existing Series E Eight and Series III Ten, employing a rigid chassis frame and independent front suspension. Owing to the war, and rather in the fashion of the old 18 hp Six in 1928, these cars were never produced, and in fact Alec Issigonis joined the Cowley team and sought to introduce his own ideas in terms of unit body construction and different forms of suspension for the Morris and Wolseley ranges, which would form the basis for cheaper production costs and gradually, during some twenty years' development, better cars. Quite how the MG 'one-and-a-quarter-litre', or Y-type, came into being in this climate, perhaps we will never know for certain, but in 1947 this attractive saloon of traditional styling was introduced and was to lead to the next generation of MG sports cars in the fifties.

The YA Saloon was introduced in 1948 and proved to be the starting-point for the TD Midget. It was a nicely styled car based on the body shell of the Series E Morris 8.

Interior fitments were of a very high standard. Note the sun visors, sliding roof and adjustable steering column, all features which at that time were novel.

The Y-type featured a very rigid box-frame chassis of all-welded construction – similar in construction to the R-type frame, it will be noted. Front suspension was mounted on a very strong cross-member, to which was bolted a twin lever-arm shock absorber, which doubled as the upper wishbone link. The lower link was pivoted on the cross-member, and a coil-spring was interposed. The stub axle was carried on a kingpin running in threaded trunnions, top and bottom. Steering was by rack and pinion, the gear being carried on the cross-member, ensuring a 'one piece' feel, which was certainly *not* a feature of all early independent suspension systems! If this sounds familiar to the MGB owner, it should: for the system was good enough in concept to last the next thirty-four years, even if the detail design was changed.

Rear suspension was by semi-elliptic leaf springs, shackled at the rear, with lever-arm dampers, while the frame passed under the axle as on the Midgets, rather than being swept over the axle as on the more mundane Cowley designs. The chassis design thus ensured a good solid base, allowing the suspension to 'work', thus providing the car with a good ride and handling.

The engine was the trusty XPAG unit as used on the Midget, but with only a single carburettor, and the gearbox an improved version of that fitted to the TC, 'improved' referring to the synchromesh and the general oil-tightness, for the ratios were wider, as befits a somewhat heavy saloon car of limited power.

The bodywork, although compact in size, was very well appointed in the traditions of the VA, and offered an excellent value-for-money package. The actual body shell was shared with the Series E Morris and Wolseley 8 models, but was improved with the more shapely mudguards and the MG grille. An opening roof panel was standard, as was the opening windscreen, both of which helped to keep the interior cool in summer, although there was no provision for a heater for keeping warm in winter: car heaters were still a few years away in the future!

During 1948 a tourer version was introduced, with a folding top and sidescreens, very similar in layout to the pre-war tourers. Known as the 'YT', this car featured the twin-carburettor engine of the TC, and was quite a bit lighter than the saloon, although its performance was only marginally better. But the day of the four-seat open car was well and truly dead, and most of these were exported to warmer climes. The model passed into history in 1950, relatively unloved and unmourned. Strangely, though, there is now a great following for the model, so perhaps the car was forty years ahead of its time?

In 1951 the saloon was improved considerably with revised rear suspension, dispensing with the Panhard rod and introducing a hypoid final drive, which made this unit much quieter, while smaller wheels were fitted, which made the car more attractive in profile and improved the handling by reducing the oversteering tendency of the YA. A heater was at long last offered, although as an optional extra! Now known as the 'YB', this car earned a deserved reputation for being a good sporting saloon, with positive handling attributes, which in turn allowed it to win its spurs in the growing saloon-car racing classes.

In 1953, amid cries of outrage and worse, a new saloon car was introduced which revived the Magnette name. The Z-series was a totally new concept for MG, but its prime importance was in its introduction of the BMC B-series engine to the MG range. The old XPAG engine was looking distinctly 'old hat', with its external oil pipes and oil pump, and was even at that time known for its ability to leak oil generously, even when driven fairly gently! I have already mentioned in the previous chapter that a proposed new MG sports car was passed over in preference for a car bearing the Austin name, and perhaps a charitable view of this is that the newly formed conglomerate company wished to standardize power units, and that the proposed model needed development time for changing engine and transmission. This interpretation may have some truth behind it, but two years later they introduced a saloon car with two badges, the MG Magnette which featured a B-series engine, and Wolseley 15/50 with the XPAG unit!

Calling this new model the 'Magnette' caused cries of derision from those

Post-war Saloons

The Series E Morris Eight was introduced in 1939 and continued after the war through to 1948. They shared the same main body section as the 1¼ litre MG, but very little else!

The 1952 YB model 1¼ litre saloon, displaying the improved looks given by the use of smaller wheels and restyled wings.

The YT Tourer somehow was not attractive as the saloon, and proved to be the last four-seat open MG produced.

The Tourer was decidedly 'sporting' with its fold-flat windscreen.

The weather equipment provided adequate protection , but most of the models were exported to warmer countries than Great Britain!

Above: The ZA Magnette, displaying its standard fog lamps. Its performance and handling had few peers in 1953 and the car continued in production with few modifications to 1959.

The ZB Magnette was changed only in detail from the ZA, but managed to keep its good looks.

who thought of the deeds of the old K3 Magnettes of the thirties and ignored the fact that the racing car was derived from a saloon car! In fact the new Magnette not only broke new ground for MG but also set a new standard for British sporting saloons, and stepped towards performance and handling which had previously only been available in the products of Italy. The new Magnette, coded the ZA, featured a unit construction body, independent front suspension, rack-and-pinion steering, and semi-elliptic leaf-sprung rear suspension. There were no components interchangeable with any other MG model, and it looked indeed as though badge engineering had arrived at Abingdon. In fact it was the first of a new breed of cars based on more modern components and using modern production techniques, in this respect mirroring the development pattern of the past.

The B-series engine derived from an Austin design of the early post-war era, and was originally a 1300 cc unit used in the A40 model, the first new post-war Austin car. It had been increased in size to 1500 cc in 1951, and had proved to be a very durable unit, with a respectable specific power output. It had pushrod-operated overhead valves, but improved foundry techniques made it a much cleaner unit than the Morris engines in terms of oil leakage, a problem which had been largely ignored before the war. It was mated to a four-speed gearbox, with synchromesh on the top three ratios, the clutch being operated hydraulically, which finally disposed of the crazy Nuffield compensated linkage of complicated lever and rod operation. Final drive was via a long two-piece propeller shaft to a rear axle unit enclosing hypoid gears. Suspension was independent at the front by coil spring and double unequal length wishbones, but unlike the Y-type the shock absorber was a telescopic unit enclosed by the spring. At the rear, semi-elliptic

Front view of the ZB – it looked good from any angle!

168

springs were used with the live axle, and these were damped by telescopic shock absorbers.

The bodywork was very well appointed in the MG saloon tradition, complete with varnished woodwork, and at last the car featured a heater as standard, although this was by no means common on cars in its price range in 1953! As a heater it was a pretty rudimentary affair, and although it had an impressive control panel, actual control of the output was difficult, while there was no associated de-mist facility, so that the car misted up internally when the heater was in use... but at that time there was nothing better in use, even in much more expensive cars.

The Z-Series Magnette was, in the context of its time, an excellent car providing a really good specification, coupled with a performance which few other saloon cars could rival. Over the next few years the specification was improved in detail, becoming the ZB in 1956, and the 'Varitone' in 1958, with duo-tone colour scheme. During its currency a proprietary automatic clutch system, known as 'Manumatic' was introduced. This was a conventional clutch which was operated hydraulically according to the demands of engine inlet manifold vacuum, engine speed, and a micro-switch on the gearlever. The whole thing was designed to do away with the conventional clutch pedal as a step towards a fully automatic transmission system, these not being suitable for use with engines as small as 1500 cc in the mid-1950s! Unfortunately the Manumatic was dependent upon too many signals from various components, over which the driver had no control, for smooth operation, and once wear had taken place it was very unpredictable in operation, to say the least, and it disappeared into oblivion.

In 1958 the worst excesses of BMC badge engineering began to make their

The well-equipped driver's compartment — only a rev counter was missing. Heater controls are hidden by the steering wheel.

The 'ZB Varitone' was the final form of the model, its two-tone colour scheme making it arguably the best-looking!

effect felt. The Z-series was by this time five years into production, and the actual production at Abingdon was causing problems, for MGA production was increasing rapidly while space was being sought for a new small sports car, so that space at the small Berkshire factory was at a premium. To move production of the Magnette did not make sense, for in any case a new saloon model would soon be launched. What could be better than an MG version of the new saloon?

Economic sense the new model made, but as a replacement for the Z-series it was a non-starter. The basic Austin A60 and Morris Oxford saloon was styled by the respected Italian body design house of Pinin Farina, and it was characterized by having plenty of interior space, a large luggage boot and a comfortable ride on a smooth road. It had rather poor steering geometry, and a worse suspension layout. BMC Design Office at Longbridge made an attractive MG grille, and fitted out the interior with wood trim; they even put a twin-carburettor version of the engine under the bonnet, and called the creation the Magnette Mark 3, but in truth it was more of a Frankenstein monster! Introduced during 1959, the car was derided and unloved by press and MG enthusiast alike, but as a top-of-the-range model it sold well enough.

In 1961, an attempt was made to improve the appeal of the car. The body was improved in detail, while the suspension and steering geometry were improved immeasurably and the engine was increased in size to 1622 cc. Now known as the Magnette Mark IV, the car was in fact far superior in almost every respect and could be hustled along in a brisk manner. In this form the Magnette name survived until 1968 when it was quietly dropped.

Of the saloons thus far discussed, the Y and Z types were truly of the MG tradition, but the Longbridge-designed Farina models were rather far

The Mark III Magnette was a car which few liked from the aesthetic point of view — and it failed to live up to the standards of performance and handling set by the Z-series. It was the first MG since 1930 not to have been built at Abingdon.

Right and below: The Mark IV Magnette, displaying the large boot which helped make it an excellent family car. In truth, however, it was a top-of-the-range BMC car rather than an MG, as if underlining the fact that it was not built in Abingdon.

The MG 1100 was a success in spite of its ancestry — but the car's handling was superior to most sports cars.

In 1967 the 1100 was replaced by the MG 1300, which was more powered and better appointed.

removed from the ideals of fine handling and good performance, even if by the standards of their day they were not actually bad cars. It was to be another series of cars which was to bring back these ideals to the MG name.

Way back in 1946 Alec Issigonis had been responsible for the design of the first post-war Morris car, the Minor, and its larger brother, the Oxford. Issigonis was a great innovative engineer, who would always start a design with a clean sheet of paper and a new pencil. So it is hardly surprising that when the British Motor Corporation started work on a new series of cars for

The two-door MG Sedan built for the American market, where it was not successful, that market not being ready for small saloons for another five years!

The MG 1300 in its final two-door form.

The WSM MG 1100, a late attempt at restyling, but only this one was built.

the 1960s during the mid-1950s, a radically new design was produced. Basically three sizes of car were envisaged: a tiny car in the old Austin Seven mould, a mid-range model, and a large commodious saloon. All three would have most of the carrying capacity given to the four occupants, with adequate room for their luggage. The new basic principle of a wheel at each corner was established, while engine sizes were to be 850 cc, 1100 cc and 1800 cc for the three cars. The cars all caused problems both in design and production, and later in service, but there is no denying that these three car models set new standards in motor engineering that every other manufacturer has copied.

The Mini is one of the motoring phenomena, alongside the Model-T Ford and the original Volkswagen. It is not surprising that sporting versions of the Mini were produced; what was surprising was that the MG name was not put on these.

The mid-range 1100 series, coded ADO16, was the best-selling car in Britain for several years. Introduced in 1961, it had only been in production for a year when an MG version, with better appointments, a twin-carburettor engine and a smart MG grille, was announced. With all-round independent suspension, working on an inter-connected pressurized fluid displacement system known as 'Hydrolastic', it restored really high standards to the road holding and handling departments of the MG saloon. The engine was mounted transversely in the frame, with the gearbox integral with and below it. Drive was through the front wheels. The whole build of the car was very low, but internal room was surprisingly great, performance was excellent, with fuel economy undreamt of even five years previously in a car of this sort of performance potential, and if anyone doubts that the car had good performance, let it be said that it was as quick as any of the preceding sports models!

By 1967 the 1100 was beginning to look a little dated and the performance standards were rising due to competition from other saloon cars. The whole range was face-lifted, and uprated. The MG version was given a 1275 cc engine and a two-door body was offered as an option. Instrumentation was improved, as was trim, and the model was henceforth known as the MG 1275, but almost immediately became the 1300. A four-speed automatic transmission was offered as an option, but in this case the engine only had a single carburettor.

For 1969 the four-door option was dropped from the MG range, as was the automatic transmission, and the model was finally dropped in 1971 in favour of the Austin GT, which the newly formed Leyland Group saw as the way out of a proliferation of marque names. Most people mourned the passing of the MG model and it was to be ten years before another MG saloon was offered.

The MG saloon range ceased to be regarded as 'true' MGs once production of them was stopped at Abingdon, but it must be recorded that all of them sold well, offering the traditional package of good value for money and a tempting offer for the MG enthusiast who had become a family man. Was this not the principle established by Cecil Kimber when the old Magna and Magnette saloons were built?

Fascia of the Magnette Mark III, displaying the good attempt to stylize the interior as an MG.

Fascia of the MG 1100 – apart from the plastic 'wood' finish, little to distinguish this from its Austin counterpart.

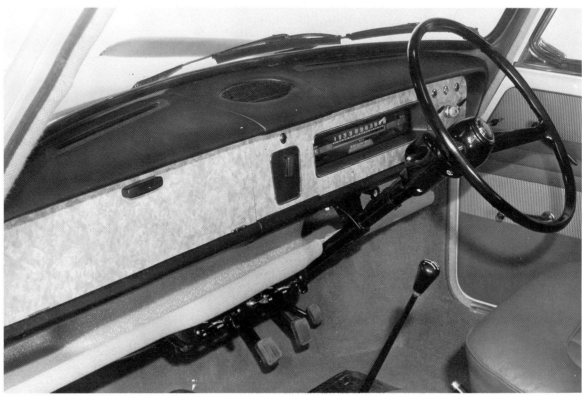

BMC publicity tried hard to give the MG 1100 a sporting connection: here posed with a BRM, with World Champion driver Graham Hill in attendance.

The power unit of the MG 1300: not especially easy to work on, except for basic servicing.

The greatly improved interior in the MG 1300, with full instrumentation and smarter steering wheel than had been fitted to the 1100 model.

A small number of Princess models were sent to America with the MG badge fitted.

9

A New Look

MG cars have always attracted enthusiasts, and one of the greatest enthusiasts for the marque was George Phillips. Phillips was by profession a photographer, and was a specialist in motor racing work. This was no coincidence since he was a keen motorist and an accomplished driver of an MG TC, which he entered in all types of racing event, including the Le Mans 24-Hour Endurance Race. The TC became gradually lighter and more specialized, and while he was not successful in the French event his general approach to preparation was of a high standard, and for the 1951 race Phil was able to convince the management at Abingdon to provide him with a streamlined body on a TD chassis. It would be nice to report that this car was a success in true 'Boy's Own Paper' style, but life is not like that, and the car failed, but that fact is immaterial. What is important about this car is that it formed the basis for the next generation of MG sports cars.

To make a traditional MG go fast it was necessary to apply a great deal of power, as is demonstrated by the fact that practically all the way from the J2, top speed of the whole range of unsupercharged road cars had been between 70 and 80 mph. Almost doubling the power output of the engine resulted in the J4 racing Midget being capable of around 95 mph in road trim, an improvement of 18 per cent. The larger-engined K3 Magnette was barely faster, in spite of better chassis design and a further increase in power of 20 per cent. On the other hand a record-breaking version of the K3, using a fully streamlined body but with only marginally more power, had achieved over 200 mph, an increase of 100 per cent, merely by reducing frontal area. This was the route being followed by racing car designers in the post-war period, and it is hardly surprising that the Phillips TD special, with around half the power of the K3, had *lapped* Le Mans at speeds in excess of the maximum speed of a TD, and indeed quicker than a K3 had ever done!

By 1952 the original car had been improved in looks, the chassis improved from the original TD, and while it was still powered by the venerable XPAG engine, there was little doubt in the minds of Sydney Enever and his design team that the car, coded EX176, would be a winner if it were to be produced for sale. John Thornley was soon convinced that this prototype was a commercial proposition, and the case for producing the new car was put to the Longbridge board of directors of the newly formed British Motor Corporation, who had to give sanction for further work on the development of any new car to proceed.

Longbridge was now the home of the Corporation's centralized design team, who were in the throes of determining which of the various design formats within the group would be used in the future. It was no small task: the Austin Motor Company and the Nuffield group had been merged, largely out of economic necessity; Austin were just about bankrupt following heavy investment in new power unit and model programmes which were not entirely successful. Nuffield on the other hand were solvent financially, but needed new power trains for their good basic designs to replace the largely pre-war engine and transmission designs. Each had large design departments and enormous production facilities and, although the market was buoyant, the cost of retooling new production lines made justification of entirely separate units out of the question. It became obvious that standardization of components was needed, followed by rationalization of products, if the new business venture was to succeed. Thus both Austin and Nuffield had their existing model programmes, as well as commitment to the future, and it is in the light of this that the decision *not* to proceed with the new MG must be judged.

At this stage it will be of interest to look briefly at the history of the Healey marque; from this point onwards there will be quite a few instances of Healey and Austin-Healey cars crossing the MG storyline! Donald Healey had been associated with car production since before the Second World War, having worked for Invicta, then Triumph, but in 1945 had set up a small factory at the rear of a converted cinema in Warwick to produce sporting cars bearing his own name. Powered at first by Riley engines bought from the Nuffield group, and later by a larger unit of American origin, the cars were a moderate success, giving a good performance coupled with great refinement. Production was low, fewer than 400 units were produced even in a good year, so the facts that the cars were expensive and that the model range was complex were of no embarrassment to the limited production facilities.

Healey had always had an interest in sports cars, and while his early designs were sporting in character, sports cars they were not. The 'Silverstone' of 1949 was the first sports car bearing the Healey name, but its styling was too stark to be more than an initial test of the market. By early 1951 Healey was at work with a new shape, a new chassis, and based on the running gear of the Austin A90 'Atlantic': a lamentably poor attempt at sports car design by Longbridge. Healey submitted his design to the board of the Austin Motor Company to see if Austins would be prepared to supply the parts. Leonard Lord was so taken with the car that he persuaded his board to produce the car at Longbridge in larger quantities and at a cheaper selling price than Healey could ever envisage. As far as Austin were concerned the proposed Austin-Healey was something of a salvation, for it would use the capacity for production of the Atlantic model, which was dropped from the range, and would cost little other than royalty payments for the use of the Healey name. Contracts were duly exchanged, possibly just before the actual formation of the British Motor Corporation, and production of a few cars was completed in time for the 1952 London Motor Show, probably at about the time that Abingdon made their presentation of EX176 to the new Board of BMC.

The Austin Healey '100' was no competitor for the MG, having a 2.2-litre engine; it was simply a case of limited financial resources for sports car design and production being fully stretched, and the new MG model had to wait before entering production. In the event, although disappointing to the men of Abingdon, the decision was something of a blessing in disguise for it

The MGA as it originally appeared, but fitted here with an extra luggage rack. Note the close-fitting hood.

The MGA was offered with optional wire wheels.

enabled the new model to be fully developed with the better BMC engine and transmission than the old Nuffield units which it was originally intended to have. Prototype versions of the new model appeared at Le Mans in 1955, and the press were encouraged to write road test reports of the prototypes soon after the race. A further racing foray in the TT three months later was followed by an announcement that factory-sponsored racing was to stop, but the point had been made, and the MGA was announced in time for the London Motor Show.

The new chassis was recognizably a development from that of the TD, but was considerably stiffened amidships, with a strong boxed and braced scuttle hoop replacing the tubular item in the TD/TF. The side-members were much further apart than on the TF, allowing the passengers to sit within the frame, and giving the car a really low centre of gravity. Front and rear suspension used similar components to the earlier car, but the actual rear axle unit owed its origin to the BMC unit used in the Magnette saloon. Engine and gearbox likewise were BMC units shared with the saloon, and the clutch was hydraulically operated as on the Magnette. Sharing of components between the sports and saloon cars made production control of the two models simpler, as well as rationalizing maintenance for the dealers.

The new body was low and sleek, and owed much to work carried out in the record-breaking field, in which MG had achieved phenomenal speeds with limited power outputs. Incidentally, it was to be the last body to be engineered by the old Morris Bodies plant for MG, for the era of the separate body mounted on a chassis frame was coming to an end. It carried two people in comfort with adequate space for luggage in an enclosed boot. The hood was snug, providing rather more than the token covering previously the standard with sports car soft tops, and yet not too complicated to erect in a hurry, which had been a damning criticism of some convertibles. There was even a heater, although it was an optional extra which was not always specified: the age of the true sports car driver was not dead yet! In front of the driver's eye was a full set of instruments, while steering wheel and gear-change lever were each where they might be expected in a sports car.

The whole car showed that the MG had been modernized and improved out of all recognition when compared to previous sports models. It was as near perfect as one might expect from MG, where sports cars had been produced for the past thirty years. When it was announced in 1955 the press were eulogistic: enthusiastic comments were showered on the new car, and Abingdon entered a new phase. At no time since the 1930s had such praise been lavished on the products of the little Berkshire factory. One hundred mph was at last almost a real claim for a production sports car made in large quantity, and this was coupled with the usual helping of 'Safety Fast' handling. Even fuel economy was in a new league, with almost 30 mpg, a figure not achieved since the old M-type, and never before with an engine of a full 1.5 litres; in fact the press pointed out that roughly 30 per cent less power was required by the MGA than the TF to maintain 60 mph.

The fact that three prototype cars had run at Le Mans and the TT shortly before the official announcement of the new model certainly helped with the sales, for here was a 'real' sports car, race-bred just like the old pre-war cars.

An optional factory-fitted hardtop was offered for the first time on an MGA.

The fixed-head coupé model pioneered the larger screen for the closed version of a sports car. Wind-up windows were offered on a closed two-seat MG for the first time.

The MGA Twin Cam displaying its knock-on disc wheels, but there was little else to differentiate this model from the push rod engined car.

Right: Under the bonnet, however, things were quite different: very cramped from the servicing point of view — the distributor was under the rear carburettor, and points needed attention every 3,000 miles!

A coupé version of the Twin Cam in Mark II form: note the radiator grille.

The new model title 'MGA' even bespoke a new era, for had not the whole alphabet been used up in previous models? Everyone liked the MGA, and over 13,000 were sold during the twelve months of production, with the larger percentage of these going to America where, as expected, the car was especially well received. The simple fact of the matter was that the MGA really was a good car in the context of its time, way ahead of its rivals, the HRG and the Jowett Jupiter, both of which disappeared, together with their manufacturers, at about this time. At its price there was nothing to touch it, and it even outperformed several more expensive sports cars. The Kimber touch seemed to have returned to Abingdon.

In August 1956 a number of international class records were taken at between 140 and 171 mph, which must have embarrassed the Warwick/ Longbridge axis who struggled to get 152 with the prototype six-cylinder Austin-Healey of almost twice the engine capacity. At the 1956 London Motor Show, a closed coupé body was offered which was fully trimmed, and featured wind-up windows for the first time on an MG two-seater since the pre-war Tickford Midgets, a sign of things to come, even if the body styling was not as inspired as that of the open car. The little coupé however, was shown to be capable of a genuine 100 mph, the first unsupercharged production MG to be so.

Just over a year later a specifically developed car, powered by a supercharged twin-cam engine, became the first 1.5-litre car to exceed two miles a minute. The twin-cam engine was felt to be a desirable addition to the sports car range, and the MGA Twin Cam was introduced in 1957. The Twin Cam was intended to be a competition version of the MGA, and while it was recognizably an MGA, it was rather special under the skin. The first sign of a double ohc engine had been at the 1955 TT race, when two cars had sported this type of engine; what the press did not spot at the time however, was that there were actually two engines, quite different from each other. One had been worked from a clean sheet of paper at Longbridge, largely the work of Bill Appleby and his team. Appleby had worked with Murray Jamieson on the twin camshaft Austin racing car before the war. The other had been a modification of the B-series unit, worked up by Eddie Maher and his team at the old Morris Engines Plant at Coventry where the old Riley cars had been built. Even ten years later Appleby felt aggrieved that his engine had been turned down in favour of 'the Coventry lash-up', and was sure that, had his engine been used, the emission problems of that later period would have been solved in a simpler manner. Be that as it may, it was Longbridge that decreed that the Coventry engine be used, on the basis that the B-Series block assembly could be employed. The capacity of the engine was increased to 1588 cc, which was shortly to be the standard capacity for the pushrod B-Series unit.

To complement the new engine, the gearbox ratios were improved, and the final drive ratio raised. Dunlop disc brakes were used on all four wheels, posing the well-known conundrum of making an effective and reliable parking brake, which was not altogether effectively solved! In addition Dunlop disc wheels were used, but with centre locking, like the familiar wire-spoked units. These wheels had the dual merit of being light but

The MGA 1600 Mark II was the final form of the MGA.

immensely strong, and requiring far less maintenance than the older but well-loved 'wires'. The car was otherwise indistinguishable from the MGA, and a mistake was made by the marketing men in pushing the car as an up-market version, with 100 mph being available. It was not too long before the design error of using a 10 : 1 compression ratio was discovered, for even in the days of five star petrol, pistons did not take kindly to the heat output produced at the low gas speeds found under road conditions, especially when the car was driven at 30 mph in top gear! The compression ratio was dropped in production to 8.8 : 1 and the Twin Cam then became the true top-of-the-range model.

Almost concurrently with the introduction of the Twin Cam, the MGA was uprated to 1588 cc, and its front brakes were equipped with discs. Sundry minor improvements were introduced at the same time, and thus was born the MGA 1600.

In 1959 EX181 reappeared, this time with the engine opened out to 1506 cc, in order to take it into the 2-litre class (Class E) and this time it exceeded 250 mph by a comfortable margin. Things were riding high at MG: production was booming in response to demands for cars from all parts of the world. Production of the Austin-Healey Sprite had started, and production was now exclusively of sports cars, with the Magnette Mark III being built at Cowley. With everything going well it was hardly surprising that development appeared to stagnate for a time, although this was far from the truth.

During the following year the Twin Cam was quietly dropped from the range, its performance bonus not being sufficient to justify the extra complication. In 1961 the MGA 1600 Mark II was introduced, with the engine increased in size to 1622 cc, in line with other BMC models, and again minor changes were made to the appearance of the car, although perhaps not for the good! However, the performance from the new engine gave the car a new lease of life, with 16 per cent more power and a torque curve to match, enabling the rear axle ratio to be raised to that of the Twin Cam, while the road performance was not far short of the more exotic cousin. Indeed, the last fifty or so Twin Cam chassis were fitted with 1622 engines, and marketed as the 'MGA 1600 Mark II de Luxe' model – quite a mouthful for a Company which prided itself on its short model names!

It seemed as though the MGA would carry on in production for years yet. It was a good car, well loved, but creature comforts were falling behind some of the opposition, in particular the Sunbeam Alpine which was a direct competitor. In fact the sports car market was widening in its appeal, and a whole new brand of owners were appearing who demanded all types of creature comforts which hitherto had not been seen as necessary, so that while the opposition vehicles might not have been sports cars in the old-fashioned sense, they were what the buying public actually wanted. Thus the game of annual updating of models was born, coupled with some genuine improvements to the car.

There were over 100,000 MGAs produced, a milestone commemorated by the factory to ensure that all staff were aware of the fact.

UMG 400: the 1952 Le Mans TD from which the MGA was evolved; here seen on test with George Phillips at the wheel.

The MGA was a nice car to drive, with the ability to be used in competition with little modification; indeed the company extended its range of tuning advice and equipment as a result of its own competition experience. On the road it was a thoroughly practical car when judged by the standards of its contemporaries, and considerably more economical to run than its predecessors, demonstrating what enormous strides were being made in the motor industry in the late fifties. Total production of the MGA passed the 100,000 mark in the spring of 1962, more than the previous total production of cars at Abingdon. Yet shortly after this, less than eight years after its introduction, a successor was being announced.

The MGA chassis in production form (actually a 1600): compare the layout of this with that of the TF on p. 159.

The 1960 Wimbledon Champion, Darlene Hard, here pictured with an MGA which was afterwards shipped to the States for her.

A New Look

The rival Austin twin ohc engine built for the MGA, but not put into production. Ten years later the chief designer, Bill Appleby, was claiming that this engine would have been less troublesome and given emission levels to meet the requirements of the late 1960s.

The special supercharged 1500 cc engine built for the record-breaker EX181. The author has one of the connection rods from this engine.

A factory demonstrator car on test at the press release of the Twin Cam at Chobham.

One of the most famous Twin Cams. Starting life as the prototype, this car went on to be raced in the early 1960s by John Sharpe, fitted with a prototype MGB engine.

10

Modern Midgets:
from Sprite to Spitfire

As recounted in the previous chapter, the Austin-Healey had appeared almost as an accident, owing to contracts signed by the Austin Motor Company before the formation of the BMC. It was justified by the new Corporation as being the sports car for the Austin network to sell, since the MG was not available to them, an example of the muddled thinking which was to beset the sales and production policies of the next twenty-five years and more.

During the early 1950s quite a number of budding motor engineers tried their hands at building a small production sports car which would emulate the pre-war MG Midget models. Some of these, like the Buckler, were pure specials. With these cars, the buyer purchased a chassis frame of advanced design which could be built into a car by the keen amateur, using proprietary suspension components manufactured either by the specialist or by one of the major manufacturers. These cars then accepted a wide range of power unit options, including the MG XPAG unit. The whole car was covered with

The original 948 cc Midget was a pretty little car which sought the market at one time filled by the M, J and P-type Midgets.

The hood was a definite improvement over earlier Midgets, but in side view it was as ugly as that of the M-type!

The Mark II Midget was considerably changed in mechanical specification, but apart from wind-up windows was difficult to distinguish from the Mark I.

a proprietary glassfibre body shell, and presented the capable enthusiast with a cheap way into 'new' car ownership. It must be said, however, that many of these projects were never completed and some of those which were left quite a lot to be desired!

There were others, like the Dellow and Lotus, which were uncompromising competition cars. In between lay the genuine attempts to build a road car, typified by the Fairthorpe. All such manufacturers, however, relied on the owner to finish the car, since it allowed all parties to benefit from a loophole in the then-current laws relating to the taxation of new cars: in short, the cars were in effect tax-free, saving around a third on the purchase price!

It was within this framework that Midlands motor enthusiast Jack Turner, who was also a brilliant and innovative engineer, was already at work building a number of specialized cars for the sporting motorist, mainly on the one-off basis. Good though these cars were, only one of Turner's creations was ever taken seriously and that was a small sports car based on the Austin A30. In this venture he was backed by Midlands enthusiast John Webb, who happened at the same time to be racing an old K3 Magnette. The A30 was a small saloon car, dubbed at the time of its introduction by the popular press as the modern Austin Seven. Powered by the 803 cc A-series engine, and mated to a gearbox most kindly described as typically 'Austin' with its four widely spaced ratios, it was a jolly little family car with independent front suspension and a good turn of performance to rival, but not equal, that of the Issigonis-designed Morris Minor. As a possible sports car, it was as appealing as the pre-war Austin Seven!

The Turner Sports used A30 front and rear suspension, as well as the engine and transmission, the engine being mildly tuned and fitted with twin SU carburettors. All this was mounted on a simple tubular ladder frame and covered by a glassfibre bodyshell. Probably around twenty or thirty of these cars were built, one of their customers being the entertainer Petula Clark, whose car was painted bright pink! In fact the model was quite handsome but the financial backing was insufficient and it was not produced in large enough quantities to worry the car-producing giants or to exploit the market which existed.

There can be little doubt that Donald Healey did not miss the commercial possibilities of the Turner Sports, but it took a couple of years for him to produce the design of his small sports car, based on the floorpan of the A30 instead of a conventional chassis. This was the master-stroke of his design, since it allowed the body to become integral with the chassis, giving greater rigidity to the overall structure, as well as reducing tooling costs. It is not generally realized that the original name for the new sports car was to have been the Imp, but this name had already been claimed by the Rootes group for their new small saloon, as yet unannounced, so that it became known as the Sprite to the chagrin of the Riley enthusiasts. It was an immediate winner, and production was shifted to Abingdon, where Enever and his men re-engineered much of the detail work to ease production difficulties.

The frame consisted broadly of two side-members separated by a flat floor, but with a bracing member running parallel with these at the centre and forming the transmission tunnel. At the front a bracing was built up forming the scuttle, while two longerons stretched forward of this, closed with a transverse cross-member. To the rear was a box which formed the boot without an opening lid. Front wings were integral with the forward hinged bonnet.

Front suspension was mounted on the foremost cross-member, and was derived directly from the A30, which by this time had grown up into the A35, with a large wishbone forming the lower link and the hydraulic lever-arm damper the top link, with a coil spring mounted between. Rear suspension was by stiff quarter-elliptic springs, and damped by lever-arm shock absorbers. The engine, by this time of 948 cc, was mounted between the forward chassis extensions, and the four-speed gearbox with much

The hood line of the Mark III Midget provided the car with good looks whether up...

... or down.

The cockpit of the Mark III Midget was spartan, but well enough equipped to ensure good sales.

improved ratios and a neat remote control gearlever was hidden in the long tunnel. The rear axle was pure A35 with hypoid gears. Mercifully the brakes were not derived from the A35 but the Morris Minor, and were hydraulically operated with a simple cable-operated handbrake.

Naturally there was no fixed roof, the two bucket seats being covered with a neat soft-top which stowed in the rear compartment, reached by tilting the seats forward. The hood was made snug by fitting removable side-screens in place on top of the doors in a traditional fashion. In front of the driver was a vertical steering wheel, while instrumentation was similar to that of other sports cars of the period. The gear-stick came, as journalists put it, neatly to the hand on the central tunnel right beside the rim of the steering wheel.

The car was the answer to the criticism that no one was producing a true sports car of under one litre, but from the MG enthusiast's point of view it had the wrong name. With production based at Abingdon, it was not long before the engineers began a critical appraisal of the car. The bonnet unit was a very expensive piece to produce, and suffered in that if it was damaged in a road accident, even a minor parking bump, the entire unit needed replacing, to the detriment of the insurance premiums! Also, there being no boot lid did produce sales resistance. These two factors combined to ensure that by 1961 a revised bodyshell was produced. A sign of the times was that people had started to criticise the soft-top which rattled and leaked when the car was driven at speed: no one had ever thought of using the hood when driving fast until this period but both the MGA and the Sprite were now coming under fire. It was a reasonable case since there were sprots cars with usable hoods on the market: so why could not MG, the 'home of the sports car', make one?

The Mark II Sprite was announced in April 1961, followed a month later by the MG Midget. Still powered by the 948 cc engine, and with virtually unchanged suspension front and rear, the bodywork was considerably better looking. The front wings were now bolted to the chassis structure, and a simple alligator jaw bonnet replaced the old 'frog eye' Sprite unit, with only slight loss of accessibility, but being much cheaper to repair following minor accident damage. At the rear the general shape followed the style of the day, allowing the rear light clusters to be mounted prominently, and with a flatter rear deck, a proper opening boot lid was provided. The hood was not improved on this model, incidentally, and the good old-fashioned side screens were retained. The bulk of the re-engineering was carried out at Abingdon by Enever and his men, one or two of the Abingdon diehards harbouring thoughts that the new car might just carry the name MG, but this was not to be and the Sprite Mark II was announced just a few days before the new MG Midget, the latter car being a de luxe version with slightly better equipment and costing some £40 more. Although there was little difference between the new models MG enthusiasts were quick to take the new car to their hearts.

An uprated Midget was announced in 1963, featuring an engine capacity increase to 1098 cc, coupled with the improved gearbox with a really good set of ratios. With this increase in performance came the introduction of disc brakes at the front, and wire-spoked wheels as an optional extra. All this of course meant the loss of the 'under one litre' car, but was necessary in view

The 1971 home market Midget cockpit, showing the rocker switches and simpler instrumentation.

The 1971 USA market Midget cockpit, with safety dash and instruments packed in front of the driver.

The 1971 home market Midget had distinctive wheels.

For 1972 the wheels were changed to Rostyle pattern and round wheel arches were featured. Stylists had replaced engineers, it seemed!

of the introduction of the Triumph Spitfire to the market place, which was to prove a direct rival to the Midget throughout the rest of its production life. The increased power of the 1100 cc engine showed up the deficiencies of the rear suspension, which offered little lateral location of the axle, and therefore a marked tendency to oversteer. Enever's men worked hard on this, and the revised rear suspension, using semi-elliptic rear springs, formed the principal change on the introduction of the Mark II Midget early in 1964, the equivalent Sprite being the Mark III, just to confuse the next generation! At the same time however, creature comforts were being looked after, and the body was revised. A new windscreen was fitted, and the doors were provided with drop-glasses in place of the old-fashioned side curtains, these running between concealed channels at the rear and the BMC quarter lights, inaptly named 'no draught ventilators' by the sales copywriters of the day.

The Mark II Midget was by this time a firm favourite in all types of club motor sporting event, just as the old J, P and T-types had been in previous eras. Those still running the older cars referred to the new cars as 'Tin Midgets', but we admired the way in which the new cars were able to be thrashed unmercifully for hours on end. It was found necessary to increase main bearing size for the crankshaft with the introduction of the Mark II, something which went almost unnoticed at the time.

Good though the performance was, an increase was required, because this was now the era of the small hot saloon, and in particular the Mini Cooper. These little cars offered real sports car performance and handling, but with the convenience of four seats and a solid roof which did not leak when it rained... well, the roof did not, even if the screen seals were less than watertight! The men at Abingdon, along with almost everyone else at the time, were most impressed with the Mini and they had even experimented with an open MG derivative, ADO34, but this failed to impress Longbridge, and rather than badge-engineer an MG saloon version, as they had with the Wolseley Hornet and Riley Elf, Longbridge Design allowed MG to use a 1275 cc engine in the Midget, derived from the rally-winning Mini Cooper S unit. The new model was announced in time for the 1965 London Motor Show as the Midget Mark III.

The enlarged engine initially brought a little spot of trouble since, even against the advice of Appleby, it had been decided to use a crankshaft of the same material as the 1100, but this was found to break just as easily as had that of the J2 in an earlier age. The problem was solved initially by using a nitrided crank as in the Mini Cooper S, and later by using cranks made of different material from the original, but the problem caused a minor hiatus at the time. With the introduction of the new engine came a revised bodyshell, which featured at last a proper folding hood, designed to be used in the erect position! Rear suspension was uprated and much detail improvement was seen inside the cockpit. The only feature not improved was the heater, which even in 1965 was behind the times, but was to survive for another fourteen years!

The 1275 cc engine in the Midget ran through practically unchanged until 1974, although the Sprite was quietly deleted in 1968. Each year from 1966 it had become necessary to meet increasingly stringent safety and emission

The 1974 model car featured 'safety' bumpers and raised ride light.

regulations imposed by zealot legislators in the USA and elsewhere, and while I do not hold brief for those who condemn moves to improve the environment, it must be admitted that annual changes did tend to divert the attention of designers from the important tasks of designing the next generation of cars on to a holding operation which sapped resources. From 1966, therefore, an annual updating of the American-market car occurred, while the domestic models tended to show stagnation of design. Owing to the large content of American- market cars in their production, Abingdon had been provided with a test-house in the production stream for testing the exhaust emissions of new cars, and this unit, known as the Air Pollution Control Centre (APCC), became the first such production unit in Europe, and possibly in the world. I had a large hand in the design and operation of this unit, and, opened in 1966, it was fitting that it was started under the aegis of Reg Jackson, who was to retire two years later, very proud that MG should have built it. It was regarding the APCC that the first contacts were made between the Canley and Abingdon staff actually prior to the formation of British Leyland.

By 1972 the Midget was very old-fashioned; it still sold well, chiefly because of its enthusiastic and loyal following and to a large measure because it happened to do its job well. New projects were started, of which the most promising was probably EX234, but because of the effort being put into keeping the older cars on the market, there was insufficient funding for a new model.

There was of course another factor: during 1968 the British Leyland Corporation had been formed. During 1964 BMC had bought out the ailing Jaguar Car Company, which had suffered itself in buying out the old Daimler Company. The move was to cost the new combine – British Motor Holdings – dear, for it rapidly degenerated from a major manufacturer, enjoying the larger part of the national car sales, to an under-financed giant which, with poor management and over-active politically motivated 'unionism', went from bad to worse. The Leyland Group, led by commercial-vehicle salesman extraordinary Donald Stokes, was prevailed upon by a Government more noted for political ideals than actual attainment to head up what was, in effect, a nationalized motor industry, to be named the British Leyland Motor Corporation, bringing together most of the respected marque names in Britain, including, as it happened, MG and Triumph.

Stokes had heard of Triumph; after all, it was one of the companies which he had bought in forming the original Leyland Group. Not being particularly interested in cars at all, he seemed not to have heard of MG, and those of us at Abingdon were aghast when we heard him say on television something to the effect that Triumph was the only British sports car! At a stroke it seemed that forty-odd years of achievement were to be replaced by a post-war upstart! This is not what happened, of course, and it was soon common knowledge that the men of Abingdon and Canley were working together.

Triumph were producing a range of cars which included a small sports car called the Spitfire, a direct competitor for the Midget. This is not the place to

Under the bonnet of the 1974 model was fitted the 1500 cc engine, which owed its origins to the Triumph range.

discuss the relative merits of the two cars, but it is probably fair to say that while the Midget appealed to the young man with sporting aspirations, the Spitfire appealed more to those who wanted to use their car for touring only: in truth, two different markets which only overlapped by a small degree. The motoring press were at pains to show that either the Midget or the Spitfire was doomed, depending upon their particular bias, and I think that everyone was taken by surprise when the 'new' Midget was announced for 1974!

The Midget was updated, with revised bumper bars and ride height to conform with the safety requirements regarding potential tailgate accidents in the USA. At the same time the 1500 cc Spitfire engine and gearbox were fitted, which enabled the Corporation to reduce the workload on emission engineering. The job of installing the new engine was a real 'shoe-horn job' and under-bonnet space became very short... not that there had been much room for working before! The engine was viewed with some suspicion by MG enthusiasts, while the gearbox, with synchromesh on bottom gear (would you believe it!) was regarded as 'sissy' by the diehard MG man!

It was the old story again, of course, and while the 1500 engine was not the best sports car engine in the world, it did give the car a long-legged cruising ability coupled with a very spirited performance capability. While the standard 1275 car had been hard pressed to reach 100 mph, the new 1500 could do so with ease, but this was now an academic point, since such speeds were by this time illegal in most countries and absolute performance was no longer a criterion upon which to judge a motor car; indeed the whole idea of a sports car was becoming outdated.

The Midget underwent few further modifications during its life; the rear axle ratio was raised for the 1976 model, but it finally went out of production during 1978, by which time over 250,000 units had been built – without doubt the best selling Midget ever! In its final form the Midget had lost a lot of its character, and was no longer a sports car in some respects. Its straight line performance was good and, despite contemporary criticism, the handling was not really impaired. The engine, rather in the manner of the TA unit some forty years previously, did not revel in being used at high crankshaft speeds, while the gear ratios were fairly widely spaced, which meant that the engine *had* to be 'revved' to get smooth progression: the result was a number of burst engines and wrecked gearboxes, which gave the car an undeserved amount of criticism.

Personally, I feel that the Midget had grown from 948 cc to 1275 cc gracefully, but needed replacement at that juncture, when the design was twenty years old. Further development of the model on the same chassis was doomed, and it is a pity that more resources were not made available for sports car design back in 1966. The essential elements of the Midget were present as long as the old A-series engine was there, and it was capable of being tuned to give far greater performance. Once the 1500 cc engine was fitted the performance was there immediately, but the engine was somehow 'softer' and less forgiving if driven really hard: this being the difference between the earlier Midget and the Spitfire, of course!

The original 1959 Austin-Healey Sprite, which was the inspiration for the long line of MG Midgets through the 1960s and 1970s.

Fascia of the Mark I Midget: a delightfully simple but uncluttered layout.

A comparison of grilles: the MGA and the Midget, in production concurrently — few guessed that the square look would soon take over from the shapely 'A'.

The last series of Midget.

The Triumph Spitfire from which the engine of the Midget 1500 was derived. The Spitfire was the direct competitor of the Midget, but never sold in the same numbers.

11

MGB: the Last of the Sports Cars

Towards the end of the 1950s it was becoming obvious that a new model was needed to replace the successful MGA model. Which direction to follow presented a difficult choice: the MGA was a success, but it was based on a chassis frame with a separate body, and every car designer was sure that this design route was old-fashioned – the resultant car was needlessly overweight, which detracted from the overall performance, surely the *raison d'être* of the sports car. But then the design of an open-top car using a monocoque construction was not simple if one were to provide doors for the passengers' entry and exit! Such provision allowed for an unacceptable amount of body movement, which ultimately affected handling and sports cars were not to be compromised in this area.

The pointer for an intended route was given with the Midget, née Sprite, but to be fair it is likely that the initial work for the MGA replacement had already started when the Sprite appeared: the Design Office project number for the MGB was ADO23, while that for the Sprite/Midget was ADO41/47. Sydney Enever always maintained that the starting point for ADO23 was EX181, the two-mile-a-minute record-breaker of 1957, but this is surely the car designer's equivalent of poetic licence! There are strong connections with the MGA to be found in the later car especially in the basic underframe and running gear.

The floorpan was in two parts separated by three parallel longitudinal tubes, of which the centre one formed the transmission tunnel. At the front was formed a steel box scuttle, with tall sheet-steel extensions rising from square section extensions. The front suspension was carried at the forward end of these, while the front wings were bolted to the vertical sheets, which thus formed the inner wing valances and ensured considerable strength at the front, at the same time forming a 'box' to house the engine. At the rear of the floor section was built up another scuttle which formed the rear boot, while box-section chassis members under this carried the rear springs and formed a rigid base for the boot. The rear wings and valances formed a semi-stressed skin to make a rear 'box'. The doors closed the vertical spaces between front and rear boxes.

The overall length of the car was actually a couple of inches shorter than the MGA, with shorter wheelbase, but the track remained the same. The front suspension was carried on a removable cross-member, similar in style to the fixed cross-member of the MGA chassis, and although similar in layout, with the shock absorber forming the upper link and the lower wishbone identical to that of the earlier car, the actual stub axles and kingpins were quite different, and much simpler to maintain. The rear

A very early MGB: this car was actually around the factory until the late 1960s, having been a demonstrator, then a development car for the emission control work, finally ending its days as a factory 'tug' before being broken up.

suspension was still by semi-elliptic springs, not because Abingdon were not interested in independent rear suspension, but for the simple reason that it had not been possible to demonstrate that any system tried was sufficiently better to justify the complications of manufacture maintenance. It is interesting to reflect that it was more likely that a de Dion layout would have been favoured, which was the system which Rover eventually adopted for their new saloon model of the same period. Certainly the few mass-produced sports cars of the late fifties and early sixties which were equipped with independent rear suspension were not renowned for either good handling or supreme cornering ability!

The choice of engine was an important one. Unlike the space under the bonnet of the MGA, there was plenty of room in the new car. Several layout projections were made, including a V4 and an in-line small six unit; these were naturally being designed at Longbridge with sedan cars principally in mind, but Abingdon were allowed to evaluate the prototype units for their applications. The V4 had many merits, in that it was short, and comparatively light, but it did have terrible vibration periods which were unacceptable, something that Ford found when they tried such a unit. The six-cylinder engine has never been very successful in the British market and there was little chance of this unit finding favour in a Morris Oxford or similar car, in spite of its undoubted merits of perfect balance and superior torque characteristics to an equal-sized four in the same state of tune. A six-cylinder engine was eventually adopted which had a much larger capacity for an additional model, as recounted in the next chapter.

The engine fitted to the MGB was therefore the much-loved B-series unit, but now opened out to 1800 cc. The crankshaft still ran in three main bearings, and although it came in for some criticism from the technical press, few customers complained and most admired the enormous torque the engine developed at very low crankshaft speeds. It had a high compression ratio and a long stroke, and with its twin 1½-inch SU carburettors gave a very respectable 94 bhp. It is difficult to keep in mind that this engine started life as a 1200 cc unit, for in 1800 cc form it was easily the best yet produced. Oil consumption and specific fuel consumption were particularly good by the standards of the day.

A diaphragm clutch was used for the first time on an MG, taking the drive to the gearbox; still with but three synchronized, widely spaced gears, it transmitted power to the strong, if somewhat noisy, rear axle by open propshaft. The lack of synchromesh on bottom gear was at the dictate of BMC's Chief Engineer, Alec Issigonis, so often an innovator but in this matter behind the times. Whatever the faults of the transmission it was robust and cheap to replace. It also had the merit of a very sweet gear change, and the broad torque curve of the engine made the gaps in the ratios less noticeable than they might have been.

Instrumentation was up to the now normal MG standard, while seating was conventional, providing plenty of leg room for the tallest of people. The heater supplied (by now it was an optional *non-fitment*) was still somewhat rudimentary but up to the standards of 1962, even if the controls were ... well ... idiosyncratic! The hood was a real masterpiece, being both snug when fitted, and easy to erect or stow, and what is more it stayed in place at all speeds of which the car was capable. The hood was still removed for stowage, and a tonneau cover was available when the hood was stowed: Abingdon still regarded the hood as something to be used occasionally in inclement weather, rather than a roof to be removed when the sun shone, whatever the customer thought!

The initial road tests showed an excellent performance and praised the handling of the car. Top speed was significantly over 100 mph, while fuel consumption was reported to be in the 25–30 mpg bracket, even when driven hard. There was no doubt that the MGB represented a genuine improvement over its predecessor in every respect. The whole car represented the state of the sports car art when it was introduced, and it was as well received as its predecessor had been. It drove well, handled well, was economical, and while it was not a really radical new design most of those who tried the car liked its good road manners. Of those who would have had MG build a small, highly sophisticated production design, there were none who appreciated the factors which influenced a large car producer in his choice of vehicle. Any car built by a large combine would have to use components which were readily available, to enable development of the

The rear view of the original MGB model, showing what a good-looking car it was. The boot was partly occupied by the spare wheel, and the optional luggage rack was a useful extra.

Another early MGB, this one seen taking part in an MG Car Club race meeting in the early 1970s. At the time of writing it has been in the same family since 1965.

specialist elements of the car to be maximized: failure to do this in the mid-thirties had resulted in Kimber having his knuckles rapped, at least metaphorically, and in a rapid change of policy in 1935. By the late fifties the major cost of car design lay in the chassis and body design; mechanical components therefore had by necessity to be readily available from the store shelves to keep manufacturing costs within bounds. The fact that the Abingdon people were able to design such a good car from such unpromising material as that provided by the BMC is a tribute to their ability, and should certainly not be sneered at in retrospect.

In 1963 an overdrive was offered as an optional fitment to the gearbox, and during the same year a coupé-style folding hood and wire wheels became available as factory-fitted options. The following year the engine crankcase was revised, five main bearings being provided for the crankshaft, chiefly it must be said for the new saloon car, the BMC 1800, which was to prove the largest of the front-wheel-drive variants. This was to provide a much smoother-running engine capable of running at higher sustained crankshaft speeds.

The problem of the fixed-head coupé was exercising minds at Abingdon, it always being conceded that the MGA Coupé was hardly a good-looking car. Attempts to make an MGB Coupé were proving equally difficult and it was the styling studio of Pininfarina which finally solved the puzzle. In 1965 the MGB GT was announced. It was one of the classic car shapes, with a large windscreen, large rear quarter lights and an opening tailgate, hinged along its top edge. Almost certainly the first of the now-fashionable 'hatchback' cars, this body style was immediately successful. It was very heavy, since money was not made available to retool the underframe, but this did result in a very rigid body. The GT was as well received as the tourer had been; it proved marginally faster and more economical on fuel, although acceleration was not quite as good. Sales of the new version quickly overtook those of the tourer, especially on the home market, and a whole new market was opened up.

The following year saw the first effect of the wave of safety and emission regulations which were being forced through the legislature in America, and which would have profound effects on the production of cars, not only at MG, but throughout the world. A whole series of rules and regulations were enacted which specified the ways in which cars should be built to protect their occupants in the event of an accident, and others to protect them from the effects of the exhaust gas output which was inseparable from the use of a combustion engine. So far as MG were concerned, initially there was little which needed to be done from the safety point of view. Indeed, even the emission standards were met for 1965–66, but this was to prove the start of an annual round of model-changing and updating which may have improved the environment but virtually halted the development of genuine new models which could have achieved better results had resources not been, in effect, wasted.

Meanwhile work was underway in the Transmission Design Department for a new gearbox for the range of commercial vehicles fitted with the B-series engine, and Abingdon were quick to seize on this for the MGB and

A 1971 MGB USA-specification car, displaying the factory-fitted hardtop.

for the new MGC. Much more robust than the old unit, it featured synchromesh on all gears, and a better set of ratios than hitherto, although still with a gap between second and third, a problem which beset BMC gearbox designers as well as their predecessors in Austin and Morris. People have often wondered why this should be so, especially when the Midget had such a good set of ratios in its gearbox, but the reason is that all new cars were obliged by legislation to be able to restart on any incline in the UK, and the fact that Wrynose Pass has a slope of 1 in 2.5 did impose a constraint on the gearbox ratios. The new gearbox also featured an improved overdrive unit, which was not only lighter and more reliable, but cheaper too. With the new gearbox came a new rear axle unit, too, which was quieter and stronger, based on designs of the Salisbury Company.

For the 1967 London Motor Show, the MGB Mark II was introduced, together with the additional new MGC model, which will be discussed in the next chapter. The Mark II featured a revised bodyshell in both tourer and GT forms to accommodate the new gearbox, which we knew in the factory as the wide-centre body. Advantage was taken of the increased transmission tunnel width to offer an automatic gearbox option, using the Borg-Warner Type 35 unit, which was felt to widen the car's appeal in the USA. This proved a fallacy, and the automatic was dropped from the range after less than two years.

In 1968 came the formation of the British Leyland Motor Corporation, already discussed in the previous chapter, and for the time being there was little interference in the running of the Longbridge-Abingdon design operation. There was a good deal of co-operation between Solihull, where the Rover-Triumph Design Department was based, and the old BMH company relating to safety and emission law compliance; in fact this had been going on for some time and was now formalized on an in-house basis.

The MGB GT — this car was the production prototype.

Rear view of the GT: the first of the hatchback cars, predating the Renault and Maxi models by three years!

The 1972 model MGB GT with the recessed grille, greeted at the time with some reservations: the 'yawning' B, we called it!

To us at Abingdon it seemed that while the position of the Midget and the MGC might not be secure owing to in-house competition, that of the MGB was assured since there was no direct competitor within the group, either in production or planned. And so it proved: the MGB would, it seemed, continue until such a time as a suitable replacement was approved, but in the meantime all available design time needed to be spent on the bread-and-butter saloon car models to counter the much improved products of Dagenham which were eroding 'our' traditional market. What actually happened of course was a succession of inept decisions at director level concerning saloon car production, of which the most crass was the public announcement that British Leyland was to move 'up-market' and not fight the market-place battle for sales. To follow this with a production 'lemon' like the Marina, which was patently aimed at the low-price end of the market and was such a poor attempt, was to cost the Company dear both in sales and in sympathy with the gentlemen of the press, something which was not put right for a whole decade; while that is another story, within its framework lies one of the many reasons why sports car design stagnated. Without the bread-and-butter cars, production of a sports car could not be financed, and with that market shrinking as a result of direction from the top level it became obvious that a new sports car would be shelved.

This problem was compounded by the need to meet the annual changes in legislative requirements which also cost large sums of money as well as diverting important design effort. Each autumn came a round of minor modifications for the home market together with an increasing welter of other market requirements which caused a whole profusion of production problems which were overcome by the men of Abingdon with no real difficulty. A misguided accountant in the USA succeeded in 'proving' to politicians that since one domestic car had unsafe handling characteristics, then the buying public needed to be protected from the products of the demon car manufacturers, and the subject of vehicle secondary safety became one in which all manufacturers had to take a close interest. A whole series of laws were passed with which new cars had to comply, and these laws were revised annually. Naturally no government could be seen not to take this well-intentioned effort to heart, but each one seemed set on proving that it had the 'safety' of the motor vehicle at heart and produced its own set of regulations; there were even inter-state differences in the USA which all went to fuel my suspicion that Parkinson's Law was true, and that every government department was generating its own assurance of a future! You think I am overstating the case? In 1969 we produced separate market designations for the UK, EEC countries (Britain was not 'in' at that time), France and Germany (who were), Denmark, Sweden, Norway, the USA, California, Canada (yes, three separate models for North America), Australia, Japan and Saudi Arabia, with other markets to special order! Some of the differences were very minor, and could have precipitated a diplomatic incident had we got the specification wrong, but we never did, so far as I know.

With the importance of safety aspects came the start of the 'recall' situation, where if an irregularity was found in production it had to be declared to the government body involved, all owners contacted, and their vehicles modified at company expense. At MG we had few of these, but it did make us all especially careful about quality control systems, and by the mid-seventies those we had at MG were being looked at closely by BL, who were in the process of setting up systems across the whole company. To give some idea of the annual changes, I list below some of the more important by model year; they usually appeared in production in the autumn in time for the London Motor Show. Some years there were no real changes apart from the ability to comply with a small change in emission regulations, and the principal difference with the previous year's model would be the range of colours!

For 1973 a revised grille was offered, known at the factory as the 'eggbox'

An automatic gearbox was offered as an option for the MGB in 1969: the selector control was reminiscent of the preselector control on the K Magnette.

1968: Negative earth, alternator, pre-engaged starter, two-speed wipers, octagon spinners for the wire wheels, and collapsible steering column.
US: Sidemarkers, energy-absorbing steering column, dual circuit brakes, air pump emission control system, and paddded dash.

1969: Vinyl trim, head restraints and improved hood.

1970: Mark 3 revised rear lights, recessed grille, revised interior with centre console and face-level ventilation, Rostyle wheels, flush interior door handles, and rocker switches on dash.
US: Illuminated sidemarkers.

1971: Apparently there were no changes, although no doubt a new range of colours was introduced!

1972: HIF carburettors which brought a storm of protest, but which were in fact much better than their predecessors, giving better economy and emission levels. The Mark III bodyshell was introduced at this time.
US: Chrome deleted from wiper arms and blades, glovebox fitted to the padded dash – Abingdon had found that their original design in this area far exceeded the requirements on 'safety' which highlights just how difficult it was to comply with paper standards set by bureaucrats.

1973: Brushed nylon trim.
US: Anti-run on valve, massive rubber over-riders were fitted which were nicknamed at the factory with reference to a well-endowed film actress of the time!

1974: Raised ride height, 'rubber' bumpers which, for the domestic market, were actually a soft ABS plastic material, and a single 12-volt battery was fitted at last: the twin 6-volt units being a carry-over from the old pre-war Magnette days! The bumpers fitted for the US and Swedish markets were actually an energy-absorbing unit which was much heavier.

1975: Jubilee edition GT model celebrating fifty years of MG production, and the brake servo was made standard.
US: Single CD Stromberg carburettor was fitted, together with a catalytic converter exhaust; this had the result of really dropping the performance of the American-market cars, which hitherto had only suffered marginally with the emission control features. This hardly seemed to matter for a country where the national speed limit was 55 mph.

1976: Front and rear anti-roll bars were fitted, which restored the handling of the MGB to something near its previous 'Safety Fast' standard. The electric fan was standardized, deleting the engine-driven and somewhat noisy unit previously fitted.

1977: Single-wipe facility for the screen wipers, zip-out rear window for the hood, and improved fuel tank.
US: Larger instrument faces with speedometer calibration to 80 mph maximum, although the car was actually capable of higher speeds than this. Twin cooling fans were fitted to the radiator.

1978: No changes.

1979: LE models were introduced in limited edition, ostensibly to celebrate fifty years of production at Abingdon, but in fact ended the series of cars.

1980: End of production.

During the last few years of production, development of variations of the MGB was continued. With the impending arrival of a new range of engines, it was inevitable that MG applications should be tried. During 1975–76 at least one car was, under full test, fitted with the O-series engine and this was showing great promise. A similar application was planned for the Marina/Ital range, and it seemed likely that the new engine plant at Longbridge, coupled with a change of Chief Executive at British Leyland, resulted in development of the MGB being stopped during 1978. By the time production was finished at Abingdon over half a million MGBs had been produced, easily the most successful sports car design to date, and could probably have continued in production had it not been for a number of reasons concerning the internal politics of British Leyland.

The fact was that BL had spent a fortune developing the TR7 model, which was proving a sales liability; the MGB was easily outselling the new car in 1977 and probably continued to do so into 1978. There was a strong need in BL to prove to the Government, who were supplying the money from taxpayers' funds, that they had made the right decision in producing the TR7 and other models which were not selling particularly well. On the basis that anything can be proved with statistics, and if production is curtailed sales will fall, the rate of production at Abingdon was cut, and so figures were produced to prove that the MGB model and Abingdon plant were a financial liability and ought to be axed. In fact demand for the MGB was still high in the important American market, and the car was in compliance with all known legislation for at least three years, and while it was obvious that the model could not go on in production indefinitely, surely the market should have been fed with the product it wanted? Instead it got what the BL board was told it should have! The decision to close the plant was blamed on Michael Edwardes personally, but with the information supplied to him it was the only decision he could have reached: had the data been supplied in other ways, there is little doubt that Abingdon could have become the Sports Car Division of BL Cars... but that is another story!

There were a number of misguided efforts to save the Abingdon plant but all were doomed because they required the purchase of the manufacturing rights to the name MG and the full co-operation of the BL Cars group to supply the bulk of the parts. Both of these requirements were at best a forlorn hope, but quite unrealistic, and the famous plant was closed in 1980, just fifty years after Kimber had opened it. However this did not spell the end of the MG name, for BL Cars had now been made aware of the love and affection which the motoring public held for the marque, and they actually had a new car ready for production.

A 1976 model MGB in left hand drive form, but with no safety equipment: presumably destined for Europe.

The engine compartment of the 1976 model MGB with the maligned SU HIF4 carburettors.

The Lancashire police bought a lot of MGs over the years: here is a 1963 MGB equipped for police duty.

The milestone of a quarter million MGBs was celebrated by British Leyland, and here George Turnbull, Managing Director of the Austin Morris Division, poses with the car in the factory.

A 1975 model GT, displaying the fact that the safety bumpers enhanced the side profile, especially at the front. A statement which proves beauty to be in the eye of the beholder?

A full range of touring modifications were available to the owner, this being a Stage 6, full race engine — as raced by the Factory!

A 1980 model MGB; what
was to prove the last of
the annual update
models.

Last of the line: the LE
MGB of 1980, this is a
wire wheel version
although that with alloy
wheels was more popular.

A styling exercise by Aston Martin during an unsuccessful bid by that company to buy MG.

12

Variations on a Theme in B

One of the main problems with building a successful sports car is that the temptation always exists to increase the engine size and therefore to exploit the excellent handling of the basic model more fully. Oddly enough, MG has seldom done this, preferring perhaps to develop the basic design only by small amounts before replacing the old model with a new one.

Back in the mid-thirties, the K-type Magnette engine had been increased from 1100 cc to 1300 cc, which improved the performance potential of the car, but since the model was replaced within the year with a superior chassis design no conclusions could be drawn from the exercise. The TF had been increased from 1250 to 1500 cc, but again the model had been replaced very quickly. The MGA had been increased from 1500 cc to 1600 cc with great benefit, so that as early as 1963, shortly after the introduction of the MGB, it is perhaps not altogether surprising that a larger capacity for the new model was being investigated.

The first choice for a larger engine fell to a 2-litre six-cylinder prototype which was being developed in Australia for a saloon car to be sold for that market and which was actually considered while the MGB was still in prototype form. However, the plot was complicated by the fact that Abingdon was building the Austin-Healey 3000, which had grown out of the original Healey 100. A pretty car, it had a considerable following, and it was felt that the revised sports car should be capable of carrying the Austin badge, as well as the octagon. The 3-litre engine fitted to the Austin-Healey was rather long in the tooth, and so work had commenced on its replacement – which of course also had to be suitable for a large saloon car. Two litres was considered too small for this application, and as ever at this phase of the history of the British Motor Corporation, contingencies of expense started to rear their ugly head.

It was decided that the new engine had to have the same bore and stroke as the unit it replaced, so that there should be as much interchange of components as possible. It need hardly be said that this lofty ideal was not achieved, and the new engine was completely redesigned, bearing no resemblance whatever to the older unit it replaced. To add insult to injury it was not a greatly improved unit either. It *was* a lot smoother, having seven main bearings in place of the four of the earlier unit, and it was a lot quieter in running. However, specific power was disappointing, as was fuel consumption. It took a considerable time to develop the engine into a usable form, which delayed the large-engined MGB, or ADO52 as the project was officially called.

The prototype chassis for the new car had existed since early in 1964, and

The MGC was easily distinguished from its smaller-engined sister by the 15-inch wheels, and the hump on the bonnet, but this was not enough for the press, who gave the car a very poor reception.

The under-bonnet of the MGC, (this one a home-market car) left no doubt that this was a power-house! The power produced was insufficient for the high overall gearing, however, making the car a high-speed cruiser rather than the fierce sports car the press expected.

In GT version the MGC was particularly handsome.

was even licensed. It looked for all the world like an ordinary MGB, and apart from the mellow exhaust note was very hard to detect on the road. In fact it was not at all similar to the MGB apart from outward looks, and one feels that the original intent was perhaps to change the exterior shape for production; however, that is conjecture.

The front suspension used torsion bar springs, first employed on an MG in the R-type racing car of the thirties, which had been successfully applied to a wide variety of Nuffield cars since, the most famous being the Morris Minor, which was still in production; but it had also appeared on the original post-war Morris Oxford, the Morris Six and Wolseley 4/50 and 6/80, as well as on the Riley RM series. It would be fair to say that there was a good deal of experience with the suspension type within the Corporation, and the undoubted advantages which it gave the cars in terms of suspension control, coupled with a good ride, made the medium a strong contender for sports car suspension in the early 1960s.

To make a suitable mounting for the spring bars, the entire front of the chassis frame was redesigned, and for some time it was assumed that the rear suspension would be some form of de Dion system. The Rover Company had introduced their 2000 model using this system, which was proving successful, but this car was in a higher price bracket than was envisaged for the new MG and eventually it was cost constraint, coupled with the need to ensure that the car was basically simple to maintain for its prime American market, that resulted in the decision to retain semi-elliptic leaf springs and a live axle at the rear. Fifteen-inch diameter wheels were standardized for the new car, as opposed to fourteen for the MGB, both disc and wire types being available.

Meanwhile engine development was changing horses with great rapidity, and it was impossible for Abingdon to get a firm specification for their new car without knowing what form the new engine would take! It had been hoped that the saloon car application would be transversely mounted as in the Mini, 1100 and 1800 ranges, but eventually the conventional mounting was decided upon, and this meant that the same engine installation could be used in both the saloon car and the sports model. When Abingdon saw it they were dismayed. It retained all the worst points of the old C-series engine: it was long, tall and heavy. Furthermore its maximum power output was only marginally better but its torque curve was not as good! It *was* smoother in running, and was capable of runnning at high crankshaft speeds. However, to get it under the bonnet it was necessary to put in a power bulge which spoilt the lines of the car somewhat, and the original intent for a new body shape got lost probably on cost grounds.

A new all-syncromesh gearbox was used and a much stronger rear axle was employed, which together gave the car a much lower cockpit noise level than had previously been the norm for MG sports cars! A Borg-Warner automatic gearbox was available as an optional extra with the selector lever mounted on the transmission tunnel, reminiscent of the preselector lever fitted to the K-type Magnettes.

The rest of the car was to all outward appearances pure MGB, but the new model was introduced in 1967 as the MGC. Shortly before its announcement

The MGB GT V8 as it originally appeared. With more power than the MGC, the V8 got the press response which the earlier car had needed... its performance was much better on the same overall gearing.

six pre-production cars had been run at Silverstone for considerable mileage, and apart from brake pad and tyre replacement no major problems were recorded. We were able to get the middle gear of the automatic gearbox more than a little excited when we continually engaged this at around 80 mph for engine braking, and this resulted in the specification of a gearbox oil cooler as standard for this model. The fact was, however, that we were circulating the circuit at speeds in line with those achieved at that time by highly modified MGBs, and this was with standard production cars running on ordinary road tyres! We felt that the car lacked real acceleration, and could do with a lower axle ratio to make it *feel* like a sports car, but praised the way in which it circulated so quickly but quietly.

When the first road test reports appeared, we could not believe that the press had driven the same cars – which in fact they had! The general handling of the car was panned, it was said to suffer from terminal understeer, and to be an unworthy successor to the Austin Healey 3000, which was discontinued. The press did not like the fact that the car was so similar in appointments to the MGB, and felt that it should have been a little more 'modern' in its interior appointments; on the whole we probably agreed with them on that! What we found difficult to believe was that the handling was *that* bad!

Having driven considerable distances in the MGC, I cannot agree that the understeer is 'terminal': I have never failed to get round a corner in a MGC. A look at the weight balance of the car, 53 : 47, will show that there is a preponderance of weight at the front, but this is less than most saloon cars of

This somewhat cramped under-bonnet of the V8 recalled that of the MGA Twin Cam — but the distributor was more accessible!

In 1974 model form, the MGB GT V8 looked set for a long life, but it ran for less than two more years, killed off by inter-plant politics in British Leyland.

the period, and of most pseudo-sports cars. It is likely that two factors contributed to the contemporary feeling that the car was nose-heavy. Firstly, the car looked like an MGB, and it was expected that everything else would be like the smaller car. Secondly, I think that it is likely that the press were lulled into a false sense of security by the quiet running of the car, which was at a far better level than any other sporting car to that date. These two points combined, and drivers simply found that they were travelling faster than they *thought* they were, with the result that the next corner was not 'on' in any car! Certainly cruising at 100 mph-plus was possible in this car: it is the only MG in which I have lapped the MIRA test circuit at over 100 mph, whereas one had to wear ear-plugs to drive the Austin Healey 3000 to approach that speed! Furthermore the understeering characteristic of the car could be countered by application of power at all road speeds.

The MGC was produced in an American Federal market form, parallel with the MGB, and featured emission control on the engine, by air pump and closed circuit breathing, as well as all the safety fittings. One of the items fitted in this latter context was a complete dual braking system, including twin servos, which made the under-bonnet space somewhat limited. This in turn gave problems with high under-bonnet temperatures, and small cooling fans were fitted to keep temperatures in the carburettor float chambers low! Early in its production life the rear axle ratio was dropped and the car became very pleasant to drive. A couple of experiments were tried using fuel injection systems, and these were fairly successful; with a little more development time there is no doubt that the car would have been given real performance potential.

The poor reception the press gave the MGC undoubtedly shortened its production life. The introduction of the new model was followed by the formation of the British Leyland group, as detailed in the previous chapter, and the fact was that the MGC and the Triumph TR6 were competing for the same sector of the sports car market. There was considerable feeling against anything at all emanating from the old BMC part of the corporation at the time, and it took only a month or so for the Board to make a decision on the future of the model. The MGC was dropped from the range in 1969, whereas the TR6 continued, with little change in specification, until 1976.

As early as 1967 a couple of V8 engines were received at Abingdon from Coventry. Of Daimler origin, the 2.5-litre unit was outwardly promising, having been fitted to the Daimler SP250 sports car and to a saloon based on the small Jaguar, carrying the Daimler badge. However, this unit was suffering a poor reliability record in warranty and was shortly to be dropped from production. The 4.5-litre unit from the Majestic was even less promising, but layouts were worked out, when not surprisingly it was found to be too bulky. Work on these cars was being carried out under the supervision of Terry Mitchell, and one day at lunch he let drop that what he really wanted was the 'nice little alloy unit in the Rover'. Of course that was not possible: Rover was part of the Leyland group which also owned the Triumph name... Triumph were producing their own V8 engine for the Stag model, and it seemed likely to us that the newer Triumph design would probably be the longer-lived unit.

The Rover V8 was born out of a Buick design of the late fifties, and was notably light and gave a good specific power unit, with pushrod-operated overhead valves, but it did employ hydraulic tappets which make it a noticeably quiet running unit. It was fitted to the large saloon car and to the Range Rover, and was being made in large quantities. The problem of how to get one to Abingdon was solved by the formation of British Leyland; the problem of getting the engineering passed by the Board was a greater poser. It is usually assumed these days that it was the private venture of Ken Costello sometime in 1971–72 which precipitated Abingdon into producing the

V8-engined MGB, but this is not true. Costello was an enthusiast who ran a tuning business and was a successful club racer in Minis. The first Abingdon experiments were taking place well before Costello's work was being publicized; indeed, the prototype car at Abingdon was first registered during 1970. One of the reasons that Costello stole a march on the manufacturers was precisely the reason that Abingdon was able to develop its range so quickly in the thirties: no corporate 'red tape' to deal with! While Abingdon was dealing with the problems of type approval and minor details like making the bulkhead accept the much wider engine, Costello was able to shoehorn the engine into place on a custom-built basis, and had modified a couple of dozen cars between 1971 and 1973. The Abingdon version was announced in August 1973, just two months after the press had tested a Costello car – it is hardly surprising that the myth arose.

The MGB GT V8, to give the model its full name, was a natural extension of the MGB. The engine fitted naturally into the bay and mated easily to the MGC specification gearbox, although the ratios were altered slightly. The propshaft and rear axle were derived from the MGC. Suspension was similar to the four-cylinder car, although spring rates were changed. The engine was in a basic state of tune, as fitted to the Range Rover, but it delivered 137 bhp, compared with the smaller engine's 94, so that a healthy improvement in performance was expected! One of the minor points hardly ever appreciated is that the engine will run happily on low octane fuel, since the compression ratio is 8.25 : 1.

The road wheels were of a new design, since failure of the standard Rostyle and wire types occurred under test conditions. The centres were alloy castings while the rims were of steel, chromium-plated for production. These wheels proved exceptionallly strong and were the only really distinctive feature of the V8 when viewed from the roadside. Relatively wide-section tyres were specified for the V8. Bodywork was of the current standard for the MGB GT, although the bulkhead had to be modified to

The MGC, here fitted with optional hardtop, at the press release: this was one of the cars which we at Abingdon had driven around Silverstone at speeds in excess of those attained by racing MGBs at the time – and the press said they didn't go!

The MGC GT – another of the cars we had driven at racing speeds for a month prior to release.

accept the wider unit, a change incorporated into all subsequent MGB bodyshells. The instrument panel and the minor controls were improved a little, with the wiper switch and overdrive control appearing under the steering wheel opposite the indicator control. Discreet V8 emblems were fitted to the left-hand front wing and the boot lid. Tourer versions were engineered, but were never submitted for type approval, since it appeared as though Rover would only supply a limited number of engines to Abingdon.

The press received the car well, in spite of the current feeling amongst certain sections that whatever British Leyland did was wrong, and public reaction was good. With a large part of production of MGs going to the States it was logical that a ready market would be found there and six prototype American specification models were sent to the States for dealer reaction. This was ecstatic, but it did not take Leyland long to realize that sales of the new MGB would be at the cost of lost sales on the Stag, which was not selling too well in the States, and the US model was stillborn, the excuse being that there was no capacity for the increased production of the engine. The

The engine of the special MGC GTS, which was raced with some success.

production of the V8 was thus limited to the UK market only and its price put it in high demand, always outstripping production.

In 1976 the V8 was fitted with the dreaded rubber bumpers and the changed ride height necessary for compliance with American and Swedish safety legislation, even though there was no intention to market the model there, but with so many components in common with the four-cylinder cars it was inconceivable that the V8 could deviate materially from the basic specification.

The MGB GT V8 was in most ways a better car than the Stag: it was quieter, faster, more economical, cheaper to buy and to run, and from the production point of view was more profitable. It even cost less in warranty. Its minus points were that it was not as well appointed, nor was there as much space inside, and from the point of view of the Leyland Board it had the wrong badge for a successful model! By 1977 Rover were about to introduce their new saloon model, coded SD1, and the forward-planning people decided that demand for this car would be so high that the MG could no longer stay in production. This proved to be a wrong decision, like so many made at this pre-Edwardes period, but it was too late.

The Triumph Stag, a Michelotti styled car which caused the demise of the MGC, and probably did not help the V8, but even without in-house competition the Stag was not a sales success.

13

MGs from Longbridge

The first prototypes of what we expected to be the Mini replacement car were seen during 1975, and no doubt it had been in development for some time prior to this. Quite when the decision to produce a badge-engineered MG version was taken is not at all clear, but it may have coincided with the announcement by Ford of sporty versions of its Fiesta model. The sporty Mini had of course carried the Cooper name, which coupled the model name with a then successful racing car manufacturer. By the late seventies the Leyland name was being used on Williams Grand Prix racing cars, but this was principally to advertise trucks! The once-respected name of Cooper Cars was no longer carried on a racing car and in any case the use of a name from outside the Corporation would lead to contracts and additional costs, and so the good idea of capitalizing on the MG title was hit upon – certainly one of the brightest ideas to come from the Leyland group since its formation. It is not beyond the realms of possibility that all the fuss which arose at the closure of the Abingdon factory from members of the MG Car Club and others had some bearing on the decision to continue with the MG Marque name. To be fair, BL Cars was begining to master its problems, under the inspired guidance of its Chief Executive, Michael Edwardes, and the Metro was to prove the first in a series of good new models which were to turn the fortunes of the company back to happy times again.

The Mini-Metro was announced in 1980 and was quickly seen as a good car in the small car range, but was not to displace the Mini, which continues in production to the time of writing. Powered by the ever-faithful A-series engine, mounted transversely as in the Mini, with the gearbox in a unit mounted under the engine, the Metro was available in a variety of engine and body specifications, ranging from very cheap to quite expensive.

The following year saw the introduction of an MG version, greeted by some devotees of the marque with the usual cries of derision. Sporting a polished alloy rocker cover, for the first time since the pre-war TB and WA cars, the engine was nevertheless a good performer of proven pedigree. A nice exterior finish was specified, and alloy wheels shod with a low-profile tyre were featured, all of which distinguished the car from its cheaper stablemates. If the gearbox ratios were not ideal, at least the car could be hustled along in a way to give joy to any true MG driver. Kimber might not have approved of the cheap plastic interior and stylized instruments, but all the flair of a contemporary-designed sporty car was present, and it was not long before the MG Metro 1300 was being seen at Car Club meetings, competing alongside its illustrious forebears. Much more importantly, the MG Metro was an instant sales success, boosting sales of the model to a degree that must have given great satisfaction to BL, as well as finally bringing home to their Sales and Marketing Department the true value of a marque name which had been for so long, if not exactly reviled or despised, certainly ignored.

Exhaust-driven turbochargers were becoming fashionable on production cars following a considerable effort being put into their development for Grand Prix racing. There has always been a liking for the notion of getting a power increase for little input, and turbochargers had been fitted with this end in mind to diesel engines for many years. The turbocharger is simply a supercharger driven by fast-moving exhaust gases expelled from the engine, and at first sight it appears that no power is necessary to drive it that is not already wasted. The earliest experiments in turbocharging were probably made at the turn of the century, and in the 1920s Captain Halford had attempted to produce a Grand Prix car fitted with one, but this was not successful owing to the difficulty of keeping the hot exhaust gas from heating up the cool intake charge, a problem which no adequate technology was available to solve until the mid-1960s! The use of the turbocharger on compression ignition engines was much more successful, and by the 1970s every truck producer offered a turbo option to his range.

The interest in use of the turbo in petrol engines was first rekindled by the German BMW company during the 1960s, but it was the Renault company which first used them for Grand Prix racing to exploit an alternative power unit of 1½ litres supercharged to the hitherto more normal 3 litres unblown. Engine-driven superchargers had fallen from grace in the early 1950s owing to the disparity of engine sizes in the then-ruling Grand Prix Formula, and then later when alcohol fuels were banned from the Formula. Renault persevered for a number of years before making the engine reliable enough to compete with the unblown engines, and by the late 1970s most serious Grand Prix teams were using the small blown engine in preference to the large unblown one. Controversy raged as to the ethics of using turbochargers but it must be considered a great technical achievement to extract over twice as much power from an engine of half the capacity of its competitors! So far as road cars are concerned, however, the application of the turbocharger was largely made to increase the sporty appeal of otherwise mundane saloon cars, and the turbo only boosts the power by a modest amount in the interests of long-term reliability.

The MG Metro was proving a sales success, and few of the general public expected a higher performance version, but the MG Metro Turbo came just a year after the introduction of the unblown car. The new car provided a top-of-the-range model to the Metro series of cars, and the car was distinguished from the cheaper MG model by its better interior trim, somewhat garish exterior embellishments and very low-profile tyres. Fitted with a turbocharger, the engine output was increased by a useful margin, but the inadequacies of the wide gearbox ratios now became highlighted, especially if the turbo was not producing its full designed measure of boost.

The Metro was planned to be one of a series of new cars to be introduced by BL Cars for the 1980s, the next model in size being a larger hatchback of 1300 to 1600 cc engine displacement, and to be named the Maestro. If the Turbo Metro was a surprise, then we were amazed that there should be an MG

**MGs from
Longbridge**

version of *this* new car, and introduced right at the start of the new model, underlining the great sales success of the MG Metro. No extra makeweight to the range, the MG Maestro 1600 was a new model in itself, with a more powerful engine, and a close ratio five-speed gearbox. The engine was a development of the E-series unit which had been fitted to the much-maligned Maxi range, and now code-marked the R-series. A long-stroke engine, with overhead camshaft driven by chain, it developed a good torque curve, but this was slightly spoiled by the fact that the new MG featured twin dual-choke carburettors which were notoriously difficult to keep in tune, making low speed running rather uneven, to say the least! The rest of the car showed the flair for detail design displayed in the smaller model, and the MG Maestro was to prove a popular addition to the range.

Next in line for model introduction came the saloon version of the Maestro, named the Montego. Initially seen as having the same basic power unit and drive train of the Maestro, but featuring a traditional saloon car body with a separate luggage boot, the MG version featured not the 1600 cc R-series power unit but a 2-litre S-series engine and a new close ratio gearbox, which was a pleasant surprise. The S-series engine was developed from the O-series, which at one time Abingdon had hoped to fit to the MGB, in which the overhead camshaft was driven by an internally toothed rubber belt. The

By 1987 the MG Metro had changed its wheel styling, and was fitted with a sunroof as standard, but was nevertheless still recognizable.

The Metro Turbo, introduced in 1982, with its distinctive Turbo side flash.

new engine also featured electronic ignition and electronic fuel injection, both controlled from a microchip, which ensured that the engine always had the correct timing and fuel to meet the demands of the driver. The whole car, styled the 'MG Montego EFi', was a good package offering a high degree of operational economy with very good road performance at a reasonable price. The computer-age MG had arrived, and yet at a price to make the car attractive to those who might have bought an SA in a previous era.

Almost coincident with the introduction of the MG Montego was introduced the 'Maestro 2000 EFi' featuring the same engine and transmission in the hatchback as fitted to the Montego, and replacing the somewhat troublesome 1600 unit.

If we were amazed by the announcement of the Metro Turbo, we were all astounded in 1985 by the introduction of the Montego Turbo! Here was the fastest production MG of all time, but able to carry four adults and their luggage over large distances at a level of comfort and at a relative price never before available to MG drivers! Surely this was the attainment of Cecil Kimber's original idea some sixty years previously? I can imagine certain MG traditionalists rattling their sabres at this suggestion, but I make no apologies, for whether they like it or not there is a very large measure of truth behind the suggestion.

To bring the story up to date the three models continue in production during 1988 with but detail changes, MG being the only marque name surviving in the company currently known as the Rover Group. What will happen to the MG marque when the current models finally cease production cannot be foretold, but one hopes that it will continue to display the sporting side of a worthy production range rather than giving way to an ephemeral GT or 'sport' or weak model title such as 'vitesse'.

**MGs from
Longbridge**

In the early 1980s an attempt was made to revitalize the old Competitions Department and through the efforts of this a saloon car racing challenge based on the Metro model was set up. This has proved a successful series, but arising from this was an attempt to establish the Metro as a rally car. Competition in this field has moved from the modified standard cars of the sixties to a breed of highly developed homologation specials, featuring large engines, four-wheel drive and all sorts of devices undreamed of twenty years previously. The Metro developed for this type of competition was coded 6R4, and was a mid-engined four-wheel drive saloon, bearing a passing resemblance to the Metro, but in fact based on the Maestro floorpan! The engine was a V6 unit derived from the Rover V8 engine which was fuel-injected, and the whole package was offered in limited production at a price of around £25,000. As a competition car, the MG Metro 6R4 was only a mild success, winning but one major rally, but it was eventually legislated out of contention by a change in the international rules just at the time its development was taking the car into contention.

The journalist Frank Page wrote an article comparing the Metro Turbo with the K3 MG; this is the car once driven by Richard Seaman. The performance of the two cars was surprisingly similar, except for fuel consumption and comfort!

To my way of thinking, each phase of MG car development has brought about a car which may not in itself be a great classic car, but one which has given a high measure of sporting appeal, transportation for its occupants, and at relative value for money almost unrivalled by market competitors. The present current models from Longbridge display these characteristics to a high degree, and I suggest that Kimber would have been as proud of these models as he undoubtedly was of the 18/80 models, or the S-V-W types. The only regret that I have is that the cars are no longer assembled at Abingdon by the descendants of those who built the earlier cars.

DUR 220Y

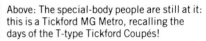

Above: The special-body people are still at it: this is a Tickford MG Metro, recalling the days of the T-type Tickford Coupés!

Left: The 1986 model Turbo shows little change from its elder brothers.

C116 AYX

The MG Maestro 1600, as introduced in 1983, offered a high-performance hatchback car which earned an undeserved reputation for being difficult to tune.

The MG Maestro 2.0 EFi is a better car in terms of performance than the 1600, but retains the body features which made the earlier car so popular.

The power unit of the Maestro 2.0 EFi, which it shares with the Montego model.

The MG Montego 2.0 EFi as introduced in 1984, a good family car with genuine high performance.

By 1987, and now called the MG Montego 2.0i, the car continued in production.

The MG Montego Turbo in its early 1985 form offers genuine high performance for a modest price.

The power house of the Montego Turbo, which makes the car the most powerful and best performing production MG ever.

The Metro 6R4 in its Clubman form, offered for sale to the public on a limited basis. With a mid-engine layout and coil spring suspension, this car owes little to the Metro, where the V6 engine is derived from the V8 unit once fitted to the MGB GT V8.

The rally version of the 6R4, fixed with spoilers and a much more powerful engine, which made it a genuine international rally contender.

The power plant of the 6R4 competition version, dominated by the exhaust silencers and air cleaners. At least the oil filter is accessible!

14

Racing and Record-breaking

To say that MG cars have always been raced is not altogether true, for certainly the side-valve cars were not at all suited to this task. This did not stop enthusiastic owners taking part in races, however, and it is almost certain that cars were run at Brooklands in low key club meetings in the late twenties. The first record of a racing success by an MG driver was a win at Buenos Aires late in 1928 using a side-valve car. Recently a letter was received by the editor of the MG Car Club magazine, *Safety Fast*, giving details of this win, which if not important in itself was to prove the spring from which many successes flowed. Participation in racing by keen owners of MG cars has followed on from this early start, but in this brief chapter we are more concerned with the official participation in racing and record-breaking by the works, or in works-supported cars.

So far as we can tell with any degree of certainty, actual works-owned cars were always a rare occurrence; more often cars were given to 'owners' or sold on a heavily discounted basis, but in general the owners were expected to pay for work carried out by the works Racing Department. To dispel another myth, by and large there were no special parts for works cars: all MG entries used parts from the normal works stores. A K3, for instance, did use special valves and rocker bushes, and the bearing metal was a higher specification than standard, but there were no differences in crankshaft, connecting rods, cylinder block or cylinder head: all these parts were standard production, normally crack-tested and possibly polished. By the 1950s there was an official book of tuning available for keen owners to enable them to achieve performance at a known level without the need for costly experimentation, a practice followed right through to the late 1970s, and this book was backed by a supply of approved parts for use.

The motivation of Cecil Kimber towards the race track started with the introduction of the 18/80 model, which was soon to win spurs in rallies and trials. No record exists of a Mark I being raced prior to 1930, but the introduction at the Double Twelve race of the Tigress model demonstrated that MG were entering the business of racing with a serious contender. That this car was not sucessful in the event mattered little, because a team of lightly modified M-type Midgets scooped the Team Prize and showed a commendable level of reliability, obtaining much more publicity than if the Tigress had won the race outright!

For the next five years MG cars were to dominate the small-car classes, both 750 and 1100 cc capacities, with their little Midget and Magnette cars, building an enviable reputation in the process. In the smaller class the

MG was to win its first race in 1927, with a 14/28 driven by Cires at San Martin, near Buenos Aires.

opposition was invariably provided by the Austin Seven, which had dominated the class until 1931 with highly modified versions of the famous 'baby' car, but by the early 1930s the racing Sevens bore as much resemblance to their progenitor as did the MG Midget to the Morris Minor! In the 1100 cc class, opposition was much sterner, coming from the continental teams of Amilcar and later Maserati, but by 1934 the Magnettes were a force to be reckoned with. The cars from Abingdon continued to be successful right up to the outbreak of the war, although less so on the international front after the ohc models had ceased to be built.

In addition to racing successes, between 1931 and 1939 the marque held every international speed record for the two classes, as well as the prestigious 'first' to achieve 100, 120, 130, and 140 mph in the smaller class and 120, 150, 180 and 200 mph in the 1100. Perhaps the most amazing record-breaking run was that of Lieutenant-Colonel A.T.G. Gardner, using a rebodied EX 135, Captain George Eyston's old car, which he bought in 1937. Using a tuned version of the old K3 engine, he succeeded in achieving in excess of 203 mph over the measured kilometre and mile distances in the 1100 cc class at Dessau in 1939. By a small adjustment in engine size, much easier said than done for this involved an *overnight* rebore of the cylinders, the first to attain 200 mph in the 1500 cc class was achieved with a speed of 204 mph, using a capacity of 1106 cc!

After the war record-breaking continued, with a special six-cylinder 750 cc engine, and by permutating the available cylinders the car took records in the 750, 500 and 350 cc classes in 1946–47. Following the feast of record-breaking, for 1948 a prototype Jaguar engine was installed, and a number of records were taken in the 2-litre class. One car thus simultaneously held records in no less than six capacity classes! Even this was not the end, for the car came back in 1949–50, again raising records in the two smallest classes; then in 1951, using an XPAG engine, it took more records in the 1500 cc class. Finally in 1952, using a special ohc 2-litre Wolseley engine, it took its own records, held using the Jaguar engine, in the 2-litre class.

By the early 1950s MG cars were being used in all types of club racing,

EX120, the first 750 cc car to exceed 100 mph, here pictured with Reg Jackson, who prepared the car, Fred Kindell, then his right-hand man, Ernest Eldridge, who sponsored the attempt, Cec Cousins, in overall charge of MG personnel, Gordon Phillips, who did much of the chassis preparation, and with George Eyston in the car. Note the battered radiator cowl, hastily made at Montlhéry by Jackson in an attempt to keep the engine warm.

EX120 near the end of its historic hour attempt – it crashed shortly after, leading to the famous incident of a 'lost' driver!

Racing and Record-breaking

while TC and TD cars were used in the TT and other national class races with success in their own capacity class. How this led to later and better models has been discussed elsewhere, and, after this, actual works participation in racing diminished, as did the suitability of production cars for international competition. It was left to amateur-level competition to show the public what MG cars could attain through events organized by the MG Car Club, who provided competitions for all types of MG and other Clubs, such as the British Racing and Sports Car Club. Racing successes continued internationally at Club levels in Australia, South Africa and, of course, the USA.

After its début at the fateful Le Mans and Dundrod races of 1955, the MGA was successful at club levels, but occasional entries by the BMC Competitions Department ensured that a Team prize win at Sebring in 1956 and 1957 kept the MG name in front of the all-important American-market press. Dick Jacob's private team of two Twin Cams won their class in the Autosport BARC Championship in 1959 and 1960. The British Motor Corporation officially did not support racing at all, but one special car based on the Twin Cam was built for a group of MG Car Club members to compete at Le Mans which it did from 1959 to 1961 inclusive, winning the 2-litre class in 1960.

In 1957 a record-breaker designed by Sydney Enever and his team and based on the Twin Cam was prepared. Coded EX181, this car, powered by a 1500 cc engine became the first car in its class to better 240 mph, achieving

Some of the official team who drove the Midgets in the Double Twelve race at Brooklands in 1930. From the left are: Eric Chapple, Cecil Randel, an unidentified mechanic, Robin Jackson, George Roberts and another mechanic. In addition cars were entered for Victoria Worsley and H.H. Stisted, with a sixth car also being run.

245.64 for the flying kilometre, so bettering Goldie Gardner's 204.2 which had stood for twenty years! Two years later the same car, now bored out to 1506 cc took records in the 2-litre class at speeds up to 254.91 mph, thus becoming the fastest MG to date.

During the 1960s Midgets and MGBs figured in racing results at international level; perhaps the most significant results were the class win at Le Mans in 1963 by Hopkirk and Hutcheson in a near-standard MGB, and its return the following year to take the Motor Trophy for the first British finisher, although it was not fast enough to beat the special sports racers at 99.9 mph finishing speed for the 24-hour race. Many class and category wins were achieved all over the world, but the most significant win was an outright victory in the 1966 84-hour Marathon which was run at the Nürburgring; nominally a rally, this event was a thinly disguised race in which reliability counted far more than ultimate speed. Among the Midgets, the team of two special GT cars owned and inspired by Dick Jacobs, but built at Abingdon, had several successful seasons, running in 1966 and 1967 as official works entries after Jacobs had finished with them.

During the 1980s, following the introduction of the Metro, British Leyland gave its support to a national series of races using modified Metro cars, which proved successful as a supporting race at large meetings, and has now progressed to using turbo cars. All the allowable modifications are supported by detailed instruction sheets from Cowley and the racing is close and hard fought.

At the present time, racing at minor club level for MG cars of all ages is provided by the MG Car Club, with their series of championships for various ages of cars in various states of tune and degrees of modification. Although other clubs have attempted to provide occasional races for MG cars, there is no denying that it is the MG Car Club alone which is able to support five meetings a year in which the grids comprise almost solely MG cars providing a spectacle covering the entire MG historical spectrum.

The victorious team of C-type Midgets which won the 1931 Double Twelve race outright on their return to Abingdon. The entire works personnel turned out for this picture.

Above: EX127 — Magic Midget, the first 750 cc car to exceed 120 mph, and to achieve 100 miles in the home, here seen at Pendine Sands.

Right: Reg Jackson in Magic Midget, displaying what a smooth shape he achieved with the small car.

The MG K3 Magnette was the model which really first caught the imagination of motoring enthusiasts abroad when the cars won the Team Prize and the 1100 cc Class Award in the 1933 Mille Miglia.

Nuvolari drove a K3 to victory in the 1933 TT ahead of Hamilton's J4, which suffered from a bungled pit stop.

Nuvolari and Hounslow congratulate each other at the end of the race, while Reg Jackson displays his usual reluctance to be photographed and contemplates his feet!

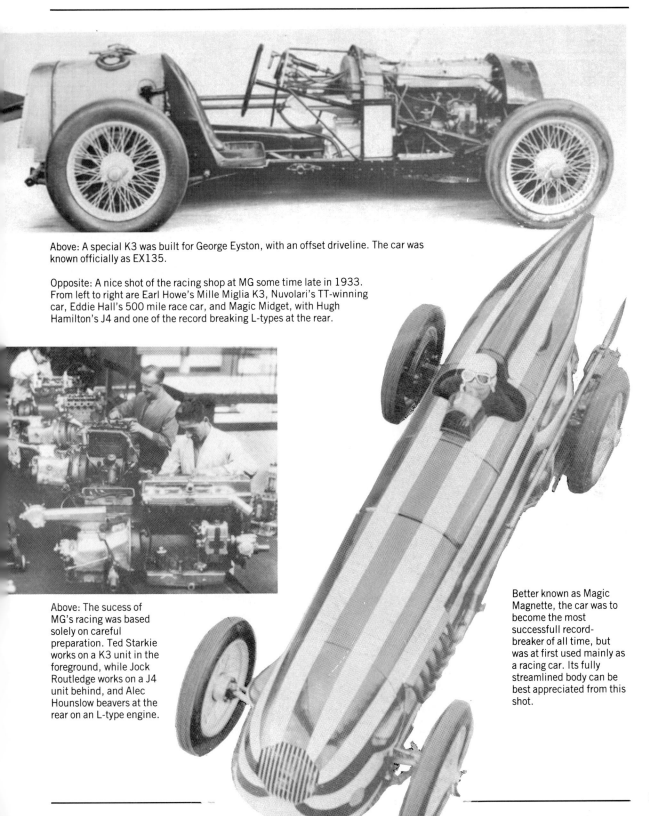

Above: A special K3 was built for George Eyston, with an offset driveline. The car was known officially as EX135.

Opposite: A nice shot of the racing shop at MG some time late in 1933. From left to right are Earl Howe's Mille Miglia K3, Nuvolari's TT-winning car, Eddie Hall's 500 mile race car, and Magic Midget, with Hugh Hamilton's J4 and one of the record breaking L-types at the rear.

Above: The sucess of MG's racing was based solely on careful preparation. Ted Starkie works on a K3 unit in the foreground, while Jock Routledge works on a J4 unit behind, and Alec Hounslow beavers at the rear on an L-type engine.

Better known as Magic Magnette, the car was to become the most successfull record-breaker of all time, but was at first used mainly as a racing car. Its fully streamlined body can be best appreciated from this shot.

Right: J.C. Elwes's J4, here seen at a meeting at Crystal Palace, where it was driven by his wife Peggy.

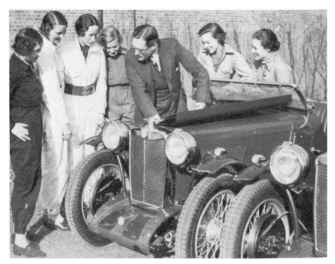

Left: P-types were raced at Le Mans in 1935, driven by a team of ladies under the strict control of George Eyston. From the left are Barbara Skinner, Barbara Eaton, Joan Richmond, Margaret Allen, George Eyston, Doreen Evans and Margaret Simpson. This was the famous 'Dancing Daughters' team.

Arguably MG's greatest TT win was that of the 1934 race, when Charlie Dodson's unsupercharged NE Magnette just pipped Eddie Hall's Bentley at a speed only 3 mph slower than Nuvolari's the year before with the K3.

Below: MG went on winning races up to the outbreak of the War. This car, driven by George Harvey-Noble, was a modified Q-type which eventually set the 750 cc class record at Brooklands at over 122 mph.

Above: Pictures of R-types racing are quite rare, but here Wal Haudley is seen cornering during the 1935 Maurice Beg race: note the angles of the wheels relative to the body!

George Eyston poses at Brooklands with his R-
type: H.N. Charles, in cap, admires his
handiwork, while Cec Cousins looks on.

EX135 as converted for its 200 mph attempts
in 1938/39, using a scientifically streamlined
body designed by Reid Railton.

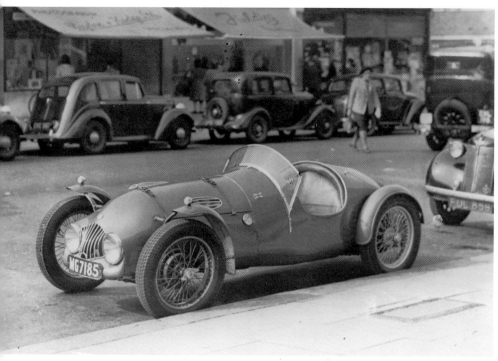

After the War racing MGs was restarted using pre-war models, but it was not long before TCs were being used. This much-modified TC was raced with great success by George Phillips.

EX135 in 750 cc trim, still using the six-cylinder engine. Goldie Gardner poses with the car.

The 750 cc engine undergoing a dynomometer check: Reg Jackson is at the front kneeling, while Syd Enever is at the rear looking at the note pad. If the engine was running, no one would have been as close!

By 1952 an XPAG engine had been fitted to the car, here seen without body in its final form. It never succeeded in bettering the figures set with the old six-cylinder engine, but did achieve over 189 mph over 5 km.

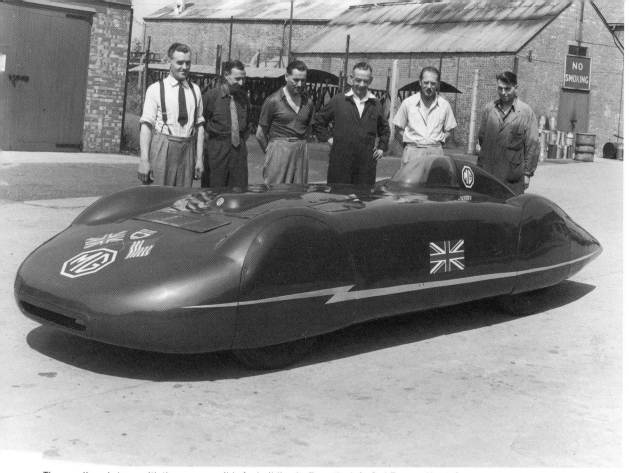

The car all ready to go with those responsible for building it. From the left: Syd Enever, Henry Stone, Alec Hounslow, John Crook, Reg Jackson and Reg Avenall.

Not everyone knows that a Y-type saloon broke records, although they were raced with success. This car, owned by Dick Benn and driven by Goldie Gardner, exceeded 104 mph. Goldie is seen here with John Thornley.

A semi-official factory team of TD Mark IIs was raced in 1950. Here are the cars after winning their class and team honours in the Dunrod TT. Drivers were Ted Lund (48), Dick Jacobs (49) and George Phillips (50).

In 1955 the MG Works Team was reconstituted and ran production prototype MGAs (EX182) at Le Mans and the Dunrod TT. Both races attracted unfavourable press, and it was fairly obvious that near-standard cars could no longer have regular success. At Le Mans the cars did win the team prize, and here Dick Jacobs is seen at the Esses. He was later to crash.

Two of the cars from the 1955 Le Mans team with those who built them. From the left: Harold Wiggins, 'Dick' Whittington, Doug Watts, Alec Hounslow, Syd Enever, Jim Cox, Cliff Bray and Gerry Wiffen.

By 1958 racing was left largely to privateers. Here Alan Foster drives his ZB Magnette at Silverstone. He eventually won the 1600 cc saloon car championship.

259

EX181 did not appear until 1957, but did achieve two miles a minute with Stirling Moss driving.

The MGA Twin Cam team which ran at Sebring in 1962; although all three finished the 12-hour race, they were outclassed.

When the MGB replaced the MGA, BMC Competitions Department raced the cars in selected events, including Le Mans, where it ran with distinction, winning the Motor Trophy for the 1st British finisher in 1964.

The MG 1100 was raced by Dick Jacobs's team in 1964. Alan Foster and Andrew Hedges shared the car at the 6-hour Touring Car Race at Brands Hatch, winning the 1300 cc class. Here it is seen chasing a Galaxie through the twisty part of the circuit.

Abingdon built three special Midget Coupés in 1963, two of these being raced with great success by Dick Jacobs's team until 1966, and then by competitors through 1967.

The Marathon de la Route in 1966 was won outright by an MGB driven by Andrew Hedges and Paddy Hopkirk, finished 10th overall at Sebring in 1968 and 1st in class.

The MGC GTS fitted with MGB engine, in which form it ran in the Circuit of Mugello.

In the 1980s MG Metro racing became popular with competitors and spectators. Here four well-known MGB racers — from the left, Barry Sidery-Smith, Neville Marriner, Mike Foster and Malcolm Beer — pose with a typical car of the 1984/85 period.

The MG Maestro challenge followed for Club drivers; here four cars contest the Cobb-Campbell complex at Thruxton circuit in 1986.

15

Rallies and Trials

The earliest trials success for an MG car was for Cecil Kimber in the 1925 Land's End Trial, driving his car now referred to as 'Old Number One' and taking a gold medal, and although two other 'golds' were taken by other Morris Garages cars, it was this success to which Kimber himself used to attribute the start of the MG sports car. The side-valve cars were not altogether suitable as competition cars, although they were more suitable for the rally and trial event than for racing or speed work, so successes did not follow in great profusion.

I suspect that all readers will know what a rally event involves, but a trial, or more correctly a 'reliability trial', may need a little elaboration. A typically British event, the trial enjoyed considerable vogue in the 1920s and 30s, in essence being a rally with special tests at specific places, the tests being in general very steep hills with sharp bends designed to sort drivers' abilities. The trial of the pre-war period had more in common with the present-day stage rally, and while the pre-war rally was merely a long-distance driving event its difficulty should not be underestimated, for frequently there were no roads on which to drive in many of the continental events. Even in Britain many of the roads were not metalled, so that the Wrynose Pass or Bwlch-y-Croes became a formidable object when driving a 1930s car!

By 1929 the 18/80 was being run in the Monte Carlo Rally, and one took the third fastest time for the Mont des Mules Hillclimb, the subject of one of Reg Jackson's many funny stories, as Francis Samuelson's 'man' on this event, and killing for ever for him any liking for rally events! It was the following year that in rallies as well as in racing the Midget overshadowed its larger brother by winning the 1100 cc class award and breaking the class record.

In 1932 came another win in the Mont des Mules, this time with a car which was to prove very effective in a different competition field, for it was the original prototype K3 Magnette. 1933 saw the J2 Midget winning many awards in trials, while in 1934 this position was consolidated by winning several of the more important events outright, and the formation of the famous 'Cream Cracker' team. On the international front a Glacier Cup was won on the Alpine Trial.

In 1935 an MG came closer to winning the Monte Carlo Rally outright than at any other time, but this was not to be, the Magnette crashing during the final driving test when all it had to do was complete the course to win! At home the newly formed 'Three Musketeer' team of MG Magnettes won the Welsh Rally outright and the Team award.

During 1935 the Cream Cracker team were provided with specially prepared PB Midgets, supercharged, and fitted with lightweight bodies;

these cars were surprisingly near standard, and proceeded to dominate the domestic trials scene. Early in 1936 the Musketeer team were provided with special Magnettes, which in reality were compendium cars built of Midget, Magna and Magnette components. Much more specialized than their 'Cracker' stablemates, these cars proved to be very formidable opponents, athough in fact they were quite difficult to drive, being very powerful but rather long for their beam. These two teams became so formidable that fellow competitors complained about unfair competition, ignoring the fact that it was the works teams of Austin and Singer which had started the whole thing ... but then the Austins and Singers were not so successful! In 1936 the Cream Crackers won the MCC Team Championship.

For 1937 both teams used modified T-series Midgets, the cars being recognizably near standard, the Crackers again winning the Team Championship. For 1938 more highly modified cars were provided, the

Crackers having large-engined cars, powered by engines from the VA, but over-bored to give a capacity of 1750 cc, using pistons which were to appear in the WA the following year – a minor case of competition improving the breed, perhaps? The Musketeers had supercharged T-series cars of normal capacity, but using special crankshafts. Things were not altogether happy in the teams, dissention raging as to the best formulation for success; while they each won several events the large-engined opposition were more difficult to beat, and when the leading lights of the teams left at the end of 1938, it was obvious that without the results of previous years the teams had dubious press value and they were disbanded during 1939.

The larger saloons and tourers from the S-V-W range were successful in rallies in the pre-war period, proving the value of these cars as long-distance cars in a grand touring tradition.

After the war all types of MG were entered for rallies and trials, although the latter were becoming more specialized, favouring purpose-built cars driving in freak plots. All post-war T-series cars featured in rallies, with a few Y-types also winning class awards. It is difficult now to put events into a roll of honour, since many of the events once considered of importance are no longer so thought, but TDs in particular won a considerable number of class awards in rallies in the period of 1950–53. Even the maligned TF was successful in rallies, the first international event entered by former show-jumping star Pat Moss at the wheel of a TF.

The Z-series Magnette and MGA were successful in international rally events, Nancy Mitchell winning the Ladies European Championship in 1956 and 1957 using these cars, but it was mainly class wins which brought success to Abingdon throughout the fifties, sixties and seventies, latterly with the Midget and MGB.

Several privateers brought success in smaller national events, but by the 1960s rallies had become stage events, which favoured more modern saloon cars with better ground clearance than that provided by the products of Abingdon. This did not stop Midgets and MGBs winning awards in international rallies until well into the late 1960s, but usually as private entries in events not attended by the works teams.

In the 1980s the breed of highly specialized Group B cars saw the MG name carried on the Metro 6R4, a mid-engined homologation special which was very fast and extremely promising, but the whole of Group B was killed off by legislation in late 1985, and the 6R4 won only one international rally, the Circuit of Ireland in 1985.

As with racing so with trials: at the present time competition is provided by the MG Car Club at club level so that the ordinary MG owner may drive his car in competition, trials now being in the main of the 'Production Car' type, but the evergreen Motor Cycling Club still run their Classic Trials, the Exeter in the winter, the Land's End in the spring, and the Edinburgh in the autumn, in which MGs frequently figure among the award winners.

A much publicized stunt in 1930 was 100 consecutive ascents of Beggars Roost, during which the engine was not stopped. H.S. Linfield of *Light Car* was the driver.

Not really a rally or a trial, but this 18/80 Mark I was photographed by Kimber in typical trials country. The model is Mrs Kimber, and the car EX101 – the prototype.

No series of pictures of trials 18/80s would be complete without Morgan Marshall with his beloved 'KX', here seen at an MG Car Club event at Cheddar in 1981. Marshall covered over 350,000 miles in his car, including many of the MCC Classic Trials.

Richard Seaman started his astonishing activities in this F-Magna, here seen in an Alpine Trial in 1932.

The K3 Magnette started its competitive career in the Monte Carlo Rally, this prototype car breaking FTD in the Mont des Mules climb. The same car scored the K3's first race victory at Donnington in March 1933, driven by Ron Horton.

1935 was a good year for MG rally activities, if not wholly successful. This car was driven by Humfrey Symons and Fred Kindell in the Monte. The author has owned the car since 1961 and has covered over 90,000 miles in it

The same car in 1984 at a club trial.

Countess Moy with her J3 Midget in the 1935 Paris —St Raphael Rallye Féminine.

The victorious NE cars, rebodied with K-type two-seater shells and called the 'Three Musketeers', won the 1935 Welsh Rally outright and took the team award.

J.E.S. Jones with his P3 Midget of the famous 1936 Cream Cracker team, during the Abingdon Trials. These supercharged cars were almost without equal that year.

Sam Nash with 'Aramis' of the 1936 'Three Musketeers' team. Later in the year these cars, based on a Magna chassis, with supercharged Magnette engines and Midget bodies, were driven by non-works drivers.

For 1937 both teams had TA Midgets, and here 'Gof' Imhof prepares to tackle a climb.

In 1938 each team had modified TAs, the 'Crackers' powered by stretched VA engines, and the 'Muskets' by blown T-type engines. Ken Crawford here tackles New Mill in the 1938 Land's End in the Cracker.

'Mac' Macdermid in the blown Musketeer
at the same time. These cars had special
crankshafts to cope with the
blown power.

An SA Tickford during a Scottish Trial in
1938, closely followed by a P-type.

The 1962 Monte Carlo Rally and another MG — this time a Midget, driven by Mike Hughes and winning the 1,000 cc GT class.

Right: Nancy Mitchell, here seen with the ZB Magnette she drove in the 1958 rally season.

This MGA won the 2,000 cc GT class, driven by the Morley Brothers in the 1962 Monte.

To prove that any MG makes a rally car — a Mark III Magnette in the Southern Rhodesia rally in 1960, driven by Mr and Mrs J. King.

In the 1980s we had to wait for the spectacular Metro 6R4 for any attempt at rally success in international events. Here Dai Llewellyn drives at Sutton Park at the start of the 1986 RAC Rally — but he later retired.

16

Putting in the Magic

Within the motor industry in Great Britain a great deal of respect was held for the men who built MG cars at Abingdon, while among MG enthusiasts there is something approaching hero worship applied to their deeds. It is easy to become dewy-eyed listening to the reminiscences of those who worked at the Abingdon factory in the early days, and remembering happy times, but I will try to give some idea of what it was like to work there. In this I am indebted to the many former employees who gave me their thoughts to record, as well as to the written testimonies of many who are no longer with us.

Back in the late 1920s, shortly after the opening of the Edmund Road factory, Kimber sought to separate the products of his little plant from those of the parent Morris empire, no doubt to satisfy a small snob value but principally to widen the appeal of the cars to people who would not associate Morris cars with performance cars. He produced a small booklet which detailed the production processes and invited customers to the factory to see their new cars being built. These booklets were sent to all those who enquired after MG cars, and given to visitors to the factory, who were not made unwelcome. Certainly the additional work put into the cars made them quite different from the track-assembled Morris cars, although no secret of the origin of parts used was made.

At this time, to which we now refer as the 'vintage' period I gather that people worked at the MG as much because it was a job as for any other reason. It must be remembered that while the embryonic factory was finding its feet there was a trade recession and many car manufacturers were failing: Morris Motors were surviving, but they were not taking on new workers, and their survival was a result of ruthless cost cutting and highly competitive pricing in the market place. The starting of another car manufacturer in Oxford, of all places, in such a trading climate, offering slightly modified Morris cars at inflated prices, could not have been seen to offer much by way of job opportunity, but by 1928 there were perhaps thirty regular employees on the payroll. It was the introduction of the Midget which really caused the increase in workforce and the huge increase in numbers of cars built, ultimately resulting in the move to Abingdon and the firm establishment of MG as a motor manufacturer in its own right.

In the early 1930s a magazine article was written entitled 'Putting in the Pep' which dealt with production at the MG factory and detailed the state of the art at that time, emphasizing that many of the parts used were to MG design, and hardly mentioning the parent Morris company. This article, reprinted, was widely distributed through MG sales agencies and did much to establish the identity of MG Abingdon as something separate from Morris Motors, Cowley.

Morris Garages had a number of service depots, including this one in Merton Street. That in Longwall Street was where the earliest MGs were built.

In the 1920–40 period it was considered important to have a job and those who had were proud of the fact and were intensely loyal to their employers. To be part of something which was at the forefront of competition, and building a car which was every young man's ideal, was especially exciting, and this feeling of belonging to something special existed at Abingdon right up to the time the factory closed in 1980. One of the points which struck a new and young member of staff on joining the company in the early 1960s was the number of people who had spent a lifetime of work there, and one felt that there was a sense of permanence about the factory and a happy atmosphere in which everyone had a place and a job to do.

During the Second World War the men at MG were involved with the war effort, making parts for aeroplanes and guns, and overhauling light tanks and other machines: no job was considered beneath them, and unconsciously was born a formal inspection procedure which was developed between 1945 and 1960 to ensure that cars were built to the specification, and as far as possible properly tested before the customer took delivery of his new car. In the early 1960s a new generation of university-trained engineers brought more modern ideas and techniques including statistical assessment and improvement of production rates, and by the 1970s, when it was dictated that modern quality control techniques would be applied, we at MG were genuinely surprised at how near to the mark we were, and our techniques were studied by other plants since they were relatively cheap to introduce!

This is not to say that quality control builds cars: it does not; at best it merely ensures that what is built is to specification. The actual production processes were simple, having been laid down in the late 1930s and not changed significantly since. Previously, cars were built in the same way as they had been in the vintage period, with pattern parts being held by a tool room or sub-contractor, and new batches being called up against reference numbers. Very few drawings existed until 1933, and it was at the time that H.N. Charles first came to Abingdon on a permanent basis that drawings were considered necessary. With the closing of the Racing Department in 1935 considerable effort was put into retrospectively drawing parts of all the earlier models. But the earliest models were never drawn in detail at all, which may be a reason why until the 1960s the early side-valve cars were largely ignored by MG historians.

Production of cars became easier with the introduction of the SA, TA and VA models, at least in the sense that parts were drawn *before* they were sourced, but the increase in paperwork undoubtedly slowed the introduction of new models to the market place, so that when production of the Midget was changed from the J to the P series in 1934, it took less than two months to effect the changeover and reach full production rate. Two years later, when the T series took over from the P, the model change took over six months,

A 14/40 about to be dispatched from Edmund Road: the first (and only) purpose-built factory for MG production.

The service bay at Edmund Road – it is just possible to see the production line right at the rear of the shop.

and another two months before production rate was satisfying demand in the sales rooms. At least the production team had drawings from which to work, specifications showing which parts were called up, and those parts were actually available in the stores for a production run.

Right up to the closure of the factory, actual production methods did not change significantly. Cars were built in three phases: body and trim being the first, chassis mounting the second, and rectification the third. Each of these phases was subdivided in stages to contain approximately ten minutes of work per operator. Although the cars were built on 'lines', one behind the other, these were not motorized as in the large manufacturers' plants, and cars were passed along the line by manual pushing from stage to stage. At each stage a gang of operators carried out their allotted tasks before passing the job on. The number of men in each stage was determined by a Process Control Department using data supplied by Design and Inspection Departments, and worked out on the basis of the time required to carry out the jobs at each stage, attempting to complete as many operations as possible without having operators impeding the progress of each other. At the end of each phase was an inspection stage in which all faults were recorded on a build card. After completion of the first two phases of build, the car would be road-tested and then it would be passed to Rectification where all recorded faults would be corrected, and Final View Inspection would give the car an 'OK' ticket, or not!

During the mid-1960s a Quality Engineering Department was set up which not only monitored overall quality standards, but also helped to improve attainable quality standards by highlighting difficulties in the build process, persistent quality defects, and faulty incoming parts from suppliers, and attempting to have these re-engineered to overcome the problems. It was also the responsibility of this department to ensure that cars complied with the various territorial emission and safety standards which were causing problems. The Air Pollution Control Centre was operated as a function of this department. During the 1970s road-testing was replaced by roller dynamometer testing, also incorporating a brief emission test, which prevented cars from being run unnecessarily on the highway, which was something of a hazard in the winter when roads became heavily salted.

The foregoing should prove that really there was no more 'magic' in the building of MG cars than in the building of any other car. The success of the cars is attributable to the care taken in design, coupled with the genuine interest at all levels in the ultimate product: no 'magic' – just plain hard work. What did contribute to the very pleasant working conditions at Abingdon was the fact that the plant was quite small. At the height of the success of the MGB and Midget models, when production was raised to 1,400 – 1,500 cars per week the payroll was 1,250, representing a production rate of better than one car per employee, the figure held by British Leyland as the ideal for which to aim for the ultimate success of the company. Admittedly we did not actually build or paint the body, and by this time the trim was largely carried out at Cowley, but we were responsible for the detail design, development and final assembly, and had to provide staff to liaise with the many sub-contractors who made parts, as well as building and

The chassis finishing shop at Edmund Road. At this stage body mounting was still carried out by the coachbuilders, and chassis were driven to Coventry for this.

Right: Five 18/80 chassis about to leave from Edmund Road for Carbodies at Coventry. The front car is driven here by Tom Viner, a close associate of the author in the 1960s.

It was the success of the Midget which prompted the move to Abingdon. Here the engine is being fitted to a chassis. The stack of chassis frames in the background testifies to the success!

inspecting the cars and the parts which went into their production. With only 1,250 people on the plant, there was a fair chance that one knew many people there, and even now I am pleased when I meet one of my former colleagues, and am amazed when they recall me – this is over ten years ago! Although I finished my time with Leyland at other plants, I regret that I can barely recall more than a handful of names and faces from the tens of thousands who worked at Cowley, Canley or Longbridge.

The people of Abingdon were proud of their small car factory, and many families worked two generations at 'the MG', some even for three. Everyone

Body-mounting an M-type – compare this with pictures later in the chapter.

Bodies arrive six at a time on a truck, and cost MG £5.50 each!

at the MG was proud to be associated with the products and the fact that these were being sent all over the world. Until 1968 the MG Car Club headquarters were at the factory, and the combined factory and club magazine *Safety Fast* ensured that the workforce were kept in touch with the activities of owners all over the world.

There were times when production was not wholly MG, and the BMC Competitions Department became based at Abingdon initially with a very large MG competitions support programme, but as time progressed the sporting activities supported by the factory also included saloon car rallies, so that while the plant was always known as 'the MG' it was sometimes difficult to be sure whom we were cheering for! We were very proud to be associated with the Mini rally successes of the mid-1960s, but more so when it was an MG that had won.

The heavy hand of Leyland firstly pruned our model range and then set about 'proving' that Abingdon could not possibly be profitable. In common with the other plants, staff levels were cut, which helped to retain the profitability of the plant. Shortly after the formation of Leyland, I started a series of visits as factory representative to the States, and quickly appreciated that our models were far from dead and still had a very real demand, whatever was the picture back on the home market. It is certain that a new model was demanded but that this needed an MG badge. In fact the car produced had a Triumph badge, which was not good news, and then although it was basically a sound car it suffered with a poor reliability record, and sales never took off. Something that the Sales Department of British Leyland never appreciated was that the MGB outsold all other sports models in the Leyland range *added up together*, right up to 1977 when I left the company. Indeed shortly before I left I suggested to a member of the Sales staff at Canley that they were not interested in the truth of the sales pattern, a view supported by the fact that TR7 cars were built for stock, whereas MGs were sold to order!

If the reader thinks I am unnaturally biased towards the products of Abingdon, let me simply state that I was by this time a Leyland man trying to plan a future for the company, and dealt in statistics supplied by the Sales Department. It was when the facts came before me that I realized that the time had come to part from the motor industry, for here was one branch of it which needed to alter the truth to set its targets.

After I left I kept up my close ties with the men of Abingdon, and early in 1980 it seemed that things were set fair for another fifty years of MG cars. A small celebration was held at the factory, attended by many enthusiasts and Abingdon residents, commemorating fifty years of MG in the town. Ten days later Leyland announced that the factory would close! Early the following year all production ceased and the staff were either transferred to other duties, mainly at Cowley, or were given redundancy payments. The factory and its contents were sold at public auction, the former providing the basis of a small but highly successful trading estate. But I cannot walk around the site today without being assailed by memories of the people who worked there and the cars they built. Such happy memories, kept alive – and so well maintained today – by the many cars we produced.

18/80 & M-type
production lines side by
side at Abingdon in 1931.

The car wash at Abingdon
— cars being prepared for
shipment to dealers.

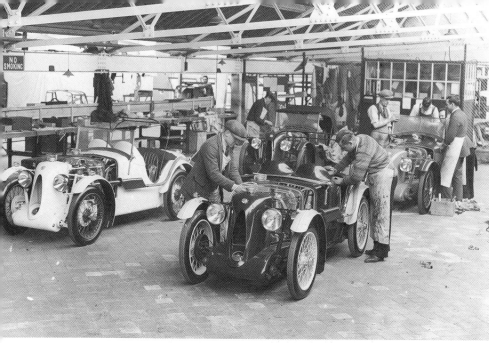

By 1931 racing cars were being built and in April no less than fourteen C-type Midgets were delivered at Brooklands for the Double Twelve race. Here four of the cars get their finishing polish.

Rows of L-type Magnas awaiting delivery in 1933.

J-type radiators in the store.

The drawing office at Abingdon in the mid-1930s. H.N. Charles is standing almost in the centre.

Below: One influence of H.N. Charles was the introduction of test equipment. Here an L-type chassis has its brakes set.

The MG High Speed Service Van, based on the M-type. The idea was not a good one at a time when commercial vehicles were restricted to 30 mph!

Below: The SA Service Van of the late 1930s. This vehicle was recovered from the remains of the BRM70, the car which the Wisdoms crashed in the Mille Miglia in 1937.

Bottom: Known as 'Bitsy', this tractor was used around the factory for ten or so years after the War. Several models went into the make-up, hence the name.

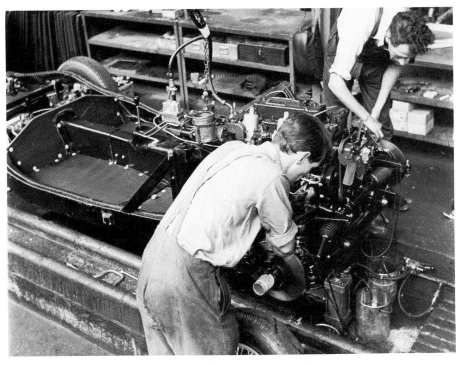

The MGA chassis line in 1962. The method of building has hardly changed since 1930!

The MGA body drop: almost identical with that of the M-type.

Midget bodies arrive six at a time on a lorry — this time in 1964.

Persuading an engine and gearbox into a Midget was not quite as easy as fitting to a chassis frame, but time taken was around three minutes!

Finishing touches being applied to a Midget at the end of the track.

After completion, all cars were road tested until 1974, after which dynamometers were used. Here a Midget leaves Marcham Road Gate for its run.

By the late 1960s technology had caught up. Here the author is seen at work with a bank of gas analysers in 1966, during emission testing in the Air Pollution Control Centre.

Humour was always present at MG — even on sad occasions. Here the last Midget is signed off in 1979.

Documentary evidence that MG Abingdon produced the best cars in BL. This board was on display in all plants and represented the index of performance model by model, as assessed by an independent team of engineers at Birmingham. This picture was taken by the author in 1979.

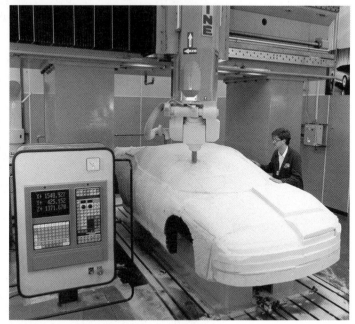

Not only is the technology new, so is the shape. A three-axis co-ordinate milling machine at work on the design project MG known as EXE.

Might this project design be the MG of the future? Who can tell, but it would be nice if the MG marque was preserved in sporting cars of this type.

APPENDIX 1

Mechanical Specifications

It is virtually impossible to list every mechanical detail of every MG produced. The reasons for this are many and varied. To start off with the details for the earlier models are scant, and in some cases contradictory. What I have attempted to list here are the details for all models in a similar layout, so that readers can compare various models, and come to their own conclusions as to what progress was made, and which is the best specification of all time ·... whatever that might mean! In some cases I have been able to provide more detail, and so some specifications are slightly longer than others.

The bald fact of the matter is that each model can only stand on its own merits within the context of its production life, and if any comparison is to be made it must be against a product of another manufacturer of the same period — and even in this case comparisons can be dangerous, since apparently similarly priced vehicles might be aiming at a different market, while a difference of what is now a comparatively trivial amount of money, say £15, might move a product of the 1920s or 1930s into a quite different sales area.

Technical specifications therefore follow for interest purposes, and to assist those who are trying to rebuild an MG car. However, I have not attempted to make a workshop manual so that in addition to the cautionary words above, I now add the following comments.

1. All data is believed to be correct, and is copied from official data issued by the MG Car Co. or its successors. If any errors have entered please let me know so that they can be corrected.
2. Tuning data is included, and based on original data, which must vary if an engine has had its state of tune changed.
3. Sparking plug recommendations have been translated to the currently available Champion range using data supplied by information available from a publication of that company. When running some of the more exotic pre-war models, other plugs may be found necessary in actual use, but the chart will supply a starting-point.
4. Recommendations for lubricants is based on contemporary information only. The use of multigrade lubricants in old engines should be treated with caution, since these *may* not be suitable for use with thick layers of babbit metal.
5. All pre-war cars are included, but only those built at Abingdon post-war are listed. I trust this will not be construed as chauvinism on the author's part!

14/28 AND 14/40

Production period	approx 1924 to 1929
Chassis	Steel channel section side members, channel section cross members.
Wheelbase	8ft 10.5in
Track	4ft
Steering	Marles gear, worm and peg type.
Turning circle	approx 35ft
Toe in	0.1875in
Grade of oil	SEA 140
Brakes	
Drum size, front	12in
Drum size, rear	12in
Method of operation	Mechanical, perrot shaft & rods
Wheels	Bolt-on wire spoked type
Rim size	19in
Tyre size	4.75/5.00 × 19
	Early cars used 28 × 4.4 B.E. tyres
Tyre pressure	Early cars: 40/45 psi
	Later cars: 30/35 psi
Engine	4 cylinder in line, side valve, detachable head.
Bore	75 mm
Stroke	102 mm
Cubic capacity	1802 cc
Power output	approx 35 bhp at 4000rpm
Compression ratio	approx 5 : 1
Firing order	1-3-4-2
Valve timing: IO	13 deg BTDC
IC	45 deg ABDC
EO	60 deg BBDC
EC	12 deg ATDC
Rocker clearance	Inlet: 0.004in Exhaust: 0.006in
Valve seat angle	30 degrees
Valve spring type	Single coil
Connecting rods	H-section, duralumin
Bigend type	Bronze bush, white metal lined
Smallend type	Pinch bolt
Gudgeon pin diameter	20 mm
Pistons	Aluminium, split skirt
Number of rings	Three
Oil pressure	2–10 psi at 30/40 mph when hot
Grade of oil	SAE 50
Sump capacity	approx 1.5 gallons
Ignition timing	Fully retarded, points just breaking at TDC
Distributor points gap	0.015 in
Sparking plugs	Champion D16
Gap	0.025in
Carburettor type	Solex
Jet size, main	115
pilot	40
Needle recommendation	n/a
Clutch	Twin plates, running in oil
Material	Cork insert
Number of springs	8
Gearbox	Three speed non-synchromesh
Ratios: Top	1.00
Second	1.72
First	3.20
Reverse	3.89
Grade of oil	SAE 50
Capacity	Approx 1 pint
Propellor shaft	Fully enclosed shaft, plain bearing u/j at front.
Final drive	Torque tube, spiral bevel gears
Ratio	4.42 : 1
MPH/1000 RPM	approx 20 mph per 1000 rpm
Grade of oil	SAE 90
Capacity	approx 3 pints
Cooling system	Thermosyphon water cooled
Capacity	Approx 3 gallons
Fuel tank capacity	Approx 12 gallons
Location	In scuttle, filler under bonnet

Body Styles	4 seat	2 seat	Saloons and others
Numbers built			
Bullnose	214	101	80
Flatnose	425	302	118

18/80

Production period	1928 to 1932	
Chassis	Channel section side members & cross members, riveted construction	
	Mk I	Mk II & III
Wheelbase	9ft 6in	9ft 6in
Track	4ft	4ft 4in
Steering	Marles box, worm and peg	
Turning circle	43ft	44ft
Castor angle		
Camber angle		
Kingpin angle		
Toe in	0.1875in	
Grade of oil	SAE 140	
Brakes	Mechanical	
Drum size, front	MkI: 12 in	MkII & III: 14in
Drum size, rear	MkI: 12 in	MkII & III: 14in
Method of operation	Cable operated, cams on backplates.	
Wheels	Rudge pattern wire wheels	
Rim size	19in	
Tyre size	5.00 × 19	
Tyre pressure	approx 35 psi	
Engine	6 cylinder in line, ohc	
Bore	69 mm	
Stroke	110 mm	
Cubic capacity	2468 cc	
Power output	Approx 60 bhp @ 3800rpm	
	Mk 111: 80/85 bhp	
Compression ratio	Approx 6 : 1	
Firing order	1 5 3 6 2 4	
Valve timing:	Mk 1 & 11	Mk 111
IO	7.5 deg BTDC	14 deg BTDC
IC	50.5 deg ABDC	56 deg ABDC
EO	41.5 deg BBDC	55 deg BBDC
EC	16.5 deg ATDC	15 deg ATDC
Rocker clearance	Inlet: 0.006in Exhaust: 0.008in	
Valve seat angle	30 degrees	
Valve spring type	Single coil	

Connecting rods	H-section steel
Bigend type	Direct metalled babbit type
Smallend type	Pinchbolt
Pistons	Aluminium, split skirt
Number of rings	Three
Oil pressure	40/60 psi at 30 mph and above
Grade of oil	MkI & II: SAE 50. MkIII: R
Sump capacity	MkI & II: 1.5 gallon. MkIII: 5 gallon
Ignition timing	Points about to break fully retarded at TDC
Distributor points gap	0.015in
Sparking plugs	Champion D16
Gap	0.025in
Carburettor type	Twin SU, 1.375in
Jet size, main	0.090in
Needle recommendation	Mk I & II: No 24 Mk III: TB
Clutch	Twin plate, running in oil
Material	Cork
Number of springs	8

Gearbox
Non synchromesh

	MkI	Mk II	Mk III
Ratios: Top	1.00	1.00	1.00
Third	–	1.306	1.206
Second	1.55	2.00	1.84
First	3.11	3.42	3.42
Reverse	4.25	3.42	3.42
Grade of oil	SAE 50	SAE 50	SAE 50
Capacity	1 pint	3 pints	3 pints

Propellor shaft	Fully enclosed shaft, plain bearing u/j at front
Final drive	Torque tube, spiral bevel gears
Ratio	4.25 : 1
MPH/1000 RPM	Approx 20 mph per 1000 rpm
Grade of oil	SAE 90
Capacity	3 pints
Cooling system	Thermosyphon, pump assisted
Capacity	Approx 5 gallons
Fuel tank capacity	Approx 15 gallons
Location	At rear of car

Body Styles

Body Styles	2/s open	4/s open
Numbers built Mk I:	2/s open	4/s open
	37	109
	Saloons	Specials
	343	12
Mk II:	2/s open	4/s open
	17	30
	Saloons	Specials
	166	23
Mk III:		4/s open
		5

THE M TYPE MIDGET

Production Period	1929/30
Chassis	Steel channel section, channel cross-members, rivetted construction: overslung
Wheelbase	6 ft 6 in
Track	3 ft 6 in

Steering	Worm and wheel, Adamant box
Turning circle	34 ft
Castor angle	3 degrees
Camber Angle	2.5 degrees
Kingpin Angle	6.5 degrees
Toe-in	0.125 in
Grade of Oil	SAE 140
Brakes	Drum brakes, mechanically operated
Drum size, front	8 in
Drum size, rear	8 in
Method of operation	Cables, with connected handbrake, early cars had part rod system, with transmission handbrake.
Wheels	Bolt on wire spoked Morris wheels
Rim size	2.50 × 19 in
Tyre size	4.00 × 19 in
Tyre pressure	Approx 30 psi
Engine	4 cylinder in line, ohc
Bore	57 mm
Stroke	83 mm
Cubic Capacity	847 cc
Power output	20 bhp @ 4000 rpm, after Engine 2024A 27 bhp @ 4500 rpm
Compression Ratio	5.4:1
Firing Order	1 3 4 2

Valve timing:	Early engine	After 2024A
IO	9 deg ATDC	TDC
IC	36 deg ABDC	50 deg ABDC
EO	43 deg BBDC	43 deg BBDC
EC	7 deg ADTC	7 deg ATDC

Cam Lift	0.200 in
Valve Lift	0.282 in
Valve seat angle	30 deg
Valve spring type	Single coil
seat tension	25 lb
rate	71 lb/in
installed length	1.406 in
free length	1.75 in
Connecting rods	H-section forged steel
Length	6.5 in
Bigend type	Direct white metal lined
Smallend type	Pinch-bolt
Gudgeon pin diameter	0.5625 in
Pistons	Cast Aluminium alloy
Number of rings	3
Compression height	1.406 in
Oil pressure	40/60 psi at 30 mph
Grade of Oil	SAE 50
Sump Capacity	8 pints, early engines 6 pints
Ignition timing	TDC fully retarded
Distributor points gap	0.020 in
Sparking plugs	D16
Gap	0.025 in
Carburetter type	Single SU HV2
Jet size, main	0.090 in
Needle recommendation	M5
Clutch	Single dry plate
Material	Ferodo
Number of springs	6
Load engaged	63 psi

Gearbox	3 speed manual
Ratios: Top	1.000
Second	1.83
First	3.50
Reverse	2.82
Grade of oil	SAE 140
Capacity	1.5 pints approx
Propellor shaft	Hardy-Spicer, with fabric couplings
Final drive	Spiral bevel gear
Ratio	4.89 : 1
MPH/1000 RPM	16.4
Grade of oil	SAE 140
Capacity	1.5 pints approx
Cooling system	Thermosyphon
Capacity	Approx 2 gallons
Fuel tank capacity	6 gallons, with tap reserve
Location	Under scuttle
Body Styles	Open two-seater, Closed two-seat Coupe, Racing two seater

Numbers built:	
Fabric two-seater	2329
Fabric Coupe	493
Panelled open car	273
Panelled Coupe	37
12/12 Replica	21
Chassis sold	82

MONTLHÉRY MIDGET: C-TYPE

Production period	1931–32
Chassis	Steel channel section side members, tubular steel cross members, bolted construction.
Wheelbase	6ft 9in
Track	3ft 6in
Steering	Adamant box, worm and wheel type
Turning circle	Approx 34ft
Castor angle	6 degrees
Camber angle	9 degrees
Kingpin angle	6.5 degrees
Toe in	0.1875in
Grade of oil	SAE 140
Brakes	
Drum size, front	Early cars 8in, later cars 12in
Drum size, rear	Early cars 8in, later cars 12 in
Method of operation	Mechanical, operated by cables
Wheels	Rudge pattern wire spoked
Rim size	19 × 2.50in
Tyre size	19 × 4.00in
Tyre pressure	approx 40 psi
Engine	4 cylinder in line, single ohc.
Bore	57mm
Stroke	73mm
Cubic capacity	746cc

	AA head	AB head	AA S/c	AB S/c
Power output	37.4	44.1	44.9	52.5
	AA head	AB head	AA S/c	AB S/c
@ rpm	6000	64.00	6200	6500

Combustion Chamber volume	AA head	AB head	AA S/c	AB S/c
	22cc	22cc	32cc	32cc
Compression ratio	AA head	AB head	AA S/c	AB S/c
	8.5:1	8.5:1	5.8:1	5.8:1

Supercharger boost pressure	AA head	AA S/c
	n/a	10/12 psi
	AB head	AB S/c
	n-a	10/12psi

Firing order	1 3 4 2 all types
Valve timing: 10	15 deg BTDC all types
IC	55 deg ABDC
EO	50 deg BBDC
EC	20 deg ATDC

	AA head	AB head
Cam lift	0.200in	0.220in
Valve lift	0.282in	0.300in
Rocker clearance: Inlet	0.008in	0.008in
Exhaust	0.010in	0.014in

| Valve seat angle | 30 degrees all types |

Valve spring type	Double	Triple	Double	Triple
Seat tension	40lb	50lb	40lb	50lb
rate	60lb in	92lb in	60lb in	92lb in
Installed length	1.406in	1.406in	1.36in	1.36in
Free length	1.75in	1.75in	1.75in	1.75in

Connecting rods	H-section, 55 ton Ni-Cr steel
Length	7.281in centres
Bigend type	White metal, direct into rod
Smallend type	Bronze bush, floating pin
Gudgeon pin diameter	0.5625in
Pistons	Aluminium solid skirt, forged
Number of rings	Three
Compression height	1.406in
Oil pressure	80/90 psi max, idle 60 psi hot
Grade of oil	Castor based, R40
Sump capacity	1 gallon
Ignition timing	Points breaking fully retarded TDC
Distributor points gap	0.015in all types

Sparking plugs	AA head	AA s/c	AB head	AB s/c
	D16	K9	L82YC	L64YC
Gap	0.025 all types			

Carburettor:	AA head	AA S/c	AB head	AB S/c
Type	SU HV3	SU HV2	2 SU HV2	SU HV3
Jet size	0.090in	0.090in	0.090in	0.090in
Needle recommendation	C	RLB	C	RLB

Clutch	Twin plate dry
Material	Mintex 'Halo' asbestos compound
Number of springs	Six
Load engaged	63 psi
Gearbox	Four speed ENV non synchromesh
Ratios: Top	1.00
Third	1.36
Second	1.96 or 1.86
First	3.58 or 2.69
Reverse	3.58 or 2.69
Grade of oil	SAE 90
Capacity	2 pints
Propeller shaft	Hardy Spicer open shaft, plain bronze bush u/j at each end
Final drive	Live axle, straight cut bevel gears

Ratio	5.375:1 (8/43) or 8/45 or 8/47
MPH/1000 RPM	15.2
Grade of oil	SAE 140
Capacity	1.5 pints
Cooling system	Thermosyphon, pump assisted
Capacity	Approx 2 gallons
Fuel tank capacity	Approx 15 gallons
Location	Rear of car, enclosed in tail
Body Styles	Open two seat, doorless
Numbers built 1931	36
1932	8

THE D-TYPE MIDGET

Production Period	1931/32
Chassis	Steel channel section, tubular cross members, riveted construction, Underslung at rear
Wheelbase	7 ft, first 100 cars, remainder: 7 ft 2 in
Track	3 ft 6 in
Steering	Adamant box, worm and wheel
Turning circle	34 ft
Castor angle	6 deg
Camber Angle	9 deg
Kingpin Angle	6.5 deg
Toe-in	0.1875 in
Grade of Oil	SAE 140
Brakes	Drum brakes, mechanically operated
Drum size, front	8 in
Drum size, rear	8 in
Method of operation	Cables
Wheels	Rudge type, wire spoked
Rim size	2.50 × 19 in
Tyre size	4.00 × 19 in
Tyre pressure	Approx 30 psi
Engine	4 cylinder in line ohc
Bore	57 mm
Stroke	83 mm
Cubic Capacity	847 cc
Power output	27 bhp @ 4500 rpm
Compression Ratio	5.4 : 1
Firing Order	1 3 4 2
Valve timing: IO	TDC
IC	50 deg ABDC
EO	43 deg BBDC
EC	7 deg ATDC
Cam lift	0.200 in
Valve lift	0.282 in
Valve seat angle	30 deg
Valve spring type	Single coil
seat tension	30 lb
rate	74 lb/in
installed length	1.406 in
free length	1.75 in
Connecting rods	H-section steel forging
Length	6.5 in
Bigend type	Direct white metal lined
Smallend type	Pinch bolt
Gudgeon pin diameter	0.5625 in

Pistons	Aluminium alloy cast
Number of rings	3
Compression height	1.406 in
Oil pressure	40/60 psi @ 30 mph
Grade of Oil	SAE 50
Sump Capacity	8 pints
Ignition timing	TDC, fully retarded
Distributor points gap	0.020 in
Sparking plugs	D 16
Gap	0.025 in.
Carburetter type	Single SU, HV2 type
Jet size, main	0.090 in
Needle recommendation	M5
Clutch	Single dry plate
Material	Ferodo
Number of springs	6
Load engaged	63 psi
Gearbox	Manual three speed
Ratios: Top	1.000
Second	1.83
First	3.50
Reverse	2.82
Grade of oil	SAE 140
Capacity	1.5 pints approx
Propellor shaft	Hardy-Spicer open shaft, plain bearing universal joints
Final drive	Spiral bevel gears
Ratio	5.375 : 1
MPH/1000 RPM	14.7
Grade of oil	SAE 140
Capacity	1.5 pints approx
Cooling system	Thermosyphon
Capacity	2 gallons approx
Fuel tank capacity	6 gallons, including 2 reserve
Location	Rear of car
Body Styles	Open and closed four-seater
Numbers built:	208
Four-seat open	
Salonette	37
Chassis	5

F-TYPE MAGNA

Production Period	1931/33
Chassis	Steel channel section, with tubular cross-members, rivetted construction underslung at rear
Wheelbase	7 ft 10 in
Tracks	3 ft 6 in
Steering	Adamant box, worm and wheel type
Turning circle	Approx 35 ft
Castor angle	6 deg
Camber Angle	9 deg
Kingpin Angle	6.5 deg
Toe-in	0.1875 in
Grade of Oil	SAE 140
Brakes	Drum brakes, mechanically operated
Drum size, front	8 in

Drum size, rear	8 in
Method of operation	Cables
Wheels	Rudge-type, wire spoked
Rim size	2.50 × 19 in
Tyre size	4.00 × 19 in
Tyre pressure	Approx 30 psi
Engine	6 cylinder in line ohc
Bore	57 mm
Stroke	83 mm
Cubic Capacity	1271 cc
Power output	37 bhp @ 4100 rpm
Combustion chamber volume	40.2 cc
Compression Ratio	5.0 : 1
Firing Order	1 4 2 6 3 5
Valve timing: IO	9 deg ATDC
IC	50 deg ABDC
EO	43 deg BBDC
EC	7 deg ATDC
Cam lift	0.200 in
Valve lift	0.282 in
Valve seat angle	0.006 in inlet and exhaust
Valve spring type	Single coil
seat tension	30 lb
rate	74 lb/in
installed length	1.406 in
free length	1.75 in
Connecting rods	H-section steel forging
Length	6.5 in
Bigend type	Direct white metal lined
Smalled type	Pinch bolt
Gudgeon pin diameter	0.5625 in
Pistons	Aluminium alloy cast
Number of rings	3
Compression height	1.406 in
Oil pressure	40/60 psi @ 30 mph
Grade of Oil	SAE 50
Sump Capacity	12 pints
Ignition timing	TDC fully retarded
Distributor points gap	0.020 in
Sparking plugs	D 16
Gap	0.025 in
Carburetter type	Twin SU, OM-type
Jet size, main	0.090 in
Needle recommendation	M5
Clutch	Single dry plate
Material	Ferodo
Number of springs	6
Load engaged	63 lb
Gearbox	**ENV four-speed manual**
Ratios: Top	1.00
Second	1.36
First	4.02
Reverse	4.02
Grade of oil	SAE 90
Capacity	2 pints
Propellor shaft	Open Hardy-Spicer plain bearing type
Final drive	Spiral bevel
Ratio	4.89 : 1
MPH/1000 RPM	16.7
Grade of oil	SAE 140
Capacity	1.5 pints

Cooling system	Fan assisted, thermosyphon
Capacity	Approx 3.5 gallons
Fuel tank capacity	6 gallons, 12 on F2 cars
Location	Rear of car
Body Styles	Open two and four seaters, Salonette
Numbers built: F1 tourer	565
F1 Salonette	370
F2	40
F3 tourer	67
F3 salonette	20
Chassis	188

THE J-TYPE MIDGET

Production Period	1932/34
Chassis	Steel channel section, with tubular cross members, rivetted construction underslung at rear
Wheelbase	7 ft 2 in
Track	3 ft 6 in
Steering	J1, J2, J3: Marles box; J4: Bishop, Worm and peg type
Turning circle	Approx 34 ft
Castor angle	6 deg
Camber Angle	9 deg
Kingpin Angle	6.5 deg
Toe-in	0.1875 in
Grade of Oil	SAE 140
Brakes	Drum brakes, mechanically operated
Drum size, front and rear	J1, J2, J3: 8 in; J4: 12 in
Method of operation	Cable
Wheels	Rudge type, wire spoked
Rim size	2.50 × 19 in
Tyre size	J1, J2, J3: 4.00 × 19 in
Tyre pressure	Approx 30 psi
Engine	4 cylinder in line, ohc. J3 & J4 were supercharged
Bore	57 mm
Stroke	J1, J2: 83 mm J3, J4: 73 mm
Cubic Capacity	J1, J2: 847 cc; J3, J4: 746 cc
Power output	J1, J2: 36 bhp @ 5500 rpm
Compression Ratio	J1, J2, 6.2 : 1; J3, J4: 5.4 : 1
Firing Order	1 3 4 2
Valve timing: IO	15 deg BTDC
IC	55 deg ABDC
EO	50 deg BBDC
EC	20 deg ATDC
Cam lift	0.22 in
Valve lift	0.275 in
Rocker clearance	J1, J2: 0.006 in; Inlet and exhaust J3: 0.008 inlet, 0.010 exhaust J4: 0.010 inlet, 0.014 exhaust
Valve seat angle	30 deg
Valve spring type	Double coil
seat tension	40 lb
rate	60 lb/in
installed length	1.36 in

free length	1.75 in
Connecting rods	H-section steel forging
Length	J1, J2: 6.5 in; J3, J4: 7.28 in
Bigend type	Direct white metal lined
Smallend type	Bronze bush
Gudgeon pin diameter	0.5625 in
Pistons	Aluminium alloy castings
Number of rings	3
Compression height	1.406 in
Oil pressure	J1, J2, J3: 60/80 psi @ 2500 rpm
	J4: 80/100 psi hot
Grade of Oil	J1, J2, J3: SAE 50; J4: R40
Sump Capacity	8 pints
Ignition timing	TDC fully retarded all models
Distributor points gap	0.015 in
Sparking plugs	L82YC
Gap	0.025 in
Carburetter type	J1, J2: Twin SU HV2; J3: Single HV3; J4: Single HV 5
Jet size, main	J1, J2, J3: 0.090 in; J4: 0.125 in
Needle recommendation	J1, J2: D9; J3: RLB; J4: OI
Clutch	J1, J2, J3: Single dry plate, J4: Double dry plate
Number of springs	Six
Load engaged	J1, J2, J3: 83 psi; J4: 63 psi

Gearbox	Four speed manual	
	J1, J2, J3	J4
Ratios: Top	1.00	1.00
Second	2.14	1.86
First	3.58	2.69
Reverse	3.58	2.69
Grade of oil	SAE 50	R40
Capacity	1.5 pints	2 pints

Propellor shaft	Open Hardy-Spicer, plain bearing Universal joints
Final drive	Spiral bevel (Straight cut on J4)
Ratio	J1, J2, J4: 5.375; J3: 4.78
MPH/1000 RPM	J1, J2, J4: 14.73; J3: 16.4
Grade of oil	SAE 140
Capacity	Approx 2 gallons
Cooling system	Thermosyphon. Water pump fitted to J4 only
Capacity	Approx 2 gallons
Fuel tank capacity	J1: 6 gallons, J2, J3, J4: 12 gallons
Location	Rear of car
Body Styles	J1: Open and closed four seaters, J2, J3, J4: open two seaters.
Numbers built: J1 Open	262
J1 Salonette	117
J2	2061
J3	22
J4	9
Chassis	23

MAGNETTE, TYPES K1 AND K2

Production Period	1932/34
Chassis	Steel channel section, tubular

	cross members, rivetted construction. Underslung at rear.	
Wheelbase	K1: 9 ft; Kt: 7 ft 10.1875 in	
Track	4 ft	
Steering	Marles box, worm and peg type	
Turning circle	K1: 38 ft; K2: 36 ft	
Castor angle	6 deg	
Camber Angle	10.5 deg	
Kingpin Angle	7.5 deg	
Toe-in	0.1875 in	
Grade of Oil	SAE 140	
Brakes	Drum, mechanically operated	
Drum size, front & rear	13 in	
Method of operation	Cable	
Wheels	Rudge type, wire spoked	
Rim size	2.75 × 19 in	
Tyre size	4.75 × 19 in	
Tyre pressure	Approx 30 psi	
Engine	6 cylinder in line, ohc: KA, KB, KD types	
Bore	57 mm	
Stroke	KA, KB: 71 mm; KD: 83 mm	
Cubic Capacity	KA, KB: 1086 cc; KD: 1271 cc	
Power output	KA: 39 bhp @ 5500 rpm	
	KB: 41 bhp @ 5500 rpm	
	KD: 48 bhp @ 5500 rpm	
Compression Ratio	All types: 6.4 : 1	
Firing Order	1 4 2 6 3 5	
Ignition timing	TDC fully retarded	
Distributor points gap	Magneto: 0.015 in; Coil: 0.018 in	
Sparking plugs	L 82YC	
Gap	0.025 in	

	KA	KB, KD
Valve timing: IO	TDC	15 deg BTDC
IC	47 deg ABDC	55 deg ABDC
EO	40 deg BBDC	50 deg BBDC
EC	7 deg ATDC	20 deg ATDC

Cam Lift	0.22 in
Valve Lift	0.309 in
Valve seat angle	30 deg
Valve spring type	Double coil
seat tension	40 lb
rate	66 lb/in
installed length	1.36 in
free length	1.75 in
Connecting rods	H-section steel forging
Length	6.5 in
Bigend type	Direct white metal lined
Smallend type	Bronze bush
Gudgeon pin diameter	0.5625 in
Pistons	Aluminium alloy cast
Number of rings	3
Compression height	1.406 in
Oil pressure	60/80 psi @ 2500 rpm
Grade of Oil	SAE 50
Sump Capacity	12 pints

Carburetter type	KA, KB	KD
	3 SU, OM	2 SU, HV2
Jet size, main	0.090 in	0.090 in
Needle recommendation	RS	L

Clutch	KA: nil, KB: Twin dry plate, KD: single dry plate
Number of springs	Six

	KA, KD: ENV preselector, KB: four speed manual	
Gearbox	**KA, KD**	**KB**
Ratios: Top	1.00	1.00
Third	1.34	1.36
Second	2.00	2.14
First	3.40	3.58
Reverse	5.07	3.58
Grade of oil	SAE 30	SAE 90
Capacity	3 pints	1.5 pints

Propellor shaft	Open Hardy-Spicer, plain bush u/j
Final drive	Spiral bevel
Ratio	5.78 : 1
MPH/1000 RPM	14.2
Grade of oil	SAE 140
Capacity	2 pints
Cooling system	Pump assisted thermosyphon
Capacity	Approx 3 gallons
Fuel tank capacity	Approx 12 gallons
Location	Rear of car
Body Styles	K1: open and closed four seater, K2: open two seater
Numbers built:	
K1 Tourer	97
K1 Saloon	74
K2	20
Chassis	35

MAGNETTE, TYPE K3

Production period	1933/34
Chassis	Steel channel section side members, tubular steel cross members, with channel section cross bracing. Rivetted construction.
Wheelbase	7ft 10.1875in
Track	4ft
Steering	Bishop Cam box, worm and peg type
Turning circle	36ft
Castor angle	6 degrees
Camber angle	10.5 degrees
Kingpin angle	7.5 degrees
Toe in	0.1875in
Grade of oil	SAE 140
Brakes	Mechanical
Drum size, front	13in
Drum size, rear	13in
Method of operation	Cable operating on backplate cam levers, 1 in 1933, 2 in 1934
Wheels	Rudge type wire spoked
Rim size	19 × 2.75in
Tyre size	19 × 4.75in
Tyre pressure	Approx 35 psi
Engine	6 cylinder in line, ohc
Bore	57mm
Stroke	71mm
Cubic capacity	1087cc
Power output	Approx 120bhp @ 6500rpm

Depth of cylinder head	3.60in
Combustion chamber volume	29.1cc
Compression ratio	6.4 : 1
Firing order	1 4 2 6 3 5
Valve timing: IO	15 deg BTDC
IC	55 deg ABDC
EO	50 deg BBDC
EC	20 deg ATDC
Cam lift	0.22in
Valve lift	0.309in
Rocker clearance	0.008in
Valve seat angle	0.014in
Valve spring type	Triple coil
seat tension	50 lb
rate	92 lb in
installed length	1.36in
free length	1.75in
Connecting rods	H section, Ni/Cr steel alloy
Length	6.5 in centres
Bigend type	Direct white metal
Smallend type	Bronze bush
Gudgeon pin diameter	0.5625in
Pistons	Aluminium alloy, solid skirt
Number of rings	Three
Compression height	1.406in
Oil pressure	80/90 psi max. Idle at 60psi hot
Grade of oil	Castor, R40
Sump capacity	2 gallons
Ignition timing	Points just breaking TDC full retard
Maximum advance	12/18 deg (petrol), 35/40 deg (dope)
Distributor points gap	0.015in
Sparking plugs	L82YC
Gap	0.018in
Carburettor type	SU HV8
Jet size, main	0.125 petrol, 0.1875 dope
Needle recommendation	VE petrol, RM6 dope
Clutch	Nil: incorporated in gearbox
Gearbox	4 speed Wilson preselector, built by ENV.
Ratios: Top	1.00
Third	1.36
Second	2.00
First	3.40
Reverse	5.07
Grade of oil	Castor, R40
Capacity	3 pints
Propellor shaft	Open shaft, plain bearing u/j at each end
Final drive	Live axle, straight cut gears
Ratio	4.89:1 (9/44): 9/52, 9/39 alternate
MPH/1000 RPM	17.85 on 9/44
Grade of oil	SAE 140
Capacity	2 pints
Cooling system	Thermosyphon, pump assisted
Capacity	Approx 4 gallons
Fuel tank capacity	23.5 gallons (1933), 27.5 (1934)
Location	Rear of car
Body Styles	Open two seater, doorless

L-TYPE MAGNA

Production Period	1933/34
Chassis	Steel channel section, with tubular cross members, rivetted construction. Underslung at rear.
Wheelbase	7 ft 10.1875 in
Track	3 ft 6 in
Steering	Marles box, worm and peg type
Turning circle	36 ft
Castor angle	7 deg
Camber Angle	9 deg
Kingpin Angle	6.5 deg
Toe-in	0.1875 in
Grade of Oil	SAE 140
Brakes	Drum, mechanically operated
Drum size, front & rear	12 in
Method of operation	Cable
Wheels	Wire spoked, Rudge type
Rim size	2.50 × 19 in
Tyre size	4.00 × 19 in
Tyre pressure	Approx 30 psi
Engine	6 cylinder in line ohc
Bore	57 mm
Stroke	71 mm
Cubic Capacity	1086 cc
Power output	41 bhp @ 5500 rpm
Compression Ratio	6.2 : 1
Firing Order	1 4 2 6 3 5
Valve timing: IO	15 deg BTDC
IC	55 deg ABDC
EO	50 deg BBDC
EC	20 deg ATDC
Cam Lift	0.22 in
Valve Lift	0.309 in
Rocker clearance	Inlet: 0.006 in; Exhaust: 0.008 in
Valve seat angle	30 degrees
Valve spring type	Double coil
seat tension	40 lb
rate	66 lb/in
installed length	1.36 in
free length	1.75 in
Connecting rods	H-section steel forgings
Length	6.5 in
Bigend type	Direct white-metal lined
Smallend type	Bronze bush
Gudgeon pin diameter	0.5625 in
Pistons	Aluminium alloy cast
Number of rings	3
Compression height	1.406 in
Oil pressure	60/80 psi at 30 mph
Grade of Oil	SAE 50
Sump Capacity	12 pints
Ignition timing	TDC, fully retarded
Distributor points gap	0.018 in
Sparking plugs	L 82YC
Carburetter type	Twin SU, HV2
Jet size, main	0.090 in
Needle recommendation	L
Clutch	Twin plate dry
Number of springs	Six
Gearbox	**Four speed manual**
Ratios: Top	1.00
Third	1.36
Second	2.14
First	3.58
Reverse	3.58
Grade of oil	SAE 90
Capacity	1.5 pints
Propellor shaft	Open Hardy-Spicer, plain bearing universal joints
Final drive	Spiral bevel
Ratio	5.375 : 1
MPH/1000 RPM	15.2
Grade of oil	SAE 140
Capacity	1.5 pints
Cooling system	Pump assisted thermosyphon
Capacity	Approx 3 gallons
Fuel tank capacity	All cars approx 12 gallons
Location	Rear of car
Body Styles	L1: open and closed four seater, & two seat Continentalcoupé; L2: 2 seat open

Numbers built:	
L1 4 seat tourer	258
L1 Saloon	97
L1 Continental	100
L2	90
Chassis	31

P-TYPE MIDGET

Production Period	1934/36
Chassis	Steel channel section, with tubular cross members, rivetted construction. Underslung at rear.
Wheelbase	7 ft 3.3125 in
Track	3 ft 6 in
Steering	Bishop Cam: Worm and peg type
Turning circle	34 ft
Castor angle	8.5 deg
Camber Angle	9 deg
Kingpin Angle	6.5 deg
Toe-in	0.1875 in
Grade of Oil	SAE 140
Brakes	Drum, mechanically operated
Drum size, front & rear	12 in
Method of operation	Cable
Wheels	Rudge type, wire spoked
Rim size	2.50 × 19 in
Tyre size	4.00 × 19 in
Tyre pressure	Approx 30 psi
Engine	4 cylinder in line ohc: PA & PB type

	PA	PB
Bore	57 mm	60 mm
Stroke	83 mm	83 mm
Cubic Capacity	847 cc	939 cc

Power output	36 bhp @	43 bhp @
	5500 rpm	5500 rpm
Compression Ratio	6.4 : 1	6.7 : 1
Firing Order	1 3 4 2	
Valve timing: IO	15 deg BTDC	
IC	55 deg ABDC	
EO	50 deg BBDC	
EC	20 deg ATDC	
Cam Lift	0.22 in	
Valve Lift	0.309 in	
Valve seat angle	30 deg	
Valve spring type	Double coil	
seat tension	40 lb	
rate	60 lb/in	
installed length	1.36 in	
free length	1.75 in	
Connecting rods	H-section steel forging	
Length	6.5 in	
Bigend type	Direct white metal	
Smallend type	Bronze bush	
Gudgeon pin diameter	0.5625 in	
Pistons	Aluminium alloy, cast	
Number of rings	3	
Compression height	1.406 in	
Oil pressure	60/80 psi @ 2500 rpm	
Grade of Oil	SAE 50	
Sump Capacity	8 pints	
Ignition timing	20 deg BTDC	
Distributor points gap	0.015 in	
Sparking plugs	L 82YC	
Gap	0.025 in	
Carburetter type	Twin SU, HV2	
Jet size, main	0.090 in	
Needle		
recommendation	M6	
Clutch	Single dry plate	
Number of springs	Twelve	
Gearbox	Four speed manual	

	PA	PB
Ratios: Top	1.00	1.00
Third	1.36	1.36
Second	2.32	2.14
First	4.18	3.58
Reverse	4.18	3.58

Grade of oil	SAE 90	
Capacity	1.5 pints	
Propellor shaft	Open Hardy spicer, plain bearing	
Final drive	Spiral bevel	
Ratio	5.375 : 1	
MPH/1000 RPM	14.73	
Grade of oil	SAE 140	
Capacity	1.5 pints	
Cooling system	Thermosyphon	
Capacity	Approx 2 gallons	
Fuel tank capacity	4 seater: 10 gallons	
	2 seater: 12 gallons	
Location	Rear of car	
Body Styles	Open two and four seaters, Airline coupé.	

Numbers built		
PA 2 seater	1396	
PA 4 seater	498	
PA Airline	28	
PB 2 seater	408	
PB 4 seater	99	
PB Airline	14	
Chassis	57	

MIDGET QA TYPE

Production period	1934
Chassis	Steel channel section side members, Tublare cross members, tubular cross bracing, riveted construction
Wheelbase	7ft 10.1875in
Track	3ft 9in
Steering	Bishop Cam box, worm and peg type
Turning circle	Approx 35ft
Castor angle	6 degrees on axle, +2 deg taper pack
Camber angle	10.5 degrees
Kingpin angle	7.5 degrees
Toe in	0.1875in
Grade of oil	SAE 140
Brakes	Mechanical
Drum size, front	12in
Drum size, rear	12in
Method of operation	Cable, cam levers on backplates
Wheels	Rudge type, wire spoked
Rim size	18 × 2.50in
Tyre size	18 × 4.75in
Tyre pressure	Approx 40 psi
Engine	4 cylinder in line, ohc
Bore	57 mm
Stroke	73 mm
Cubic capacity	746 cc
Power output	113 bhp @ 7200 rpm
Combustion chamber	
volume	Approx 30 cc
Compression ratio	6.25:1
Firing order	1 3 4 2
Valve timing: IO	15 deg BTDC
IC	55 deg ABDC
EO	50 deg BBDC
EC	20 deg ATDC
Cam lift	0.22 in
Valve lift	0.309 in
Rocker clearance	Inlet: 0.008in, Exhaust 0.014in
Valve seat angle	30 degrees
Valve spring type	Triple coil
seat tension	50 lb
rate	92 lb in
installed length	1.36in
free length	1.75in
Connecting rods	H section Ni/Cr steel
Length	6.7 in centres
Bigend type	Direct white metalled
Smallend type	Bronze bush
Gudgeon pin diameter	0.5625in
Pistons	Aluminium alloy, solid skirt
Number of rings	Three
Compression height	1.406in
Oil pressure	80/90 psi max, idle 60 psi hot

Grade of oil	Castor R40
Sump capacity	1.25 gallons
Ignition timing: basic	TDC, points just breaking
Distributor points gap	0.015in
Sparking plugs	L 57R, or as required for conditions
Gap	0.018
Carburettor type	SU HVB
Jet size, main	0.1875in
Needle recommendation	RM @ or RM3
Clutch	Twin plate non operating
Material	Ferodo MR
Number of springs	Six
Load engaged	90 lb
Gearbox	4 speed Wilson preselector, built by ENV. Two types available

	Type QA	Type QH
Ratios: Top	1.00	1.00
Third	1.36	1.31
Second	2.00	1.84
First	3.40	3.10
Reverse	5.07	4.15
Capacity	3 pints	5.25 pints
Grade of oil	Castor R40, both types	

Propellor shaft	Open shaft, needle roller bearing u/j at each end.
Final drive	Live axle, straight cut gears
Ratio	4.5:1 (8/36): 8/33, 8/39
MPH/1000 RPM	18.5
Grade of oil	SAE 140
Capacity	2 pints
Cooling system	Thermosyphon, pump assisted
Capacity	Approx 2.5 gallons
Fuel tank capacity	19 gallons
Location	Rear of car, enclosed
Body Styles	Open two seater, doorless
Numbers built	8

N-TYPE MAGNETTE

Production Period	1934/36
Chassis	Steel channel with tubular cross members, rivetted construction. Underslung at rear: N & KN types

	N	KN
Wheelbase	8 ft	9 ft
Track	3 ft 9 in	4 ft
Steering	Bishop Cam worm and peg type	
Turning circle	30 ft	38 ft
Castor angle	8 deg	6 deg
Camber Angle	10.5 deg	10.5 deg
Kingpin Angle	7.5 deg	7.5 deg
Toe in	0.1875 in	0.1875 in
Grade of Oil	SAE 140	SAE 140

Brakes	Drum, mechanically operated
Drum size, front & rear: N-type	12 in
Drum size, front & rear: KN	13 in
Method of operation	Cable

Wheels	Wire spoked, Rudge type

	N	KN
	N	KN
Rim size	2.50 × 18 in	2.75 × 19 in
Tyre size	4.75 × 18 in	4.75 × 19 in
Tyre pressure	All models approx 30 psi	

Engine	6 cylinder in line, ohc
Bore	57 mm
Stroke	83 mm
Cubic Capacity	1271 cc
Power output	56 bhp @ 5500 rpm
Compression Ratio	6.2 : 1
Firing Order	1 4 2 6 3 5
Valve timing: IO	15 deg BTDC
IC	55 deg ABDC
EO	50 deg BBDC
EC	20 deg ATDC
Cam Lift	0.22 in
Valve Lift	0.309 in
Rocker clearance	Inlet: 0.006 in; Exhaust: 0.008 in
Valve seat angle	30 deg
Valve spring type	Double coil
seat tension	40 lb
rate	60 lb/in
installed length	1.36 in
free length	1.75 in
Connecting rods	H-section steel forging
Length	6.5 in
Bigend type	Direct white metal
Smallend type	Bronze bush
Gudgeon pin diameter	0.5625 in
Pistons	Cast aluminium alloy
Number of rings	Three
Compression height	1.406 in
Oil pressure	60/80 psi @ 2500 rpm
Grade of Oil	SAE 50
Sump Capacity	12 pints
Ignition timing	20 deg BTDC
Distributor points gap	0.015 in
Sparking plugs	L 82YC
Gap	0.025 in
Carburetter type	Twin SU, HV2
Jet size, main	0.090 in
Needle recommendation	3
Clutch	Single dry plate
Number of springs	Twelve
Gearbox	Four speed manual

	NA/ND/KN	NB/NE
Ratios: Top	1.00	1.00
Third	1.36	1.36
Second	2.32	2.14
First	4.18	3.58
Reverse	4.18	3.58
Grade of oil	SAE 90	
Capacity	1.5 pints	

Propellor shaft	Open Hardy spicer, plain bearing universal joints: NB had needle roller u/j.
Final drive	Spiral bevel
Ratio	N: 5.125; KN: 5.375
MPH/1000 RPM	N: 1565; KN 14.18

Grade of oil	SAE 140		Rocker clearance	Inlet: 0.008in, Exhaust: 0.014in
Capacity	N: 1.5 pints; KN 2 pints		Valve seat angle	30 degrees
Cooling system	Pump assisted thermosyphon		Valve spring type	Triple coil
Capacity	Approx 3 gallons		seat tension	50 lb
Body Styles	Open two and four seaters, coupé and saloon		rate	92 lb in
			installed length	1.36in
Numbers built			free length	1.75in
NA 2 seat	176		Connecting rods	H section Ni/Cr alloy steel
NA four seat	234		Length	6.7in centres
NA Allingham	16		Bigend type	Direct white metalled
NA Saloon	1		Smallend type	Bronze bush
NA Airline	6		Gudgeon pin diameter	0.5625in
ND two seater	24		Pistons	Aluminium alloy solid skirt
NE Racing	7		Number of rings	Three
NB two seat	98		Compression height	1.406in
NB four seat			Oil pressure	120 psi max. Idle at over 80 hot
Chassis	48		Grade of oil	Castor R40
KN Saloon	173		Sump capacity	1.25 pints
Chassis	28		**Ignition timing: basic**	TDC points just breaking
			Distributor points gap	0.015in
			Sparking plugs	L 57R, or as required for conditions

MIDGET RA TYPE

			Gap	0.018in
Production period	1935		**Carburettor type**	SU HV8
Chassis	Steel box section Y-frame, welded construction. Front and rear suspension independent by torsion springs, and wishbones.		Jet size, main	0.1875in
			Needle recommendation	RM2 or RM3
			Clutch	Twin plate non operating
			Material	Ferodo MR
Wheelbase	7ft 6.5in		Number of springs	Six
Track: Front	3ft 10.375in		Load engaged	90 lb
Rear	3ft 9.5in		**Gearbox**	4 speed Wilson preselector, built by ENV
Steering	Cam Gear worm and peg type			
Turning circle	28ft		Ratios: Top	1.00
Castor angle	5 degrees		Third	1.31
Camber angle	10.5 degrees		Second	1.84
Kingpin angle	7.5 degrees		First	3.10
Toe in	0.1875in		Reverse	4.15
Grade of oil	SAE 140		Grade of oil	Castor R40
Brakes	Mechanical, Girling system		Capacity	5.25 pints
Drum size, front	12in		**Propellor shaft**	Open shaft, needle roller bearing u/j at each end
Drum size, rear	12in			
Method of operation	Cable pulling on expanders in drums		Final drive	Diff gear chassis mounted, c/v shaft drive to each wheel
Wheels	Rudge pattern wire spoked		Ratio	4.50:1 (8/36), other ratios available
Rim size	18 × 3.00			
Tyre size	18 × 4.75		MPH/1000 RPM	18.5
Tyre pressure	Approx 40 psi		Grade of oil	SAE 90
Engine	4 cylinder in line, ohc		Capacity	1.5 pints
Bore	57 mm		**Cooling system**	Thermosyphon, pump assisted
Stroke	73 mm		Capacity	2.5 gallons, approx
Cubic capacity	746 cc		**Fuel tank capacity**	21 gallons
Power output	113 bhp @ 7200 rpm		Location	Rear of car, external
Combustion chamber volume	Approx 30 cc		**Body Styles**	Monoposto
			Numbers built	10
Compression ratio	6.25:1			
Firing order	1 3 4 2			
Valve timing: IO	15 deg BTDC		## TWO-LITRE: SA-SERIES	
IC	55 deg ABDC			
EO	50 deg BBDC		**Production Period**	1936/39
EC	20 deg ATDC		**Chassis**	Steel channel section, channel-section cross members, rivetted construction, overslung at rear.
Cam lift	0.22in			
Valve lift	0.309in			

Wheelbase	10 ft 3 in	Capacity	2.25 pints
Track	4 ft 5.5 in	**Propellor shaft**	Open Hardy Spicer, needle roller
Steering	Bishop Cam worm and peg type		universal joints
Turning circle	40 ft	**Final drive**	Spiral bevel
Castor angle	4 deg	Ratio	4.75 : 1
Camber Angle	10 deg	MPH/1000 RPM	18
Kingpin Angle	8 deg	Grade of oil	SAE 90
Toe in	0.1875 in	Capacity	2 pints
Grade of Oil	SAE 140	**Cooling system**	Thermosyphon, pump and fan
Brakes	Lockheed hydraulic system		assisted with thermostat
Drum size, front & rear	12 in	Capacity	Approx 4 gallons
Method of operation	Fluid displacement, cable	**Body Styles**	Saloon, fourseat Tourer, folding-
	handbrake		head coupé
Wheels	Rudge type wire spoked	Numbers built:	
Rim size	3.25 × 18 in	NA 2 seat	176
Tyre size	5.50 × 18 in	Saloon	1945
Tyre pressure	Approx 30 psi	Tourer	90
Engine	6 cylinder in line, pushrod ohv	Tickford coupé	696
Bore	69.5 mm (Early engines:	Chassis	14
	69.0 mm)		
Stroke	102 mm		
Cubic Capacity	2322 cc (Early engines: 2288 cc)		
Power output	78 bhp @ 4200 rpm		
Compression Ratio	6.5 : 1		
Firing Order	1 5 3 6 2 4		
Valve timing: IO	11 deg BTDC		

TA SERIES MIDGET

IC	59 deg ABDC	**Production Period**	1936/39
EO	56 deg BBDC	**Chassis**	Steel channel section, boxed front,
EC	24 deg ATDC		tubular cross members, rivetted
Valve Lift	10 mm		construction
Rocker clearance	Inlet & Exhaust: 0.015 in , cold	Wheelbase	7 ft 10 in
Valve seat angle	45 deg	Track	3 ft 9 in
Valve spring type	Triple	**Steering**	Bishop Cam, worm and peg type
seat tension	101 lb	Turning circle	37 ft
Connecting rods	H-section steel forging	Castor angle	6 deg
Length	204 mm	Camber Angle	10.5 deg
Bigend type	Direct white metal	Kingpin Angle	7.5 deg
Smalled type	Pinchbolt	Toe in	0.5 in
Gudgeon pin diameter	18 mm	Grade of Oil	SAE 140
Pistons	Aluminium alloy cast	**Brakes**	Lockheed hydraulic system
Number of rings	Three	Drum size, front & rear	9 in
Compression height	42.5 mm	Method of operation	Fluid displacement, cable
Oil pressure	60 psi hot at 2000 rpm		handbrake
Grade of Oil	SAE 40	**Wheels**	Rudge type wire spoked
Sump Capacity	20 pints	Rim size	2.50 × 19 in
Ignition timing	7 deg BTDC	Tyre size	4.50 × 19 in
Distributor points gap	0.015 in	Tyre pressure	Approx 30 psi
Sparking plugs	L 87YC	**Engine**	4 cylinder in line, pushrod ohv
Gap	0.025 in	Bore	63.5 mm
Carburetter type	Twin SU D3, downdraught type	Stroke	102 mm
Jet size, main	0.090 in	Cubic Capacity	1292 cc
Needle		Power output	50 bhp @ 4200 rpm
recommendation	CH	Compression Ratio	6.5 : 1
Clutch	Single plate, oil-immersed	Firing Order	1 3 4 2
Number of springs	15	Valve timing: IO	11 deg BTDC
Gearbox	Four-speed manual, later models	IC	59 deg ABDC
	with synchromesh on 3rd and top	EO	56 deg BBDC
	gears	EC	24 deg ATDC
Ratios: Top	1.00	Valve Lift	10 mm
Third	1.38	Rocker clearance	Inlet: 0.010 in; Exhaust: 0.015 in
Second	2.13	Valve seat angle	45 deg
First	3.76	Valve spring type	Triple coil
Reverse	4.76	seat tension	101 lb
Grade of oil	SAE 90	Connecting rods	H-section steel forging
		Length	190 mm

Bigend type	Direct white metal lined
Smallend type	Pinchbolt
Gudgeon pin diameter	16 mm
Pistons	cast aluminium alloy split skirt
Number of rings	Three
Compression height	37.5 mm
Oil pressure	60 psi @ 2500 rpm
Grade of Oil	SAE 40
Sump Capacity	11 pints
Ignition timing	TDC
Distributor points gap	0.015 in
Sparking plugs	L 87YC
Gap	0.025 in
Carburetter type	Twin SU HV3
Jet size, main	0.090 in
Needle recommendation	AC
Clutch	Single oil immersed plate
Material	Cork insert
Number of springs	Twelve
Gearbox	Four-speed manual, synchromesh on third and top ratios

Ratios:	To Eng: 683	From Eng 684
Top	1.00	1.00
Third	1.42	1.32
Second	2.20	2.04
First	3.72	3.45
Reverse	3.72	3.45

Grade of oil	SAE 90 EP
Capacity	2 pints
Propellor shaft	Open Hardy-Spicer type, needle roller universal joints
Final drive	Spiral bevel
Ratio	4.89 : 1
MPH/1000 RPM	16.78
Grade of oil	SAE 140
Capacity	2 pints
Cooling system	Thermosyphon with pump and fan assist Bypass thermostat
Capacity	Approx 2 gallons
Fuel tank capacity	15 gallons
Location	Rear of car
Body Styles	Open two seater, Tickford coupé, Airline coupé

Numbers built:	
Two seater	2740
Airline coupé	1
Tickford coupé	252
Chassis	10

ONE AND A HALF LITRE: VA

Production Period	1936-1939
Chassis	Channel section, channel cross-members, rivetted construction. Both axles overslung.
Wheelbase	9 ft 0 in
Track	4 ft 2 in
Steering	Bishop Cam worm and peg type
Castor Angle	4.5 deg
Camber Angle	10 deg

Kingpin Angle	8 deg
Toe-in	0.25 in
Grade of Oil	SAE 140
Brakes	Lockheed hydraulic system
Drum size, front	10 in
Method of operation	Fluid displacement
Wheels	Rudge type centre lock wire wheels.
Rim Size	3.0 in × 19 in
Tyre size	5.0 in × 19 in
Tyre pressure	Approx 28 psi
Engine	4 cyl in line pushrod ohv.
Bore	69.5 mm
Stroke	102 mm
Cubic Capacity	1549 cc
Power output	55 bhp @ 5500 rpm
Compression Ratio	6.5:1
Firing Order	1 3 4 2
Ignition timing	TDC points just breaking
Distributor points gap	0.015 in
Sparking Plugs	L 87 YC
Gap	0.025 in

Valve timing:	To Engine	From Engine
	TPBG 1509	TPBG 1510
IO	11 deg BTDC	11 deg BTDC
IC	59 deg ABDC	57 deg ABDC
EO	56 deg BBDC	52 deg BBDC
EC	24 deg ATDC	24 deg ATDC
Valve lift	8.4 mm	8.4 mm
Rocker clearance	0.015 in	0.019 in

Valve Seat Angle	30 deg
Valve Spring type	Triple coil.
Connecting rods	Steel forging, H-section
Length	204 mm
Bigend type	White metal lined
Smallend type	Pinchbolt
Gudgeon pin diameter	18 mm
Pistons	Solid skirt aluminium alloy
Number of rings	Three
Oil pressure	60 – 80 psi at 30 mph
Grade of Oil	SAE 40
Sump Capacity	11 pints.
Carburettor type	Twin SU HV5
Jet size: main	0.090 in
Needle recommendation	CO

Clutch	To engine	From Engine
	TPBG 1509	TPBG 1510
Material	Single plate cork lined	Single plate Borg and Beck
Number of Springs	Fifteen	Six

Gearbox	Four speed synchromesh
Ratios: Top	1.00
Third	1.35
Second	1.95
First	3.38
Reverse	3.38
Grade of Oil	SAE EP 90
Capacity	1.75 pints
Propeller shaft	Hardy spicer Needle roller bearing type
Final drive	Spiral bevel gear, 4 star diff.
Ratio	5.22:1

Mph/1000 rpm	16.29
Grade of oil	SAE EP 90
Capacity	1.5 pints.
Cooling system	Thermosyphon, pump assisted with thermostatic control and fan
Capacity	19 pints
Fuel tank capacity	12 gallons
Location	Rear of car, under boot floor
Body Styles	Saloon, Tickford Coupé, and four-seat tourer
Number built	2407

THE 2.6 LITRE: WA SERIES

Production Period	1939
Chassis	Steel channel section, with cross members rivetted, overslung at rear
Wheelbase	10 ft 3 in
Track Front	4 ft 5.375 in
Rear	4 ft 8.75 in
Steering	Bishop Cam, worm and peg type
Turning circle	41 ft
Castor angle	4 deg
Camber Angle	10 deg
Kingpin Angle	8 deg
Toe in	0.1875 in
Grade of Oil	SAE 140
Brakes	Lockheed hydraulic system, tandem master cylinder
Drum size, front & rear	14 in
Method of operation	Fluid displacement, cable handbrake
Wheels	Rudge type, wire spoked
Rim size	3.25 × 18 in
Tyre size	5.50 × 18 in
Tyre pressure	Approx 30 psi
Engine	6 cylinder in line, pushrod ohv
Bore	73 mm
Stroke	102 mm
Cubic Capacity	2561 cc
Power output	95 bhp @ 4400 rpm
Compression Ratio	7.25 : 1
Firing Order	1 5 3 6 2 4
Valve timing: IO	11 deg BTDC
IC	59 deg ABDC
EO	56 deg BBDC
EC	24 deg ATDC
Valve Lift	10 mm
Rocker clearance	Inlet & Exhaust: 0.015 in
Valve seat angle	45 deg
Valve spring type	Triple coil
seat tension	101 lb
Connecting rods	H-section steel forging
Length	204 mm
Bigend type	Steel backed white metal shell
Smallend type	Pinch bolt

Gudgeon pin diameter	18 mm
Pistons	Cast aluminium alloy split skirt
Number of rings	Three
Oil pressure	60 psi @ 2000 rpm
Grade of Oil	SAE 40
Sump Capacity	2.5 gallons
Ignition timing	4 deg BTDC
Distributor points gap	0.015 in
Sparking plugs	L 87 YC
Gap	0.025 in
Carburetter type	Twin SU, H4 type
Jet size, main	0.090 in
Needle recommendation	EL
Clutch	Single dry plate
Material	Ferodo
Number of springs	Eight
Gearbox	Four-speed manual, synchromesh on top three ratios
Ratios: Top	1.00
Third	1.42
Second	2.16
First	3.65
Reverse	3.65
Grade of oil	SAE 90 EP
Capacity	2.25 pints
Propellor shaft	Open Hardy-Spicer type, needle roller universal joints
Final drive	Spiral bevel
Ratio	4.78 : 1
MPH/1000 RPM	17.89
Grade of oil	SAE 90
Capacity	2.5 pints
Cooling system	Thermosyphon, with pump and fan assistance. Bypass thermostat
Capacity	Approx 3 gallons
Body Styles	Saloon, Tourer and Coupe
Numbers built:	
Saloon	265
Tourer	9
Tickford Coupe	86
Chassis	3

THE TB AND TC MIDGET

Production Period	TB: 1939; TC: 1945/49
Chassis	Steel channel section, front boxed tubular cross members, rivetted construction, underslung at rear
Wheelbase	7 ft 10 in
Track	3 ft 9 in
Steering	Bishop Cam, worm and peg type
Turning circle	37 ft
Castor angle	TB: 6 deg; TC: 5.5 deg
Camber Angle	10.5 deg
Kingpin Angle	7.5 deg
Toe in	TB: 0.5 in; TC: 0.25 in
Grade of Oil	SAE 140
Brakes	Lockheed hydraulic system
Drum size, front & rear	9 in
Method of operation	Fluid displacement, cable handbrake

Wheels	Rudge type, wire spoked
Rim size	2.50 × 19 in
Tyre size	4.50 × 19 in
Tyre pressure	Approx 30 psi
Engine	4 cylinder in line, pushrod ohv
Bore	66.5 mm
Stroke	90 mm
Cubic Capacity	1250 cc
Power output	54 bhp @ 5500 rpm
Compression Ratio	7.25 : 1
Firing Order	1 3 4 2
Valve timing: IO	11 deg BTDC
IC	57 deg ABDC
EO	52 deg BBDC
EC	24 deg ATDC
Valve Lift	8 mm
Rocker clearance	Inlet & Exhaust: 0.019 in
Valve seat angle	30 deg
Valve spring type	Double coil
seat tension	93 lb
Connecting rods	H-section steel forging
Length	178 mm
Bigend type	Steel backed white metal shell
Smallend type	Pinch bolt
Gudgeon pin diameter	18 mm
Pistons	Cast aluminium alloy
Number of rings	Three
Compression height	45 mm
Oil pressure	40 psi min., 70 psi max
Grade of Oil	SAE 30
Sump Capacity	9 pints
Ignition timing	TDC, max advance 32 deg
Distributor points gap	0.015 in
Sparking plugs	L 87 YC
Gap	0.025 in
Carburetter type	Twin SU, H2 type
Jet size, main	0.090 in
Needle	ES
recommendation	
Clutch	Single dry plate
Material	Ferodo
Number of springs	Six
Gearbox	Four-speed manual, synchromesh on top three ratios
Ratios: Top	1.00
Third	1.36
Second	1.95
First	3.38
Reverse	3.38
Grade of oil	SAE 140 EP
Capacity	1.25 pints
Propellor shaft	Open Hardy-Spicer, needle roller bearing universal joints
Final drive	Spiral bevel
Ratio	5.125 : 1
MPH/1000 RPM	15.64
Grade of oil	SAE 90 EP
Capacity	2 pints
Cooling system	Thermosyphon, pump and fan assisted Bypass thermostat
Capacity	14 pints
Body Styles	TB: Two seater, and Tickford Coupe
	TC: Two seater only

Numbers built:	
TB Two seater	322
TB Tickford Coupé	57
TC Two seater	10000

ONE AND A QUARTER LITRE: Y-SERIES

Production Period	1947/53	
Chassis	Steel box section, box section cross members, all welded construction. Underslung at rear	
Wheelbase	8 ft 3 in	
Track		
Front:	3 ft 11.375 in	
Rear:	4 ft 2 in	
Steering	Cam Gears rack and pinion type	
Turning circle	35 ft	
Castor angle	YA/YT: 1 deg; YB: 2 deg	
Camber Angle	10 deg	
Kingpin Angle	10.75 deg	
Toe in	Nil	
Grade of Oil	SAE 90 EP	
Brakes	Lockheed hydraulic, twin Leading show on YB only	
Drum size, front & rear	9 in	
Method of operation	Fluid displacement, cable handbrake	
Wheels	Pressed steel, bolt on	

	YA/YT	YB
Rim size	3.00 × 16 in	4J × 15 in
Tyre size	5.25 × 16 in	5.50 × 15 in
Tyre pressure	Approx 25 psi all types	

Engine	4 cylinder in line, pushrod ohv	
Bore	66.5 mm	
Stroke	90 mm	
Cubic Capacity	1250 cc	
Power output	YA/YB: 46 bhp @ 4800 rpm	
	YT: 54 bhp @ 5400 rpm	
Compression Ratio	7.25 : 1	
Firing Order	1 3 4 2	

	YA/YT	YB
Valve timing: IO	11 deg BTDC	5 deg BTDC
IC	57 deg ABDC	45 deg ABDC
EO	52 deg BBDC	45 deg BBDC
EC	24 deg ATDC	5 deg ATDC
Valve Lift	6.5 mm	8 mm
Rocker clearance Inlet & Exhaust	0.019 in	0.012 in

Valve seat angle	30 deg all types
Valve spring type	Double coil
seat tension	93 lb
Connecting rods	H-section steel forgings
Length	178 mm
Bigend type	Steel backed white metal lined shell
Smallend type	Pinch bolt
Gudgeon pin diameter	18 mm

Pistons	Cast aluminium alloy
Number of rings	Three
Compression height	45 mm
Oil pressure	40 psi min at idle
Grade of Oil	SAE 40
Sump Capacity	YA/YT: 9 pints; YB: 10.5 pints
Ignition timing	TDC
Distributor points gap	0.015 in
Sparking plugs	L 87 YC
Gap	0.025 in
Carburetter type	YA/YB: Single SU, H2 type; YT: Twin SU, H2 type
Jet size, main	0.090 in
Needle recommendation	YA/YB: F1; YT: ES
Clutch	Single dry plate
Material	Ferodo
Number of springs	Six
Gearbox	Four-speed manual, synchromesh
Ratios: Top	1.00
Third	1.39
Second	2.07
First	3.50
Reverse	3.50
Grade of oil	SAE 90 EP
Capacity	1.25 pints
Propellor shaft	Open Hardy Spicer type, needle roller universal joints
Final drive	YA/YT: Spiral bevel, YB: Hypoid gear
Ratio	YA/YT: 5.143 : 1;; YB: 5.125 : 1
MPH/1000 RPM	All models: 14.5
Grade of oil	SAE 90 EP
Capacity	1.25 pints
Cooling system	Thermosyphon, with pump and fan assistance, bypass thermostat
Capacity	Approx 14 pints
Body Styles	YA/YB: Saloon; YT: Open tourer
Numbers built:	
YA Saloon	6158
YT Tourer	877
YB Saloon	1301

TD SERIES MIDGET

Production Period	1949/53
Chassis	Steel box section, box section cross members all welded construction. Overslung at rear
Wheelbase	7 ft 10 in
Track	
Front:	3 ft 11.375 in
Rear:	4 ft 2 in
Steering	Cam Gears rack and pinion type
Turning circle	31 ft 3 in

Castor angle	2 deg
Camber Angle	10 deg
Kingpin Angle	10 deg
Toe in	Nil
Grade of Oil	SAE 140
Brakes	Lockheed hydraulic, 2 leading shoe
Drum size, front & rear	9 in
Method of operation	Fluid displacement, cable handbrake
Wheels	Pressed steel disc, wire spoked type optional from 1952
Rim size	4J × 15 in (4.5J optional)
Tyre size	5.50 × 15 in
Tyre pressure	Approx 20 psi
Engine	4 cylinder in line, pushrod ohv
Bore	66.5 mm
Stroke	90 mm
Cubic Capacity	1250 cc
Power output	54 bhp @ 5400 rpm
Compression Ratio	7.25 : 1; 9.2 : 1 on TD/3 engine
Firing Order	1 3 4 2
Valve timing: IO	5 deg BTDC
IC	45 deg ABDC
EO	45 deg BBDC
EC	5 deg ATDC
Valve Lift	8 mm
Rocker clearance	Inlet & Exhaust: 0.012 in
Valve seat angle	30 deg
Valve spring type	Double coil
seat tension	93 lb
Connecting rods	H-section steel forging
Length	178 mm
Bigend type	Steel backed white metal lined shell
Smallend type	Pinch bolt
Gudgeon pin diameter	18 mm
Pistons	Cast aluminium alloy
Number of rings	Three
Compression height	45 mm
Oil pressure	40/70 psi hot at all speeds
Grade of Oil	SAE 40
Sump Capacity	9 pints
Ignition timing	TDC
Distributor points gap	0.015 in
Sparking plugs	L 87 YC
Gap	0.025 in
Carburetter type	Twin SU, H2 type; H4 on TD/3 engine

	TD & TD2	TD/3
Jet size, main	0.090 in	0.090 in
Needle recommendation	ES	LS1

Clutch	Single dry plate
Material	Ferodo
Number of springs	Six
Gearbox	Four-speed manual, synchro on top 3
Ratios: Top	1.00
Third	1.39
Second	2.07
First	3.50
Reverse	3.50
Grade of oil	SAE 90 EP

Capacity	1.25 pints
Propellor shaft	Open shaft, needle roller universal joints
Final drive	Hypoid bevel gears
Ratio	5.125 : 1
MPH/1000 RPM	14.42
Grade of oil	SAE 90 Hypoy
Capacity	2.25 pints
Cooling system	Thermosyphon, fan and pump assisted. With bypass thermostat
Capacity	Approximately 2 gallons
Fuel tank capacity	12 gallons
Location	Rear of car
Body Styles	Two seater sports
Numbers built:	
TD	28643
TD Mark II	1022

TF SERIES MIDGET

Production Period	1953/55
Chassis	Steel box section, box section cross members all welded construction. Overslung at rear
Wheelbase	7 ft 10 in
Track	
Front:	4 ft 0.1875 in
Rear:	4 ft 2.2875 in
Steering	Cam Gears rack and pinion type
Turning circle	31 ft 3 in
Castor angle	2 deg
Camber Angle	10 deg
Kingpin Angle	10 deg
Toe in	Nil
Grade of Oil	SAE 90 Hypoy
Brakes	Lockheed hydraulic, 2 leading shoe at front
Drum size, front & rear	9 in
Method of operation	Fluid displacement, cable handbrake
Wheels	Pressed steel disc, wire spoked type optional.
Rim size	4J × 15 in (4.5J optional)
Tyre size	5.50 × 15 in; 6.00 × 15 in optional
Tyre pressure	Approx 20 psi
Engine	4 cylinder in line, pushrod ohv 2 type: XPAG/TF, XPEG
Bore	XPAG/TF: 66.5 mm; XPEG: 72 mm
Stroke	90 mm
Cubic Capacity	XPAG/TF: 1250 cc; XPEG: 1466 cc
Power output	XPAG/TF: 57 bhp @ 5500 rpm XPEG: 63 bhp @ 500 rpm
Compression Ratio	XPAG/TF: 8.1 : 1; XPEG: 8.3 : 1
Firing Order	1 3 4 2
Valve timing: IO	5 deg BTDC
IC	45 deg ABDC
EO	45 deg BBDC
EC	5 deg ATDC

Valve Lift	8 mm
Rocker clearance	Inlet & Exhaust: 0.012 in
Valve seat angle	30 deg
Valve spring type	Double coil
seat tension	114 lb
Connecting rods	H section steel forging
Length	178 mm
Bigend type	Steel backed white metal lined shell
Smallend type	Pinch bolt
Gudgeon pin diameter	18 mm
Pistons	Cast aluminium alloy
Number of rings	Three
Compression height	45 mm
Oil pressure	40/45 psi hot at all speeds
Grade of Oil	SAE 40
Sump Capacity	10.5 pints
Ignition timing	TDC
Distributor points gap	0.015 in
Sparking plugs	N 9 YC
Gap	0.025 in
Carburetter type	Twin SU, H4 type
Jet size, main	0.090 in
Needle recommendation	GJ
Clutch	Single dry plate
Material	Ferodo
Number of springs	Six
Gearbox	Four speed manual, synchro on top 3
Ratios: Top	1.00
Third	1.39
Second	2.07
First	3.50
Reverse	3.50
Grade of oil	SAE 90 EP
Capacity	1.25 pints
Propellor shaft	Open shaft, needle roller universal joints
Final drive	Hypoid bevel gears
Ratio	4.875 : 1
MPH/1000 RPM	15.19
Grade of oil	SAE 90 EP
Capacity	1.25 pints
Cooling system	Pressurised system, pump and fan assisted, with bypass thermostat
Capacity	Approximately 2 gallons
Fuel tank capacity	12 gallons
Location	Rear of car
Body Styles	Two seater sports
Numbers built:	
TF	6200
TD Mark II	3400

MAGNETTE: SERIES ZA & ZB

Production period	1953/58
Chassis	In unit with bodyshell, welded steel construction. Suspension mountings all integral.
Wheelbase	8ft 6in

Track	4ft 3in
Steering	Cam Gears rack & pinion
Turning circle	36ft 6in
Castor angle	3 degrees
Camber angle	1 degree
Kingpin angle	6 degrees
Toe in	Zero
Grade of oil	SAE 90
Brakes	Lockheed system, 2 LS at front
Drum size, front	10in
Drum size, rear	10in
Method of operation	Hydraulic footbrake, cable handbrake
Wheels	Ventilated steel disc, bolt on
Rim size	4J × 15
Tyre size	5.50 × 15
Tyre pressure	Front 24psi; rear 26
Engine	4 cylinder in line, pushrod ohv
Bore	73.025 mm
Stroke	89 mm
Cubic capacity	1489 cc

	ZA	ZB
Power output	60 bhp @ 4600	68.4 @ 5250
Combustion chamber volume	39.4cc	39.4cc
Compression ratio	7.15 : 1	8.3 : 1
Firing order	1 3 4 2	
Valve timing: IO	5 deg BTDC	
IC	45 deg ABDC	
EO	40 deg BBDC	
EC	10 deg ATDC	
Valve lift	0.322in	
Rocker clearance	Inlet & exhaust: 0.015in	
Valve seat angle	45 degrees	
Valve spring type	Double coil	
seat tension	130 lb	
installed length	1.532in	1.5625in
free length	2.016in	2.047in
Connecting rods	H section forged steel	
Length	6.5in centres	
Bigend type	ZA: Steel backed babbit lined shells	
	ZB: Steel backed, Pb/In lined shells	
Smallend type	Pinchbolt locked	
Gudgeon pin diameter	0.687in	
Pistons	Aluminium alloy, split skirt, concave crown	
Number of rings	3	
Oil pressure	50psi. 15psi at idle hot	
Grade of oil	SAE 30	
Sump capacity	1 gallon, including filter	
Ignition timing	8 deg BTDC	4 deg BTDC
Distributor points gap	0.015in	
Sparking plugs	N9YC	N9YC
Gap	0.025in	0.025in
Carburettor type	ZA: Twin SU H2	ZB: Twin H4
Jet size, main	0.090in	
Needle recommendation	ZA: GM	ZB: EQ
Clutch	Single dry plate, Borg & Beck	
Material	Ferodo	
Number of springs	Six	
	Some cars fitted with	

	'Manumatic' automatic clutch
Gearbox	4 speed manual, synchromesh on top three ratios.
Ratios: Top	1.00
Third	1.374
Second	2.214
First	3.64
Reverse	4.76
Grade of oil	SAE 30
Capacity	4.5 pints
Propellor shaft	Hardy spicer open shaft, needle bearing u/j at each end
Final drive	Live axle, hypoid bevel gears
Ratio	ZA: 4.875:1 ZB: 4.55:1
MPH/1000 RPM	ZA: 15.25 ZB: 16.32
Grade of oil	SAE 90
Capacity	2.75 pints
Cooling systems	Pump assisted, pressurized system
	Thermostatic control
Capacity	10.5 pints
Fuel tank capacity	9.25 gallons
Location	Rear of car, under boot floor
Body Styles	Saloon
Numbers built	ZA: 12754
	ZB: 23846

MG SERIES MGA

Production period	1955/62
Chassis	Steel box section, welded. Cross braced, suspension mounts integral.
Wheelbase	7ft 10in
Track Front	3ft 11.5in
Rear	4ft 0.75in
Steering	Gam Gears rack & pinion system
Turning circle	28ft
Castor angle	4 degrees
Camber angle	1 degree at full bump
Kingpin angle	9.75 degrees at full bump
Toe in	Zero
Grade of oil	SAE 90
Brakes	1500/1600:2LS front, drums all round
	1600 MkII: Disc front, drum rear
Drum size, front	10in (1600 MkII, 10.75in disc)
Drum size, rear	10in
Method of operation	Hydraulic, Lockheed system
Wheels	Ventilated disc wheels, bolt on, OR: Rudge pattern wire spoked
Rim size	4J × 15
Tyre size	5.60 × 15
Tyre pressure	21psi front, 24 rear
Engine	4 cylinder in line, pushrod ohv

	1500	1600	1600 MkII
Bore	73.025 mm	75.41 mm	76.2 mm
Stroke	89 mm	89 mm	89 mm
Cubic capacity	1489 cc	1588 cc	1622 cc
Power output	68	80	93
@ rpm	5500	5600	5500

Compression ratio	8.3:1 8.3:1 8.9:1
Valve timing: IO	16 deg BTDC all models
IC	56 deg ABDC
EO	51 deg BBDC
EC	21 deg ATDC
Valve lift	0.357in all models
Rocker clearance	0.017in 0.015in 0.015in
Valve seat angle	45 degrees
Valve spring type	Double coil
seat tension	89 lb
installed length	1.575in
free length	1.922in
Connecting rods	H section forged steel
Length	6.5in centres
Bigend type	Steel backed Lead/Indium shell
Smallend type	Pinchbolt type
Gudgeon pin diameter	15/1600: 0.687in. 1600 MkII: 0.75
Pistons	Aluminium alloy, split skirt, concave crown
Number of rings	Three
Oil pressure	50psi. Idle at 15psi
Grade of oil	SAE 30
Sump capacity	7.5 pints including filter
Firing order	1 3 4 2
Ignition timing	15/1600: 7 deg BTDC
	1622 engine: 5 deg BTDC
Distributor points gap	0.015in
Sparking plugs	N9YC
Gap	0.025in
Carburetter type	Twin SU H4
Jet size, main	0.090
Needle recommendation	1500: GS 1588/1622: No 6
Clutch	Borg & Beck Single dry plate
Material	Ferodo
Number of springs	Six
Gearbox	Four speed manual, synchromesh on top three ratios
Ratios: Top	1.00
Third	1.374
Second	2.214
First	3.64
Reverse	4.76
Grade of oil	SAE 30
Capacity	4.5 pints
Propellor shaft	Hardy Spicer open shaft, needle bearing u/j at each end
Final drive	Live axle, hypoid bevel gears
	1500 1600 1600 MkII
Ratio	10/43 10/43 10/41
MPH/1000 RPM	17.0 17.0 17.3
Grade of oil	SAE 90 all models
Capacjty	2.25 pints
Cooling system	Pressurised, thermostatic control, pump assisted
Capacity	10 pints
Fuel tank capacity	10 gallons
Location	Rear of car under boot floor
Body Styles	Open 2 seat Coupe
Numbers built	1500: 58750
	1600: 31501
	1600 Mk II: 8719

MG SERIES MGA TWIN CAM

Production period	1958/60
Chassis	Steel box section, welded. Cross braced, suspension mounts integral.
Wheelbase	7ft 10in
Track Front	3ft 11.91in
Rear	4ft 0.0875in
Steering	Gam Gears rack & pinion system
Turning circle	Approx 32ft
Castor angle	4 degrees
Camber angle	1 degree at full bump
Kingpin angle	9.75 degrees at full bump
Toe in	Zero
Grade of oil	SAE 90
Brakes	Disc brakes all four wheels
Disc size, front	11in
Disc size, rear	11in
Method of operation	Hydraulic, Dunlop system: handbrake operating on rear caliper by cable.
Wheels	Ventilated disc wheel, centre locked
Rim size	4J × 15
Tyre size	5.90 × 15
Tyre pressure	22 psi front, 24 rear
Engine	4 cylinder in line, twin ohc
Bore	75.41 mm
Stroke	89.00 mm
Cubic capacity	1588 cc
Power output	108
@ rpm	6700
Compression ratio	9.9:1
Valve timing: IO	20 deg BTDC
IC	50 deg ABDC
EO	50 deg BBDC
EC	20 deg ATDC
Valve lift	0.375in
Rocker clearance	0.014/0.015in
Valve seat angle	45 degrees
Valve spring type	Double coil
seat tension	84 lb
installed length	1.78in
free length	2.54in
Connecting rods	H section forged steel
Length	6.5 in centres
Bigend type	Steel backed Lead/Indium shell
Smallend type	Bronze bush
Gudgeon pin diameter	0.875in
Pistons	Aluminium alloy, solid skirt, domed crown
Number of rings	three
Oil pressure	50/60 psi. Idle at 15 psi
Grade of oil	SAE 30
Sump capacity	13 pints including filter
Firing order	1 3 4 2
Ignition timing	TDC
Distributor points gap	0.015in
Sparking plugs	N7YC
Gap	0.025in
Carburettor type	Twin SU H6
Jet size, main	0.100in

Needle recommendation	0A6
Clutch	Borg & Beck Single dry plate
Material	Ferodo
Number of springs	Six
Gearbox	Four speed manual, synchromesh on top three ratios
Ratios: Top	1.00
Third	1.374
Second	2.214
First	3.64
Reverse	4.76
Grade of oil	SAE 30
Capacity	4.5 pints
Propellor shaft	Hardy Spicer open shaft, needle bearing u/j at each end
Final drive	Live axle, hypoid bevel gears
Ratio	10/43
MPH/1000 RPM	17.3
Grade of oil	SAE 90 all models
Capacity	2.25 pints
Cooling system	Pressurised, thermostatic control, pump assisted
Capacity	13.5 pints
Fuel tank capacity	10 gallons
Location	Rear of car under boot floor
Body Styles	Open 2 seat Coupe
Number built	2111

MIDGET

Production period	1961/79
Chassis	Fabricated steel sheet, reinforced, welded construction. All suspension points on frame.
Wheelbase	6ft 8in
Track Front	3ft 9.75in
Rear	3ft 8.75in
Steering	Cam Gears rack & pinion to 1971 Alford & Alder thereafter
Turning circle	Approx 32ft
Castor angle	3 degrees
Camber angle	0.75 degrees
Kingpin angle	6.75 degrees
Toe in	0.0625in
Grade of oil	SAE 90
Brakes	Early cars, 2LS front brakes, drum all round. Later cars disc front drum rear. Cable operated handbrake

	Drum/drum	Disc/drum
Drum (disc) size, rear	7in	8.25in
Drum size, rear	7in	7in
Method of operation	Hydraulic, Lockheed system	

Wheels	Early cars, ventilated disc wheels, bolt on. From 1971 Rostyle offered in place. Rudge type wire wheels as option throughout production.

	Disc	Rostyle	Wire
Rim size	3.5J × 13	4J × 13	4J × 13

Tyre size	5.20 × 13	145 × 13 Either type
Tyre pressure Front	18 psi	22 psi According to type of
Rear	20 psi	24 psi tyre fitted

Engine	4 cylinder in line, pushrod ohv			
	948	1098	1275	1500
Bore	62.94 mm	64.58	70.61	73.70
Stroke	76.20 mm	83.72	81.28	87.50
Cubic capacity	948 cc	1098	1275	1493
Power output (bhp)	46.6	55	65	66
@ rpm	5500	5500	6000	5500
Compression ratio	9:1	8.9:1	8.8:1	9.0:1
Firing order	1 3 4 2 all types			
Valve timing: IO	5 BTDC	5	5	18
IC	45 ABDC	45	45	58
EO	51 BBDC	51	51	58
EC	21 ATDC	21	21	18
Valve lift	0.312in	0.312	0.318	
Rocker clearance	0.012in	0.012	0.012	0.010
Oil pressure (psi at over 1500rpm)	30/60	30/60	40/70	30/50
Grade of oil	SAE 30	SAE 30	SAE 20/50	SAE 20/50
Sump capacity (pints)	6.5	6.5	6.5	8
Ignition timing (degrees)	4 BTDC	8BTDC	13 BTDC	10 BTDC
@ rpm	600	800	1000	680
Distributor points gap	0.015in	0.015	0.015	0.015
Sparking plugs	N12YC	N9YC	N9YC	N12YC
Gap	0.025in	0.025	0.025	0.025

Carburettor type	BMC engines: twin SU HS2 1500 engine: twin SU HS4: or single Zenith 150CD4T for US markets.
Jet size, main	SU: 0.090in. Zenith: 0.100in

	948	1098	1275	1500
Needle recommendation	V2	AN	AN	450

Clutch	All models, single dry plate
Material	Ferodo
Number of springs	948/1098: 6. Others 1 diaphragm
Gearbox	4 speed manual, synchromesh on three top ratios 948/1098/1275 engines; all gears on 1500

	BMC gearbox	1500
Ratios: Top	1.000	1.000
Third	1.357	1.433
Second	1.916	2.112
First	3.200	3.412
Reverse	4.114	3.753
Grade of oil	SAE 20/50	SAE 90B
Capacity	2.25 pint	1.75 pint

Propellor shaft	Open shaft, needle bearing u/j at each end
Final drive	Live axle, hypoid bevel gears

	948	1098	1275	1500
Ratio	4.22	4.22	3.909	3.7
MPH/1000 RPM	15.4	15.4	15.5	17.3
Grade of oil	SAE 90EP	SAE 90EP	SAE 90EP	SAE 90EP

Capacity	1.75pt all models
Cooling system	Pressurized pump assisted

Capacity	system thermostatic control. Approx 10 pints all models
Fuel tank capacity	948/1098: 6 gallons. Other cars: 7 gallons.
Location	Rear of car under boot floor
Body Styles	2 seater open only
Numbers built	Mark I: 948cc 16080
	Mark I: 1098cc 9601
	Mark II: 1098cc 26601
	Mark III: 1275cc 103700
	Mark III: 1493cc 73899

MG SERIES MGB

Production period	1962/81
Chassis	Unit construction body, welded steel construction, front suspension on subframe.
Wheelbase	7ft 7in
Track Front	4ft 1.00in
Rear	4ft 1.25in
Steering	Cam Gears rack & pinion
Turning circle	32ft
Castor angle	7 degrees
Camber angle	1 degree
Kingpin angle	8 degrees
Toe in	0.1875in
Grade of oil	SAE 90
Brakes	Disc front, drum rear
Disc size, front	10.75in
Drum size, rear	10in
Method of operation	Hydraulic, vacuum servo assisted as option to 1973, standard thereafter. Dual system some markets from 67. Cable operated parking brake.
Wheels	Either steel disc bolt-on, or Rudge type wire spoked. Late cars had alloy wheels as option.

	Mk I	Mk II-on	Wires
Rim size	4J × 14	5J × 14	4.5J × 14
Tyre size	5.60 × 14	165 × 14	
Tyre pressure	Front: 21psi; Rear: 24psi		

Engine	4 cylinder in-line, pushrod ohv
Bore	80.26 mm
Stroke	88.90 mm
Cubic capacity	1789 cc
Power output	Approx 94 bhp @ 5500 rpm. Later cars had power outputs which varied from market to market. The other tuning details of the unit would be confusing in a table of this type. Please refer to the appropriate Workshop Manual
Oil pressure	Approx 60psi. 20psi at idle
Grade of oil	SAE 20/50
Sump capacity	7.5 pints
Ignition timing	Varies with engine spec., see above
Distributor points gap	0.015in

Sparking plugs	N9YC
Gap	0.025in After 1975: 0.035in
Carburettor type	To 1973: Twin SU HS4 From 1973: Twin SU HIF4 USA Market also had single Zenith 175CD/5T from 1974/76
Jet size, main	SU: 0.090in Zenith: 0.100in
Needle recommendation	Various according to carburettor spec
Clutch	Borg & Beck single dry plate
Material	Ferodo
Number of springs	Single diaphragm
Gearbox	4 speed manual: synchromesh on top 3 ratios to 1965, all synchro after. Electrical overdrive optional, standard from 1975 Borg Warner 35 automatic gearbox was also available 1967 to 1973

Engine prefix:	18G- 18GA 18GB on		
Ratios:	3sp sync	4sp sync	B-W auto
Overdrive (where fitted)	0.802	0.820	
Top	1.000	1.000	1.00 − 1.33
Third o/d (where fitted)	1.10	1.133	
Third	1.374	1.382	
Second	2.214	2.167	1.45 − 1.93
First	3.640	3.333	2.39 − 3.18
Reverse	4.760	3.095	2.09 − 2.78
Grade of oil	SAE 30	SAE 20/50	TQF
Capacity	4.5 pint	4.7 pint	6 pints
	Add approx 3 pints when o/d fitted		

Propellor shaft	Open shaft, needle roller u/j at each end
Final drive	Live axle, hypoid bevel gears
Ratio	Manual: 3.909:1. Auto: 3.7:1
MPH/1000 RPM	Manual: top: 17.9, o/d: 22.1 Auto: 18.91
Grade of oil	SAE 90EP
Capacity	1.5 pints
Cooling system	Pressurised, pump assisted, with thermostatic control
Capacity	12 pints
Fuel tank capacity	Approx 12 gallons
Location	At rear of car under boot floor

Body Styles		Tourer	GT
Numbers built Mk I	1962	4518	
	1963	23308	
	1964	26542	
	1965	24179	524
	1966	22675	10241
Mk II introduced	1967	15128	11396
	1968	17355	8352
	1969	18896	12134
	1970	23866	12704
	1971	22511	12169
	1972	26222	13171
	1973	19546	10208
	1974	19713	9638
	1975	19967	4609
	1976	25860	3698
	1977	24482	4198
	1978	21703	5652

	Tourer	GT
1979	19897	3503
1980	10891	3424

MG SERIES MGC

Production period	1967/69
Chassis	Unit construction body, welded steel construction, all suspension mounts on frame.
Wheelbase	7ft 7in
Track Front	4ft 1.00in
Rear	4ft 1.25in
Steering	Cam Gears rack & pinion
Turning circle	Approx 34ft
Grade of oil	SAE 90
Brakes	Disc front, drum rear
Disc size, front	11.06in
Drum size, rear	10in
Method of operation	Hydraulic, vacuum servo assisted as standard. Dual system for USA. Girling manufacture. Cable parking brake fitted.
Wheels	Either steel disc bolt-on, or Rudge type wire spoked.
Rim size	5J × 15
Tyre size	165 × 15
Tyre pressure	Front: 21psi; Rear: 24psi
Engine	6 cylinder in-line, pushrod ohv
Bore	83.36 mm
Stroke	88.90 mm
Cubic capacity	2912 cc
Power output	150 bhp @ 5250 rpm
Compression Ratio	9:1
Firing order	1 5 3 6 2 4
Valve clearance	0.015in
Oil pressure	Approx 60psi. 20psi at idle
Grade of oil	SAE 20/50
Sump capacity	7.5 pints
Ignition timing	20 deg @ 1000 rpm
Distributor points gap	0.015in
Sparking plugs	N9YC
Gap	0.025in
Carburettor type	Twin SU HS6
Jet size, main	0.100in
Needle recommendation	ST. (Spring loaded type: BAD)
Clutch	Borg & Beck single dry plate
Material	Ferodo
Number of springs	Single diaphragm
Gearbox	4 speed manual; synchromesh on all gears, overdrive optional extra. Borg Warner 35 automatic gearbox was also available.

Ratios:	Manual	Overdrive	B-W Auto
Overdrive (where fitted)		0.820	
Top	1.000	1.000	1.00– 2.2
Third o/d (where fitted)		1.072	
Third	1.307	1.307	
Second	2.058	2.058	1.45– 3.1
First	2.98	2.98	2.39 –5.5
Reverse	2.679	2.679	2.09– 4.598

Grade of oil	SAE 90 TQF
Capacity	4.7 pint 6 pint 6 pint
Propellor shaft	Open shaft, needle roller u/j at each end
Final drive	Live axle, hypoid bevel gears
Ratio	Manual: 3.07. O/d & Auto: 3.307 Later cars: Man: 3.307, o/d: 3.70
MPH/1000RPM	Manual: top: 24.0. o/d: 27.0 Later cars: top: 22.1, o/d: 24.0 Auto: 22
Grade of oil	SAE 90EP
Capacity	1.5 pints
Cooling system	Pressurised, pump assisted, with thermostatic control
Capacity	
Fuel tank capacity	Approx 12 gallons
Location	At rear of car under boot floor
Body Styles	Tourer GT

Numbers built	Tourer	GT
1967	189	41
1968	2566	2462
1969	1787	1954

MGB G.T. V8

Production period	1972/76
Chassis	Unit construction body, welded steel construction, front suspension on subframe.
Wheelbase	7ft 7in
Track Front	4ft 1.00in
Rear	4ft 1.25in
Steering	Cam Gears rack & pinion
Turning circle	32ft
Castor angle	7 degrees
Camber angle	1 degree
Kingpin angle	8 degrees
Toe in	0.1875in
Grade of oil	SAE 90
Brakes	Disc front, drum rear
Disc size, front	10.75in
Drum size, rear	10in
Method of operation	Hydraulic, vacuum servo assisted as standard. Cable operated parking brake.
Wheels	Steel rims, alloy centre composite construction, bolt on type.
Rim size	5J × 14
Tyre size	175HR × 14
Tyre pressure	Front: 21psi: Rear: 25psi
Engine	8 cylinder in V. pushrod ohv, aluminium construction.
Bore	88.90 mm
Stroke	71.12 mm
Cubic capacity	3532 cc
Power output	137 bhp @ 5000 rpm
Oil pressure	Approx 30–40 psi at all speeds
Grade of oil	SAE 20/50
Sump capacity	8 pints including filter
Ignition timing	8 deg BTDC @ 1000rpm

Distributor points gap	0.015in	Grade of oil	SAE 90
Sparking plugs	L92YC	Capacity	6 pints
Gap	0.035in	**Propellor shaft**	Open shaft, needle roller u/j at each end
Firing order	1 8 4 3 6 5 7 2		
Carburettor type	Twin SU HIF6	**Final drive**	Live axle, hypoid bevel gears
Jet size, main	0.100in	Ratio	3.071
Needle recommendation	BBU	MPH/1000 RPM	Top: 23, o/d: 28.
		Grade of oil	SAE 90EP
Clutch	Borg & Beck single dry plate	Capacity	1.5 pints
Material	Ferodo	**Cooling system**	Pressurised, pump assisted, with thermostatic control
Number of springs	Single diaphragm		
Gearbox	4 speed manual: synchromesh on all gears. Overdrive on top gear.	Capacity	16 pints
		Fuel tank capacity	Approx 12 gallons
Ratios:		Location	At rear of car under boot floor
Overdrive	0.820	**Body Styles**	2 seat Coupe only
Top	1.000	Numbers built	1972 3
Third	1.259		1973 1069
Second	1.974		1974 854
First	3.138		1975 489
Reverse	2.819		1976 176

APPENDIX 2

Sales Figures by Year: Pre-war

These figures are at best approximate, but are the best available. Those for the 14 hp cars are corrupted by the sales of bespoke coach work by Morris Garages Ltd, the parent company of the MG, probably by a figure of 33 cars. The later figures are slightly deviant from accepted production figures, because some cars were sold second-hand from the Factory.

	14hp	18hp	ohc	SVW	T	TOTAL
1924	33					33
1925	150					150
1926	232					232
1927	341					341
1928	346	6				352
1929	158	286	479			923
1930		285	1628			1913
1931		161	1193			1354
1932		26	2350			2376
1933			2183			2183
1934			2050			2050
1935			1193	38		1231
1936			395	949	736	2080
1937			6	1322	1517	2845
1938				1888	609	2497
1939				1320	530	1850
TOTAL	1260	764	11477	5517	3392	22410

APPENDIX 3
Build Data for Pre-war Models

This data is derived from records supplied by MG Car Club, using the records of the MG Car Co. All 14 hp cars were built in Oxford, initially in small workshops around the town, and later in a part of the Osberton Radiator works from late in 1925. All activities were moved to Edmund Road in 1927, at which plant all other 14 hp cars were built. The 18 hp production was started at Edmund Road, and was transferred to Abingdon late in 1930.

14HP MODELS

				Body styles	
		4 seat	2 seat	Saloons	Specials
Numbers built	1924	3	3		7
	1925	90	33	6	21
	1926	121	65	12	34
	1927	199	109	6	33
	1928	154	135	32	25
	1929	72	58	24	4

'Specials' in the above context include some bodies built by Morris Garages Ltd on various Morris chassis, carrying the MG identity. All cars from the 1927 model year and later carried the MG guarantee.

18HP MODELS

					Body styles	
			2/s open	4/s open	Saloons	Specials
Numbers built	Mk I	1928			6	
		1929	26	59	189	9
		1930			95	
		1931	11	50	53	3
	Mk II	1929	1		1	1
		1930	15	25	113	10
		1931	1	3	30	10
		1932		2	22	2
	Mk III	1930		5		

'Specials' in this context are non-standard bodies supplied, and bare chassis supplied to specialist coachbuilders.

BUILD FIGURES BY MODEL

These figures are the actual recorded production build numbers for each model. Where there are discrepancies between these numbers and those above, they are explained by a variety of factors, but the fact remains that both sets of figures are recorded fact! It is of interest that the Nuffield-era models actually show a lower build rate than sales, and I am not sure what inference should be drawn!

VINTAGE MODELS

Model	Build	Notes
14hp 'Bullnose'	400	Includes 212 Morris Garages bodied cars
14hp 'Flatrad'	667	Includes 29 Morris Garages specials
14/40 Mark IV	187	
18/80 Mk I	501	
18/80 Mk II	228	
18/100	5	
Total build, 14 & 18hp cars:	1988	

TRIPLE M MODELS

Those not familiar with the MG Car Club term may like to read through the next three sub-headings for explanation.

Model	Build	Notes
Midget Models		
M	3235	
C	44	
D	250	
J1	380	
J2	2083	
J3	22	
J4	9	
PA	1973	
PB	526	
QA	8	
RA	10	
Magna Models		
F1	1116	
F2	40	
F3	94	
L1	486	
L2	90	
Magnette Models		
K1/KA	54	
K1/KB	74	
K1/KD	53	
K2/KB	16	
K2/KD	4	
K3	33	
KN	200	
NA	482	
NB	231	
ND	24	Includes 3 Musketeer cars
NE	7	
Total build ohc cars: 11544		

SVW MODELS

Two-litre	2738
One & Half-litre	2407
Two-six litre	369
Total build, SVW cars	5514

T-SERIES MODELS

TA	3003
TB	379
Total build, T-series cars	3382

Total build at Oxford and Abingdon, pre-war 21428 cars.

APPENDIX 4

Sales Figures for ohc Cars 1929–37

These figures represent the total sales of the ohc cars, as opposed to production figures. These are the actual sales figures of **new** cars and any deviation from accepted figures is explained by the fact that the Factory always kept a large fleet of demonstrator cars, which were eventually sold as 'second-hand'.

MODEL	STYLE	1929	1930	1931	1932	1933
M	Fabric 2 seater	473	1294	525	37	
	Fabric Coupe	6	298	173	16	
	Panelled 2 seater	–	–	123	150	
	12/12 Replica	–	–	19	–	
	Chassis sold	–	36	37	9	
	TOTAL	479	1628	877	212	
C	Racing 2 seater	–	–	35	8	
	Monoposto	–	–	1	–	
D	Open 4 seater	–	–	73	135	
	Saloon	–	–	–	37	
	Chassis sold	–	–	–	5	
	TOTAL	–	–	73	177	
F1	Open 4 seater	–	–	106	459	
	Saloon	–	–	79	291	
	Chassis	–	–	25	155	
F2	Open 2 seater	–	–	–	40	
F3	Open 4 seater	–	–	–	66	
	Saloon	–	–	–	18	2
	Chassis	–	–	–	8	
	TOTAL	–	–	207	1037	2

MODEL	STYLE	1932	1933	1934	
J1	Open 4 seater	116	146		
	Saloon	59	58		
	Chassis	–	1		
	TOTAL	175	205		
J2	Open 2 seater	735	1293	33	
	Chassis	–	22	–	
	TOTAL	735	1315	33	
J3	Open 2 seater	5	15		
	Saloon	–	1		
	Chassis	–	1		
	TOTAL	5	17		
J4	Racing 2 seater	–	9		

		1933	1934	1935	1936
L1	Open 4 seater	–	233	15	–
	Saloon	–	70	27	–
	Continental Coupe	–	25	59	12
	Chassis	–	31	4	–
	TOTAL	–	359	105	12
L2	Open 2 seater	–	85		
K1	Open 4 seater	–	74	23	
	Saloon	–	54	20	
	Chassis	–	31	4	
	TOTAL	–	159	47	
K2	Open 2 seater	–	16	4	
K3	Open 2 seater	1	16	15	
	Monoposto	–	–	1	

MODEL	STYLE	1934	1935	1936	1937
PA	Open 2 seater	970	378	37	
	Open 4 seater	390	105	—	
	Airline Coupe	19	7	1	
	Chassis	47	4	—	
	TOTAL	1426	484	38	
PB	Open 2 seater		210	195	3
	Open 4 seater		86	13	—
	Airline Coupe		8	6	—
	Chassis		5	1	—
	TOTAL		309	215	3
QA	Racing 2 seater	8			
RA	Racing monoposto		10		
NA	Open 2 seater: NA	118	57		
	NB		44	53	
	Open 4 seater: NA	164	69		
	NB		53	81	
	Airline Coupe	4	1	1	
	Allingham Coupe	6	5	5	
	Saloon	1			
	ND	21			
	NE	6	1		
	Competition special				3
	Chassis	29	18	1	
	TOTAL	349	248	141	3
KN	Saloon	57	91	1	
	de Luxe Saloon		17		
	Chassis	5	22		
	TOTAL	62	130	1	

APPENDIX 5

Sales Figures by Model: Post-war

These figures represent the total sold, model by model. They are accurate in as much as they have been supplied from various Factory records and cross-checked where possible.

TC	10000
TD	28643
Mk II	1022
TF	6200
1500	3400
YA	6158
YB	1301
YT	877
ZA	12754
ZB	23846
MGA	58750
MGA 1600	31501
MGA 1600 Mk II	8719
MGA Twin Cam	2111
Magnette Mk III	15676
Magnette Mk IV	13738
1100	116827
1300	26240
Midget Mk I	25681
Midget Mk II	26601
Midget Mk III	103700*
Midget 1500	73899
MGB Mk I Tourer	115898
MGB Mk I GT	21835
MGB Mk II Tourer	271361*
MGB Mk II GT	103786*
MGC	8999
MGB G.T. V8	2800

*Officially, the 'Mark' designation was dropped after 1970 and a new designation based on model year was introduced.

APPENDIX 6

Build Figures by Year: Post-war

These figures are generated on a year-by-year basis, to show total MG production, including those models which were not actually built at Abingdon. No account is taken of models still in production, however, since this data might be considered confidential.

	T	Y	Z	MGA	Midget	TOTAL
1945	100					100
1946	1700					1700
1947	2360	900				3260
1948	3030	1058				4088
1949	2852	2031				4883
1950	4817	2045				6862
1951	7408	1001				8409
1952	11057	679				11736
1953	8208	622	8			8838
1954	6316		3819			10135
1955	1457		8927	1003		11387
1956			7385	13410		20795
1957			6910	20571		27481
1958			9551	16663		26214
1959			1	23419		23420
1960				16981		16981
1961				6085	7656	13741
TOTAL	49305	8336	36601	C/F	C/F	

	MGA	MGB	MGC	MGB GT V8	Midget	TOTAL
1962	3049	4518			9906	17473
1963		23308			7625	30933
1964		26542			11450	37992
1965		24703			9162	33865
1966		32916			6842	39758
1967		26524	230		7854	34608
1968		25707	5028		7372	38107
1969		31030	3741		13221	47992
1970		36570			15083	51653
1971		34680			16525	51205
1972		39393		3	16243	55639
1973		29754		1069	13988	44811
1974		29351		854	11692	41897
1975		24576		489	14478	39543
1976		29558		176	16879	46613
1977		28680			14329	43009
1978		27355			14312	41667
1979		23400			9778	33178
1980		14315				14315
TOTAL	101181	512880	8999	2591	224395	

The total MG production at Abingdon post-war was therefore 853288. Even this is not the full story, because Abingdon also produced Riley cars from 1945 to 1959. From 1957 all sports cars produced by the BMC were built at the MG factory, which meant that Austin-Healey cars were built there until 1968. In addition, a small number of Morris Minor 1000 Travellers, vans and pick-up trucks were also built alongside the sports cars between 1960 and 1964. It is truly remarkable that from 1957, the factory produced more cars per year than in the entire pre-war period, 1924–39, and that this was true until 1979!

The above figures take no account of MGs built at Cowley, which number as follows:

Farina Magnette	29414
11/1300	143067
Midget (1967 only)	476
TOTAL COWLEY BUILD	172957

Bibliography

The following books have been used to corroborate material:

Combat by Barre Lyndon, William Heinemann, 1933
Circuit Dust by Barre Lyndon, John Miles Ltd, 1934
Grand Prix by Barre Lyndon, John Miles Ltd, 1935
Maintaining the Breed by John Thornley, Motor Racing Publications, 1956
MG by McComb by Wilson McComb, Osprey, 1978
MG the Art of Abingdon by John McLellan, Motor Racing Publications, 1982
Early MG by Philip Jennings, private publication, 1983.

The following magazines have been used as research sources:

The Motor and its successor
The Autocar and its successor
The Light Car
The MG Car Club magazines, *MG Magazine, Sports Car* and *Safety Fast*.

Technical data has been drawn from Factory Data Sheets in the possession of the MG Car Club, and corroborated by use of official Workshop Manuals. Where there was a deviation, I have used the contemporary data sheets as source material.

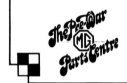